Beauty & Bounty

For John—for Everything!

Jane Ockershausen Smith

Library of Congress Cataloging in Publication Data

Smith, Jane Ockershausen.
One-day trips to beauty and bounty.

Includes index.
1. Gardens—Washington Region—Guide-books.
2. Farms—Washington Region—Guide-books.
3. Horticulture—Washington Region—Guide-books.
I. Title.
SB466.U65W387 1983 917.5 83-11676
ISBN 0-939009-03-X

EPM Publications, Inc.
1003 Turkey Run Road
McLean, Virginia 22101
Printed in the United States of America

Book design by Stephen A. Kirschner

Contents

FORMAL GARDENS

SPECIALTY GARDENS

ARBORETUMS

COLONIAL GARDENS

HERB GARDENS

WILDFLOWERS

CONSERVATORIES

JAPANESE GARDENS

COMMERCIAL GARDENS

FARTHER AFIELD FOR FLOWERS

FARMS

GARDEN PLOTS FOR RENT

PICK-YOUR-OWN FRUITS AND VEGETABLES

VINEYARDS

VIRGINIA

MARYLAND

PENNSYLVANIA

NEW JERSEY

WILDLIFE SANCTUARIES

ANIMALS

MINI-GUIDE TO PARKS

Gardens for All

As another Smith said (Alexander Smith back in the 1830s), "How deeply seated in the human heart is the liking for gardens and gardening." For many gardeners a good part of the joy of having a garden is sharing it with others. In this book there are more than a hundred horticultural treats that you are invited to share.

As you read about these gardens, farms, and vineyards, you will get an idea of what to expect on your visits and why a particular place is worth seeing. But viewing a garden is a personal experience. There are many aspects to an appealing garden. You may appreciate the over all esthetic appeal of the landscape. There may be felicitous touches: long allées through which a meandering river can be glimpsed as at Tryon Palace, North Carolina, graceful chinoiserie bridges over slow-moving canals as at the Palace Gardens in Williamsburg or the patterned symmetry of the formal parterre arrangement at Gunston Hall in Virginia or the William Paca Gardens in Maryland.

You may also appreciate a garden because of the size or number of flowers that are in bloom—the fields of daffodils at Gloucester around the Daffodil Mart, the lotus at the Kenilworth Aquatic Garden or the delicate and dazzling assortment of iris at the Presby Memorial Iris Garden.

If you are a scientific viewer you may crave exotic plants. Gardens chosen thus would include those featuring the unusual mixture, perhaps the Duke Garden Foundation for its Persian Garden, or the U.S. Botanic Garden collection. Also appealing to this type of garden fancier are those with well-marked specimens. A careful reading of the selections in this book will enable you to pick those gardens that suit your preference.

Important as it is to know what you will see at a garden, it is also vital to know when to see the garden. Many have peak blooming seasons, some are only open part of the year and all have an everchanging blooming calendar as month by month different plants come into flower. You need to be aware of the seasonal variety in order to pick the best time to schedule your visit.

A garden enthusiast may well want to start in January with the Duke Gardens, which are closed during the summer months. February is a good time to visit another indoor garden such as Kensington Orchids. In March, Dumbarton Oaks presents forsythia, the harbinger of spring. April begins the spring bonanza with a myriad of excellent choices. Flower laden trees are doubly beautiful reflected in a lake the banks of which are abloom with daffodils and azaleas as at Longwood Gardens. Daffodils and azaleas are the star attraction at the National Arboretum, Norfolk Botanical Garden, Winterthur and London Town Gardens to name just a few.

Late spring is best for viewing the delicate blossoms along the various wildflower trails; two of the best are those at Bowman's Hill in Pennsylvania and Cylburn Wildflower Preserve in Baltimore.

June's bloom is traditionally roses. The greatest profusion are the Star Rose fields in West Grove, Pennsylvania, but another attraction in that state offers a very special rose show—Hershey Gardens.

In late July or early August the garden trip to make is to the Kenilworth Aquatic Garden in northeast Washington. The brilliantly hued lotus, with flowers as large as basketballs, have to be seen to be believed.

With the advent of fall, chrysanthemums take over many gardens. Hershey has more than 4,000 plants outdoors. And all the conservatories show chrysanthemums in November as part of their series of seasonal shows.

In December you again need to direct your attention indoors and enjoy the Christmas conservatory displays. At Longwood Gardens winter seems like spring in the acres of greenhouses burgeoning with brilliant poinsettias flanked by daffodils, narcissus, and other fragrant blossoms.

Of course, many of these garden trips can be combined. You can easily spend an enjoyable day seeing the Japanese Embassy Garden, Dumbarton Oaks, and the Bishop's Garden at the Washington Cathedral with time out for lunch in Georgetown. A combination of Oatlands and Morven Park with a picnic lunch at the latter, or a stop at one of the delightful taverns in Leesburg, makes for a pleasant spring outing. A weekend foray could include Longwood Gardens, Winterthur, Nemours, and the Star Rose Garden.

Gardens can create a range of moods: playful, restful, stimulating, awe inspiring, meditative, and even practical. In fact, gardens also serve as a living catalog giving novices and experts alike valuable information. There are many teaching gardens included in this book. The stated purpose of The Scott Horticultural Foundation is just that, to show what will grow in this area. Commercial gardens like the Behnke Nursery not only sell plants, they also strive to enlighten the community about the plants that can be successfully and easily grown. One of the major educational horticultural centers in the world is the Beltsville Agricultural Center in Maryland.

This guide is a unique compendium; no other source offers a listing of this many types of horticultural sites. They are organized so that they can be enjoyed on a seasonal basis and as one-day trips from Washington, D.C. With the addition of the sections on picking your own produce, gardens to rent, and vineyards, plus the bonus chapter on East Coast gardens that can be visited on trips of two days or longer, this book provides a singular guide to horticulture in the entire middle Atlantic area.

This latest edition includes an annotated listing of all the state parks in Maryland and Virginia as well as the 11 parks within the District of Columbia.

For animal lovers there are five additional sites starting with the Aquarium in Baltimore and ending with the Zoo in Washington. And eight trips to refuges and environmental areas offer opportunities to see birds and animals in their natural habitats. Here, for family and friends, is a world of beauty, bounty, tranquility and wonder!

J.O.S.

Formal Gardens

Dumbarton Oaks

What could be more delightful than discovering a garden estate hidden amid the bustle and commercial development of Georgetown in Washington, D.C.? Its location is ideal almost any time for a handy half-day outing. When balmy spring weather proves too tempting to resist, you can escape from a city office or store for a lunch-hour respite to Dumbarton Oaks.

When you visit Dumbarton Oaks you will agree with horticulture experts who view its formal garden as one of the loveliest in the United States. The garden, designed in the early 1920s, is entered through an Orangery. Numerous terraced areas form this European-style garden. Vine covered walls make the Orangery particularly pleasing in early spring. Careful monitoring of the weather will enable you to enjoy the best of Forsythia Hill, which is planted solid with those yellow harbingers of spring, and the beginning of the delicate purple sprays of wisteria. In April another focal spot is Cherry Hill with its flowering Japanese cherries.

Near the Rose Garden is Lovers Lane Pool, a spot of especial charm. The romantic walkway past this small pool borders on nearby Dumbarton Park, part of the estate Ambassador and Mrs. Robert Bliss gave to Washington, D.C.

Early spring is the best time to visit Dumbarton Park. You'll catch the wildflowers in full bloom—crocus, narcissus, primrose, and forsythia are followed by Virginia bluebells, violets, daffodils and grape hyacinths. May blooms include wood azalea, forget-me-nots, lilies of the valley, buttercups and wild orchids. This 27-acre natural park is a delightful bonus to Dumbarton Oaks's formality.

Though spring and early summer provide the most appealing vistas at Dumbarton Oaks, areas like the Pebble Garden, where varicolored stones are arranged in geometric patterns, offer a welcome respite even during the winter.

Dumbarton Oaks is open daily from 2:00 to 6:00 P.M. April through October and from 2:00 to 5:00 P.M. the rest of the year, except holidays and during inclement weather. Admission is charged from April through October. After enjoying the gardens you may also want to explore the house where an excellent collection of Byzantine and Pre-Columbian art is on display. The house is closed on Mondays. Dumbarton Park is open daily at no charge.

Directions: Dumbarton Oaks is located at 1703 32nd Street, N.W., Washington, D.C. The entrance to the Park is on R Street between 31st Street and Avon Place.

The Bishop's Garden—Washington National Cathedral

Enter Bishop's Garden through the centuries-old Norman arch and pass into another age—that of the 12th century medieval garden. Laid out on the warm southern slopes below Washington National Cathedral, Bishop's Garden abounds with unexpected delights.

From the 800-year-old archway the garden extends along a stone path that winds through boxwood walkways. When you first enter this garden retreat you'll see a small Norman court. A second, and larger, Norman arch frames the entrance to this little court with its wall fountain and 15th century carved stone relief.

The path then leads down to the Hortulus. You step even farther back in time here, for the Hortulus suggests the era of Charlemagne and 9th century herb gardens. Flowering herbs and boxwood frame a baptismal font that came from the Abbey of St. Julie in Aisne, France. The boxwood, though not nearly as old as the font, does reflect some early American history. It was transplanted from the grounds of Hayfield Manor, a house built in Virginia by George Washington in 1761.

A choice of paths confronts you next. To the south is the Yew Walk, to the east the Rose Garden. From mid-May to early November you'll find an array of roses to welcome you in the Rose Garden. The focal point here is the statue of the Prodigal Son. A bronze sundial mounted on a 13th century capital highlights another section of the garden which is planted with herbs.

Backtracking to the Yew Walk, you'll come to the Shadow House. This picturesque, ivy-covered gazebo was built of stones from an early home of Grover Cleveland, our 22d President. These are not the only stones with a past. The Pilgrim Steps leading down to the lower level of the Yew Walk are made of stones quarried at Aquia Creek by slaves of George Washington. The stone steps were brought here from Abingdon, Virginia, the birthplace of Nelly Custis, adopted daughter of George Washington.

Though not a maze, the thick boxwood at the Bishop's Garden creates the illusion of intricate walkways, and children love to explore the winding paths. On this lower level of the Yew Walk colorful perennials border the flower-covered, stone retaining wall. Quince competes with 15th century carved panels that decorate the wall. Here you will see the Wayside Cross. Once a roadside reminder of their faith for early Christians in France, this round-headed or wheel cross is one of the few that remain from that long ago time.

Near the foot of the Pilgrim Steps is one of the yew trees after which the walk was named. This impressive 25-foot specimen has its own landing on the Pilgrim Steps. You can either return up the steps to the Cathedral or follow the path deeper into Bishop's Garden.

You should also notice one additional feature at the bottom of the Pilgrim Steps: the equestrian statue of George Washington. The bronze Washington appears to be looking toward the great Cathedral on the hill—the realization of his dreams of a "great Church for national purposes" in the nation's capital.

Also on the Cathedral grounds, but not part of Bishop's Garden, is a wooded path planted with wildflowers that are particularly enjoyable in early spring. This trail starts behind the statue of George Washington.

Another not-to-be-missed sight is the Cathedral's massive sundial. It not only measures the hours of the day but also the seasons of the church year. Nearby is the Glastonbury thorn tree. A curious legend maintains that this tree will only bloom on Christmas Day or when royalty visits the Cathedral. So far the bizarre tale has proved to be true. The only occasions other than Christmas that the Glastonbury thorn tree has bloomed were two visits by Queen Elizabeth and Prince Charles.

Associated with Bishop's Garden at the Washington Cathedral is the greenhouse, where unusual herbs are grown and sold. The Herb Cottage, a gift shop, also sells herbs and herbal products. The Herb Cottage has its own small herb garden out front.

While at the Cathedral try to include a tour of this magnificent church. If time permits stop in at the London Brass Rubbing Centre in the Cathedral's crypt. Here medieval music maintains the mood of the garden. You can get an overview of the many casts of old English brasses that are available for simple and complex rubbings. These easy to make copies of commemorative plaques are created by covering the casts with paper and then rubbing the gold, silver, bronze or black wax over the raised design.

One additional attraction is the new high-level observation gallery atop the west side of the Cathedral. While on a clear day you can't quite, as the song says, "see forever," you can glimpse the Catoctin and Blue Ridge Mountains in the distance. At 490 feet above sea level you have a fine panoramic view of the capital.

Bishop's Garden is open daily from 9:30 A.M. to 5:00 P.M. and until 6:00 P.M. during the summer months. Tours of the Cathedral are conducted Monday through Saturday from 10:00 A.M. to noon and again from 1:00 to 3:15 P.M. Tours are also conducted on Sunday afternoons. The London Brass Rubbing Centre is open Monday through Saturday from 9:00 A.M. to 5:00 P.M. The glass enclosed gallery is open Monday through Saturday from 10:00 A.M. to 3:15 P.M. and on Sunday from 12:30 to 3:15 P.M. A small admission fee is charged.

Directions: The Washington National Cathedral is located at the intersection of Massachusetts Avenue and Wisconsin Avenue just above Georgetown, in Washington, D.C.

Hillwood Museum Gardens

Though the Hillwood Museum property was originally owned and developed by Isaac Peirce, grandson of George Peirce, famous for his arboretum and park at Longwood Garden, it was Marjorie Merriweather Post who designed the gardens you'll enjoy at Hillwood today.

Mrs. Post, working with landscape architect Perry Wheeler, developed a marvelously diverse range of gardens in the 25 acres that comprise the Hillwood Museum Gardens. According to her daughter, actress Dina Merrill, "She'd think nothing of having an 80-foot tree moved merely five feet in order to improve the view." With more than 3,500 plants and trees in the gardens, this led to a great deal of rearranging before the gardens reached their present felicitous appearance.

From the portico of the house you can look out over the Lunar Lawn to the Washington Monument six miles away. The formal gardens close to the house blend into the woods by a natural arrangement of laurel, azaleas, and rhododendron, which are particularly lovely during their spring blooming season. In addition there are the flowering dogwood, cherry and crab apple trees.

A year-round pleasure is the Japanese garden, located to the right of the Lunar Lawn. A waterfall, tumbling down several levels, can be crossed by a picturesque Japanese bridge. Stone garden lanterns and dwarf conifer create a hillside facsimile of a Japanese landscape.

You'll continue back toward the house on Friendship Walk. Just off the path is an open terrace featuring a central marble medallion inscribed, "Friendship outstays the hurrying flight of years and aye abides through laughter and through tears." From here all walkways lead to the Memorial Garden. An arbor, bearing roses, surrounds the Memorial Garden. This garden contains varieties of roses and is one of two rose gardens at Hillwood. At the center of the garden is a monument containing Mrs. Post's ashes.

Just outside of the drawing room close to the house is the last and most formal garden area. Its low, close-clipped evergreens suggest the living masonry, or green walls, of the "hall" effect so fascinating to the French. Statues and fountains grace the pool area, and a Moorish water canal runs the length of the garden.

If at all possible you should plan to tour the mansion while visiting Hillwood. The interior reflects Mrs. Post's life-long interest in French art and the Russian art which she began acquiring while her husband, Joseph E. Davies, served as Ambassador to the Soviet Union from 1937 to 1938. The Russian collection is considered the finest outside the Soviet Union. In the Icon Room one can find jeweled and enameled objects by Carl Faberge, jeweler to the czars, chalices, a diamond-studded crown worn by the last three czarinas, and icons. An extensive collection of Russian porcelain and glass is exhibited in the Porcelain Room.

The furniture and decorations in the French drawing room are mostly French, including three large Beauvais tapestries and a roll top desk by David Roentgen.

The Louis XVI bedroom and formal dining room are two more of the fascinating rooms that serve as showcases for the more than 5,000 objects in Mrs. Post's collections. It is a rare experience to see a private home so lavishly furnished.

Additional points of interest at Hillwood Museum are the picturesque one-room Russian Dacha with another small Russian collection; the C. W. Post wing, which contains paintings, sculpture and furnishings assembled by Mrs. Post's father; the collection of American Indian artifacts, which Mrs. Post had exhibited at Topridge, her camp in the Adirondacks; and the greenhouse. Eight hundred orchids make the greenhouse particularly enjoyable in the slack Christmas to Easter period. You can buy plants from Hillwood at the greenhouse.

Tours of the Hillwood Museum may be taken Monday, Wednesday, Thursday, Friday and Saturday. Tours are at 9:00 A.M., 10:30 A.M., Noon and 1:30 P.M.. Admission is charged and reservations are required. Call (202)686-5807. Your tour of the house will take two hours and will begin with a half hour film that provides some background on Mrs. Post's very full life. After the mansion tour you are free to explore the gardens on your own. It is also possible to visit the gardens and all the exhibits on the estate without touring the mansion for a smaller admission fee. Call the same number as above for a reservation.

Directions: From the Beltway take Exit 33, Connecticut Avenue, south into Washington. Turn left on Tilden Street and left again on Linnean Avenue. Hillwood Museum is located at 4155 Linnean Avenue, N.W. From downtown Washington go north to Tilden Street, turn right on Tilden and proceed as above.

President's Park and White House Rose Garden

George Washington selected the site in the newly designated federal city for the President's house. All of our country's leaders, except Washington, have lived and worked there. When John Adams, our second President, moved into the just completed house, the grounds were still littered with the kilns used to make bricks for building the city.

Thomas Jefferson, always interested in every aspect of any house he was in, had sloping mounds added south of the mansion for greater privacy. From John Quincy Adams on, the Presidents or their families have planted one or more trees in this 18-acre President's Park. The tradition began when Adams planted an American elm on the south grounds. He also employed a full-time gardener and took a great deal of interest in the White House landscape, setting out many of the plants himself.

And so the Presidents and their families each began to contribute something to the grounds. Now when you walk through President's Park you can see these tangible links with our country's past.

Some Presidents made other contributions to landscaping. Andrew Johnson, the 17th President, added a fountain to the south side of the White House grounds in 1867 and his successor, Ulysses S. Grant, added one on the north side in 1873.

As 20th century development encroached on the White House additional plantings were added to preserve the natural setting of the mansion and shield it from the city. A grove of trees, primarily elm, extends from Pennsylvania Avenue along the north side of the house.

Of the three specific garden areas that comprise President's Park, the Rose Garden is the best known. The design that you see today was done in 1962 by Mrs. Paul Mellon at President Kennedy's request. But some of the roses go back to 1913 when the first Mrs. Wilson planted them. The Rose Garden was redesigned to provide space for entertaining large groups. The new design was anything but contemporary, being laid out like an 18th century American garden. Flowering crab apples spread their branches over beds planted with tulips, grape hyacinths and columbine in the spring. In the summer the beds boast roses, anemones and other favorites. Color is provided in autumn by chrysanthemums, heliotrope and salvia. The garden is framed by boxwood and osmanthus hedges.

The Rose Garden is used by the President for ceremonial occasions. French doors lead from the Oval Office into the garden. Many foreign dignitaries are greeted in the garden before entering the office for a working session. Special events have also been held in the Rose Garden. In 1976 an elegant state dinner for Queen Elizabeth II was held there alfresco. The 1971 wedding of Tricia Nixon to Edward Cox also was celebrated in the garden.

On the east side of the mansion a second garden, the Jacqueline Kennedy Garden, is used by the First Lady to receive guests. This intimate, more miniature garden is shaded and delineated by a row of lindens. Holly, crab apple and magnolia mark the eastern end. Square beds with centers of holly have spring bulbs and seasonal annuals that add color.

Finally, there is the Children's Garden, added to the grounds by the Lyndon B. Johnson family. An apple tree and goldfish ponds are the highlights of this garden planted with tulips, azaleas and colorful seasonal annuals. Children can enjoy historic President's Park every Easter Monday at the Children's Easter Egg Roll, one of the three occasions each year that the White House grounds are open to the public. A day planned with events and entertainment to please the youth, this is a Washington tradition.

The grounds are also open for free garden tours one spring and fall weekend each year. For more information call the National Park Service at (202)426-6700. They maintain the White House grounds. Or write the National Park Service, National Capital Region, 1100 Ohio Drive, S.W., Washington, D.C. 20242.

Directions: The White House is located at 1600 Pennsylvania Avenue, N.W., Washington, D.C.

Hershey Gardens

How about a little behavior modification? If you automatically think of chocolate when you think of Hershey, take a one-day trip to Hershey Gardens and get a new perspective.

These fantastic gardens were begun in April of 1936 when Milton Hershey was asked to contribute a million dollars to establish a National Rosarium in Washington, D.C. He decided to invest in a garden in his own community instead, and instructions were issued to establish "a very nice garden of roses."

During the first year of operation, 1937, more than 200,000 people came to see Mr. Hershey's "nice" garden of 12,500 roses. So pleased was Mr. Hershey with this reception that he continually expanded the garden. By 1940 there were 700 varieties of roses, with more than 25,500 bushes.

When the number of tourists reached a half million in 1941, Mr. Hershey decided to add the adjoining 17-acre field to the garden. This addition brought the number of rose bushes to 35,000, representing 850 varieties. Also planted at this time was an area of trees and shrubs highlighted by annual and perennial flowers.

During the 1960s a number of special features were added. A holly collection with 80 varieties of American, English, Japanese and Chinese hollies was included in 1966. Just one year later the Henry J. Hohman collection of rare evergreen and deciduous plants became a part of Hershey Gardens.

July color was added to the garden when 400 day lily varieties were planted in 1966. Soft spring hues were added in 1969 with flowering azaleas and rhododendron.

In the 1970s two new attractions focused on the garden's main feature: roses. The 400 rose varieties in the Old-Fashioned Rose section added in 1972–73 provide an overview of the development of the rose. Another historical feature is Mrs. Hershey's original rose garden.

The Old World is represented by the Italian Garden with its classic columns and by the grace and dignity of the English Formal Garden. The New World is exemplified by the Colonial Garden and by the Herb Collection's 100 varieties. Other areas include the Rock Garden, the All-American Rose Avenue that has an example of every All-American rose, and one of the finest arboretums in the eastern United States.

The blooming calendar at Hershey Gardens presents you first with a profusion of daffodils, over 30,000 tulips, azaleas, magnolias, flowering cherries, crab apples and dogwood from mid-April until mid-May.

Next you will see the late flowering azaleas, rhododendron and peonies from mid-May until June. Then in June the rose show begins with thousands of roses of every hue and variety, a not-to-be-missed display that continues all summer. In July the day lilies and annuals add their color to the garden. From mid-September until November the 4,000 chrysanthemums are in bloom and the roses put on their last show.

After a morning exploring the lovely gardens, take your pick of any number of other attractions. There is so much to do in Hershey that one day may not be enough. But you could tour the gardens during several blooming periods and try a different attraction after each garden visit. There's something for everyone—Hersheypark, Hershey Museum of American Life and Chocolate World.

Built in 1906 and redeveloped in 1971, Hersheypark is a multi-million dollar park with sections that represent different themes. Zoo America, the newest section of the park, exhibits plants and animals from five natural regions of the North American continent. The Everglades, the desert, the eastern forest, the western plains and mountains, and the Canadian evergreen forest are all represented.

America's past can be explored at the Hershey Museum of American Life. The history of one town's industrial growth is presented at Chocolate World, the free visitors' center for Hershey Foods Corporation. Here the story of chocolate from the tropical plantation to the finished product is told. The indoor tropical gardens include 50,000 trees, shrubs and exotic flowers. This is a marvelous setting in which to relax, enjoy a chocolate dessert and end your outing on a sweet note.

The Hershey Gardens are open from 9:00 A.M. to 5:00 P.M. in April, May, September, and October, and from 9:00 A.M. to 7:00 P.M. in June, July, and August. Admission is charged for the gardens, which are just south of the Hotel Hershey.

Directions: Take Beltway Exit 27 to I-95 north. Exit on I-695, the Baltimore Beltway. Then exit on Route 83 north to Harrisburg, Pennsylvania. Take Route 322 east to Hershey, Pennsylvania.

Longwood Gardens

Where would you expect to discover the finest garden estate in North America? In California or Florida? No. According to many experts, it is right off Route U.S. 1 in Kennett Square, Pennsylvania. Longwood Gardens is delightful year round.

Though Longwood is beautiful in any season, probably your best introduction to it would be in the spring. Along the main lake, flowering trees bend their blossom-laden limbs over their own reflections in the water. Tulips and daffodils are planted in profusion and the trails are banked with azaleas and rhododendron. In the conservatories additional azaleas and daffodils are mixed with flowers not commonly grown in this area or seen at this time of the year. A particular favorite are the delphiniums in varying shades of blues, purples and whites.

Water is a recurring theme throughout the outdoor gardens at Longwood. The main display in front of the conservatory groups six pairs of large fountains. From the center of each pair water shoots up 115 to 130 feet in the air. On Tuesday, Thursday and Sunday evenings at dusk from mid-June through August visitors enjoy a half-hour program featuring these fountains illuminated with lights in a rainbow of colors. The fountains spout up and down in tempo with musical selections. The display is as spectacular as fireworks, according to youngsters in the audience, and is considered one of the finest examples of illuminated fountains in the world.

The Italian Water Garden, copied from the Villa Gamberaia near Florence, Italy, is always fascinating. A water staircase and a rock cascade lead down to sets of fountains in tiled pools.

During the summer months concerts are also held at the Open Air Theatre, which has a six-foot-high water curtain as well as illuminated fountains.

A summer visit also gives you a chance to enjoy Longwood's roses. The walkway bordered with trellised roses is only one way in which the roses are displayed. Roses are best in June or September. Also worth noting are the wildflowers beside Longwood's waterfall. You can climb a stepping stone path through the hillside garden and across the top of the waterfall to the Chimes Tower. The Chimes Tower resembles a theatrical set and provides an appealing location for an overview of the garden.

The history of Longwood Gardens begins with the old Peirce House built in 1730 on land given to George Peirce in 1700 by William Penn. First called Peirce's Park, this estate was contemporary with George Washington's Mount Vernon and Thomas Jefferson's Monticello. During the American Revolution one of the opening skirmishes of the Battle of Brandywine occurred within earshot of Peirce's land. Later the estate would be a stop on the Underground Railway. In 1906 Pierre Samuel du Pont acquired the property as his country estate.

As early as 1921 the conservatories were open to the public. Now encompassing nearly four acres, they are one of Longwood's main attractions. Every week the display in the orchid room is changed; each display is unusual and special. Other permanent displays in the conservatories include the cacti in the Succulent House, the Rose Corridor, the Tropical Terrace Garden, the House Plant area, the unusual plant section and the Banana Collection.

In the main conservatory special seasonal displays are arranged. In November the chrysanthemums take over. The giant blooms will make backyard gardeners who shudder over fall frost reports green with envy. Some of the blossoms are as large as dinner plates. Spider mums, hanging baskets, pompon mums and exhibition mums all abound.

The conservatory also has a lovely Christmas display with a mass of poinsettia and flowering bulbs vying for attention. It's worth the drive just to walk in and smell the perfumed air. From January until March acacias, camellias and cymbidium orchids bloom. At Easter there is a special display. Every day of the year there is something to see at Longwood.

Longwood Gardens is open daily from 9:00 A.M. to 6:00 P.M. and until 5:00 P.M. November through March. The conservatories are open from 11:00 A.M. to 5:00 P.M. Admission is charged. Allow between one-and-a-half to three hours for your visit. To obtain information on special programs write Longwood Gardens, Kennett Square, Pennsylvania 19348.

Directions: Take Beltway Exit 27 to I-95 north. Continue to the Wilmington, Delaware, area. Exit on Route 141 north and continue to Route 52 north. Continue on Route 52 north to U.S. Route 1. Go left on U.S. 1 to Longwood Gardens.

Longwood Gardens Schedule of Flowering Dates

January–March	Acacias*
March–April	Amaryllis*
April–May	Azaleas*
January–April	Camellias*
November–December	Chrysanthemums*
Mid-December	Christmas Display*
March–April	Cymbidium Orchids*
Late April–May	Dogwood
Mid-March–April	Easter Display*
All Year	Orchids*
Mid-December	Poinsettia*
Mid-May	Rhododendron
June–October	Roses
February–April	Spring Flowers*
April–May	Spring Flowering Trees and Shrubs
February–March and June–October	Tuberous Begonias*
July–October	Water Lilies
April–October	Outdoor Gardens

*Conservatory display

The Winterthur Gardens

A formal garden juxtaposed with casual plantings of flowers along wooded trails, Winterthur Gardens offers the best of two worlds.

Though Winterthur's name may suggest otherwise, the best seasons in which to visit are the spring, summer or autumn. The gardens are open year round along with the Winterthur Museum. Plan your first visit for early May because the azaleas, dogwood and rhododendron make the woods seem like a fairyland.

Saucer and star magnolia, lilacs, cherries and crab apple blend their delicate colors with pastel azaleas. Along one of the wooded walks dogwood and Kurume azaleas create a wall of solid white. Winterthur is noted as one of the first gardens in North America to plant the Kurume azalea.

The Quarry Garden is one of 13 points of interest at Winterthur. Various wildflowers compete with a wide selection of primroses and daffodils nestled among the rocks.

This natural effect is evident throughout the 200-acre park. In the Pinetum, tall conifers vie with azaleas and rhododendron that flank a wide allée. The Sundial Garden, on the other hand, is a formal planting with a boxwood hedge border. Close to the Winterthur Museum is an enclosed Glade and Pool Garden that suggests 18th century France. Here, as in many of Winterthur's sections, benches provide a place to sit and enjoy the special charm of this secluded area. Bulbs, tree peonies, azaleas, dogwood and China snowballs are best enjoyed in the spring. Annuals and perennials highlight the summer garden. Autumn leaves add vibrancy to the garden and the red berries of the holly, along with the dogwood and viburnum, provide bright spots of color.

The two-and-a-half-mile tour through the garden is clearly marked, but you're welcome to digress and wander down the many meandering turf paths. Arrows will direct you to all the areas in the garden in bloom at the time of your visit. The route changes with the seasons.

Walking the grounds at Winterthur you are likely to spot a wide variety of birds who make their home in the diverse foliage. In the autumn the pond is often visited by flocks of migratory waterfowl.

This garden estate is essentially the creation of Henry Francis du Pont, who inherited it in 1927. Winterthur was named for the Swiss city where the original owner, du Pont's great-uncle, had once lived.

Winterthur Museum has 196 rooms and more than 71,000 objects that were made or used in America between 1640 and 1840. More than one visit is necessary to see all the treasures of Winterthur. One of the unreserved tours that can be taken is the Winterthur in Spring Tour, which runs from mid-April to early June. Visitors see 16 rooms normally viewed only by those with reservations, plus the 18 rooms in the American Sampler Tour that shows the decorative arts chronologically in America from the 17th century to the Empire period. A motorized tram is available to see the spring blossoms.

In summer, from late June through late September, Winterthur offers the gardens and American Sampler Tour. Autumn options begin with the Winterthur Country Fair the last Sunday in September and continue through mid-November. Offered are the American Sampler and the gardens. In the winter, tours are the same except that the motorized tram is not used in the gardens.

Visitors may want to write to reserve the two-hour guided tour offered from early January through early April and again from mid-June through mid-November. There are two versions of this tour for repeat visitors.

A seasonal celebration from late November through early January is Yuletide at Winterthur, which is also by reservation only. Holiday decorations enhance selected museum rooms.

Winterthur Museum and Gardens is open Tuesday through Saturday from 10:00 A.M. to 4:00 P.M. and on Sunday from Noon until 4:00 P.M.. Children under 12 are not admitted on the regular reserved tours. Children between 12 and 16 pay only half price admissions for reserved tours. Those under 12 are admitted without charge for all non-reserved tours. There are special rates for senior citizens, students over 12, and groups. To obtain additional information or arrange a tour, write Reservations Office, Winterthur Museum, Winterthur, Delaware 19735 or call (302)654-1548.

Directions: Take Beltway Exit 27 to I-95 north. Continue to Wilmington, Delaware. Go left, northwest, on Route 52. Winterthur is six miles from Wilmington on Route 52, between Greenville and Centreville.

Nemours

You don't have to go to France to experience the grandeur of the well-known garden masterpiece that is Versailles. A two-hour drive to the Wilmington, Delaware, area will bring you to America's version of Versailles: Nemours.

You may wonder at this transplanted French splendor. When Alfred I. du Pont began building his Louis XVI-style chateau on his 300-acre estate he wanted a garden that would complement the chateau. Thus the garden concepts of André Le Nôtre were used. His "grand design" at Versailles was a masterpiece. Le Nôtre felt that a garden should stretch in an unbroken vista and that the axis of the garden should be lined with trees or canals. Flowers played little role in Le Nôtre's design. When used, he felt they should be placed close to the house for the enjoyment of residents and guests. Water was, however, a major part of Le Nôtre's concept. At Versailles he included 14,000 fountain jets. Le Nôtre felt fountains added dignity and opulence to a garden. Though du Pont used his basic ideas at Nemours, the garden does violate one of Le Nôtre's basic principals: the view at Nemours is not continuous. It is broken at the huge colonnade midway down the main axis.

Du Pont surrounded his flamboyant estate with a high brick wall topped with broken glass to keep out intruders, "including the other du Ponts." It was not surprising, therefore, that when the gardens were opened for one day in 1932, even some family members paid the one dollar admission to see what their relative had been up to. Since 1977 Nemours has been open to the general public from May through November. Though the admission has gone up since 1932 it is well worth the fee. This garden is fantastic.

Just as Versailles is bigger than life, so is Nemours. Twelve lakes flow one into the other. The reflecting pool covers an entire acre and has 157 fountain jets. Everything including the sculpture and the columns is oversize.

In front of the colonnade that breaks the vista is the maze, though it is not a true maze as it has beds. Helleri and Canadian hemlock trimmed to six feet in a geometric pattern form this maze. At the center is the gilded statue *Achievement*. It certainly is a fitting touch to a garden estate that has to be considered an achievement by any measurement.

Past the colonnade is a sunken fountain garden. Here you will see the second focal point of the garden, the Temple of Love. Again, it is the design that is important, not the plants. But these are certainly not neglected. In the spring 58,000 tulip bulbs color the garden, and summer annuals and autumn chrysanthemums continue the show.

Towards the bottom of the garden a Children's Playhouse stands beside a small pond. Here garden gnomes create an incongruous note amid all the formality.

Before you get to the garden, which you explore on your own at your leisure, you will be conducted through the mansion itself. This 77-room chateau is furnished with American and European antiques. The stair is 17th century French wrought iron with a brass rail. The ceilings are decorated with 23-karat gold. A clock with a 19-pipe organ that was made for Marie Antoinette also is on display. Throughout the house you will see beautiful paintings, sculpture and tapestries.

A visit to Nemours must be prearranged, but it is certainly worth the effort. Tours are at 9:00 and 11:00 A.M. and 1:00 and 3:00 P.M. Tuesday through Saturday and at 11:00 A.M. and 1:00 and 3:00 P.M. on Sunday. To make reservations call (302)651-6914 or write the Nemours Foundation, Reservation Office, P.O. Box 109, Wilmington, Delaware 19899. No children under 16 are permitted on the tour.

Two other du Pont cousins have created equally exciting though quite different garden estates in this area. Nemours is only 10 minutes from Winterthur, the creation of Henry du Pont, and just a little ways past Winterthur is Pierre du Pont's Longwood Gardens. This is garden trilogy that is unequalled anywhere in the world.

Directions: Take Beltway Exit 27 to I-95 north. Continue to the Wilmington, Delaware, area. Exit on Route 202. Watch for signs to the Alfred I. du Pont Institute. Go west on Route 141 and turn left on Rockland Road. There is parking outside the gates on Rockland Road.

The Gardens at the Ambler Campus of Temple University

Though many gardening enthusiasts would heartily object to the very idea of getting a grade for their efforts, a large number of students enrolled in the Landscape Design and Horticulture Program at the Ambler Campus of Temple University do earn grades.

You don't have to enroll in the school to enjoy the gardens on campus. They are open to visitors daily without charge, although the greenhouses are closed on holidays. The peak bloom time for the gardens is from mid-May to mid-June.

The extensive gardens were designed in 1926. Since then many additional features have been added. One of the highlights of the gardens is the section of Japanese flowering cherries and English boxwood. A series of small garden areas has benches that provide the opportunity to just sit and enjoy the delights of each garden.

The Louise Stine Fisher Memorial Garden features dwarf shrubs. The central garden has four 80-foot flower borders planted with spring bulbs, perennials, biennials and annuals. Except during the winter months these borders are in bloom. Two smaller annual borders bloom from late June through the summer.

In addition to the formal garden a woodland trail is particularly appealing during the spring when flowering bulbs compete with natural wildflowers to add interest to your walk. A three-acre apple and peach orchard is another treat in the spring when it is in full flower or in the fall when the trees are loaded with fruit. The campus boasts a collection of more than 850 species and cultivars of woody plants.

The greenhouses at Ambler Campus are not large but you will find a selection of flowering plants year round. Foliage plants and vegetables are also cultivated.

Directions: Take Beltway Exit 27 to I-95 and go north to Philadelphia. At Philadelphia pick up the Route 309 Expressway. Exit at Susquehanna Road/Butler Pike. The Ambler Campus is on Meetinghouse Road between Butler Pike and Fort Washington Avenue.

Masonic Home's Garden

On 1,600 acres in Elizabethtown, Pennsylvania, the Freemasons operate a Masonic Home, where outside the Grand Lodge Hall, they have developed a lovely formal garden. Established between 1930 and 1933, the garden, winner of the Pennsylvania Garden Award in 1970, has matured and grown more lush in the 50 years since.

Laid out in a sweeping vista from the Grand Lodge Hall, the garden encompasses six and a half acres. Bordering the formal garden on both sides is an arboretum with a collection of rare and unusual trees.

Because roses are the specialty of the Masonic Home's Garden, summer is the season to visit. Twelve rose beds with more than 1,000 bushes offer a visually stunning variety of blossoms. In the area immediately in front of a large fountain, rose arbors flank a patterned walkway.

Annuals and perennials bloom throughout the summer in the 16 additional flower beds arranged throughout the garden greensward.

Water has an intricate part in the garden design. Above the large fountain there is a reflecting pool with water lilies and aquatic plants. Descending from the fountain area are two series of waterfalls.

The gardens are open daily at no charge but you need to check in at the administrative office before exploring the grounds.

Directions: Take Beltway Exit 27 to I-95 north. Exit onto I-695, the Baltimore Beltway, where you proceed to the I-83 exit. Follow I-83 north of York to the outskirts of Harrisburg. Exit eastward on I-76 and go south on Route 441 to Elizabethtown.

Specialty Gardens

Kenilworth Aquatic Garden

"Lotusland" may sound like an exotic, far away place; it really is quite near—in northeast Washington at the Kenilworth Aquatic Garden. But exotic it is. This 11-acre water wonderland has one of the most outstanding collections of its kind, more than 100,000 aquatic plants. The varieties of aquatic plants, and especially lilies, have been gathered from all parts of the world including Egypt, the Amazon, and Manchuria. There is even a Manchurian lotus that germinated from seeds 1,000 years old.

The large lily pads of a species found in the Amazon valley look like giant green stepping stones. Some are as large as six feet in diameter. If you walk quietly you are apt to spot frogs sunning themselves on these large pads and hear their croaking, which adds to the unusual ambience. Other inhabitants include turtles and even an occasional harmless snake.

The flowers, however, draw the visitors. Mid-June is the first peak bloom time, when approximately 70 varieties of day-blooming lilies can be seen. Included in this early show is a special lily, the "Louise," which costs more than $400 a plant.

The second high spot—and the one to pick if you can plan only one visit—is in late July and early August, when the lotuses bloom. Growing as tall as five to six feet, the lotus has blossoms as large as basketballs. You will rarely see flowers of this magnitude. If this isn't sufficient incentive for a visit, the night-blooming tropical lilies add their own beauty to the aquatic show. These lilies have deeper, more colorful blossoms than are customarily seen in water lilies. Their deep pink, dark blue, and purple flowers will amaze you.

Nothing else would be needed to ensure an enthusiastic return visit, but numerous other water plants can also be seen: water hyacinths, water poppies, rose mallow, water primroses, wild irises, bamboo, elephant ears, cattails, and umbrella ears, to name just some of the varieties.

Visitors often wonder how such an unusual garden came to be located at this out-of-the-way location. Contrary to what most people decide, it was not the federal government that developed this unique repository of the world's aquatic plants. It was Civil War veteran W. B. Shaw, who in 1882 planted the first water lilies here beside his home along the Anacostia River. He devoted himself to the water plants full time after his retirement. In 1912 his daughter, Helen Fowler, began managing the extensive collection. It wasn't until 1938 that the federal government purchased the gardens.

Though the gardens are open year round, the summer months are by far the best time to visit. Keep in mind, however, that some flowers in water lily gardens close during the heat of the day, so plan your visit for early morning. These same flowers reopen (along with the night flowers) in the evening, but then you have to confront the mosquitoes that inhabit any watery and marshy location. Even during afternoon visits you may want to apply an insect repellent. Hours for the Kenilworth Aquatic Gardens are 7:30 A.M. to 6:00 P.M., except during the summer months when the gardens are open until 8:00 P.M. There is no charge to visit.

Directions: Kenilworth Aquatic Gardens are located in northeast Washington. Once inside the Beltway, take Kenilworth Avenue south to Quarles Street. Bear right and cross the Eastern Avenue Overpass. Turn left onto Douglas Street and turn right for the gardens.

Franciscan Monastery Garden and Shrines

The Franciscan Monastery has an in-town Washington garden that recreates the shrines of Europe and the Holy Land. A stop here provides a welcome escape from the ordinary. Following the yellow of a springtime hillside of fresh daffodils come the reds, pinks, and soft hues of hundreds of roses.

The early spring tulip bulbs yield to Easter lilies. Adding to the color and fragrance of spring are dogwood, cherry, and tulip trees. April brings the gorgeous azaleas. Although best enjoyed in late May and June, the roses add color to the grounds throughout the entire summer. After wintering over in the greenhouses, more exotic perennials grace the garden during Washington's tropical summer months; hibiscuses, lantanas, giant caladiums, and even palms and bananas can be seen, amid the more common perennials. There are beautiful floral arrangements of religious symbols like the cross, the anchor, the heart, and the IHS.

You may well feel that you are indeed in the Mediterranean area when you see the replica of Jerusalem's Grotto of Gethsemane or of the French Grotto of Lourdes.

Don't limit your exploration to the garden alone; the monastery itself abounds with unusual features. Probably the most unusual are the underground catacombs, facsimiles of those that run for hundreds of miles beneath Rome. Burial niches and stone chapels suggest their use by persecuted Christians in ancient Rome.

Within the church, shrines of the Holy Lands are also recreated: the Grotto of the Nativity that is seen in Bethlehem as well as Mary's home in Nazareth. The monastery was built in 1898, copied after the early Franciscan monasteries in California. It was redecorated in 1949 and contains many murals and some excellent pieces of religious sculpture.

Beauty within and without make this site an inspiration regardless of your faith. The Franciscan Monastery's grounds are open daily from 8:30 A.M. to dusk. It is also open for guided tours from 8:30 A.M. to 4:00 P.M., Monday through Saturday, and from 1:00 P.M. to 4:30 P.M. on Sunday. Scheduled masses are also said in the monastery. For additional information call (202)526-6800.

Directions: The Franciscan Monastery is within the Washington, D.C. Beltway. It is located at 1400 Quincy Street in N.E., ten minutes' walk from the Brookland Metro Station and from the National Shrine of the Immaculate Conception.

Brighton Dam Azalea Garden

The largest collection of azaleas in Maryland—22,000 plants—is arranged in a lake-like setting, on the banks of Brighton Dam.

The first azaleas planted on this five-acre site came in 1949 from the Norfolk Azalea Gardens. Subsequent plants included the white Indicas from Belgium and southern India. Another import is the popular Kurume azalea that originated in Japan. The majority of the Brighton Dam plants are the multi-hued Kurume. The hardy Glen Dale azaleas were planted because they can withstand Washington's heat and the poor soil of this region.

Owned and maintained by the Washington Suburban Sanitary Commission, the garden is open at no charge during the azalea blooming, customarily from late April through May. If you can visit during the week, you can avoid the weekend crowds. There are paved walkways through the garden making it accessible to the handicapped. Benches provide the opportunity to rest while enjoying the vista.

To learn the peak blooming period call (301)699-4172. The gardens are open from 9:00 A.M. to 7:00 P.M. daily during azalea season.

Directions: Take Beltway Exit 28 to New Hampshire Avenue north (Route 650) through Colesville, Ashton, and Brinklow to Brighton Dam Road. Turn right on Brighton Dam Road and proceed for one mile. Parking is on the right and the garden entrance on the left.

Ladew Topiary Gardens

Rural Maryland has long been associated with hunting, and a drive into the countryside frequently offers pastoral vistas with sleek horses following hounds across green fields. But at the Ladew Topiary Gardens the horse and hounds are green! At what is "the most outstanding topiary garden" in the nation, this is just one of the whimsical delights.

Topiary is the art of trimming, cutting, and training trees or shrubs into ornamental shapes. The greens are trained into a wire frame and then clipped if they wander outside the patterned design. Topiary, fashionable in England since Tudor and Elizabethan times, is an art form ignored for the most part in the United States. Harvey S. Ladew was awarded the Distinguished Service Medal in 1971 by the Garden Clubs of America for his "interest in developing and maintaining the most outstanding topiary garden in America without professional help."

During the spring, summer, and autumn you will enjoy exploring this unusual spot. Fifteen unique flower gardens, each designed by Ladew himself on a special theme, surround the topiary figures and the stately topiary hedges. There is bloom in all seasons except winter. The paths at Ladew lead to delightful surprises from classical unicorns to a replica of Winston Churchill's top hat. A reindeer complete with antlers guards the front door and a dozen swans seem to ride rippling waves. Sea horses, lyre birds, a turtle, birds of paradise, and a poodle all join with the horse and hounds in this green menagerie.

The terrace gardens are arranged to look like outdoor living rooms, with the hemlock walls clipped in the shape of garlands and pyramids. But if you step through the green arches of the topiary hedges, you step into a flower garden. Pear trees have been espaliered around a rose garden that is particularly lovely during the summer months.

Harvey Ladew's whimsy is not confined to his topiary subjects; it abounds both on the grounds and in his rambling house, greatly enlarged from an 18th century farm house. For example, around one sundial are carved the words of Hilaire Belloc, "I am a sundial and I make a botch. Of what is done far better by a watch." Another source of amusement is the statue of Eve offering Adam an apple that is placed aptly in the apple orchard. The tea house, the facade of which once adorned the ticket booth at the Tivoli Theatre in London, is decorated with a picture frame around one of the clear windows overlooking the grounds.

The master of all this was a fascinating man who as a bachelor explored many unusual areas of the world and was a friend of a number of well-known figures. On an expedition in South America he had a new breed of mouse named after him. His desert adventures with the Bedouins recall one of his close friends, T. E. Lawrence, the man the world called Lawrence of Arabia. The Prince of Wales was another of his cronies both before and after the prince abdicated the throne. Framed notes from these notables decorate the walls.

One wall, however, was decorated by Ladew. In the dressing room used by his sister, Grace, he painted an entire wall, creating the illusion of a chest of drawers from which various pieces of lingerie dangled.

Always a man of wide vision, he built an oval library to accommodate a splendid oval desk when he discovered he had nowhere to put it. This room is considered one of the "100 Most Beautiful Rooms in America." A secret wall panel enabled Harvey to slip from library to card room.

When planning a visit, try for Wednesday or Sunday when both the house and gardens are open. These are the only two days you can explore the many delights of the house. The gardens are open Tuesday through Sunday mid-April through the end of October from 10:00 A.M. to 4:00 P.M., except Sundays when the hours are noon to 5:00 P.M. An admission is charged to tour the house and gardens.

Directions: Take Beltway Exit 27 to I-95 north to the Baltimore Beltway, I-695. Go left around the Beltway to Route 146 north. Continue about 14 miles to the Ladew Topiary Gardens 5 miles past Jacksonville. The address is 3535 Jarrettsville Pike, Route 146, Maryland.

Peony Hill at Seneca Creek State Park

What do you do if you have to move and you have 35,000 peonies planted on nine acres of your property? You sell it to the state as a park! That's what Mr. and Mrs. Albert L. Gloyd did with the land that became Seneca Creek State Park.

Near Gaithersburg, Maryland, this park is a floriferous "must" each year around Memorial Day. During the last two weeks in May through the first week in June these lovely peonies are in bloom—more than 250 varieties, both single and double.

The peonies, though the most spectacular, are not the only floral treats at Seneca. Keen-eyed hikers may also see rare wild orchids. In the spring the trail also surprises nature lovers with an assortment of wild flowers. The park's last distinction is less felicitous; it has the only earthquake faultline in Maryland.

Seneca Creek State Park encompasses 4,500 acres and follows Seneca Creek for about 12 miles. Once, as far back as 10,000 B.C., prehistoric man roamed this part of Maryland. The site of the oldest Indian dwelling in Maryland is in Seneca Creek State Park.

The park is open from 9:00 A.M. to 6:00 P.M. daily but budget cuts necessitate closing part of the park at times. Call (301)974-1249 to make certain the peony area, which is sometimes closed because of limited funding, is open.

Directions: Take Beltway Exit 35 to I-270 towards Rockville. Use the National Bureau of Standards-Darnestown exit and go west on Route 124 to the traffic light at Clopper Road and turn right. Continue for a short distance to the park.

Maymont Park Public Gardens

Maymont, a many-splendored park in the middle of Richmond, draws half a million visitors each year. Why not find out why?

The grounds of Maymont, the country estate of the Dooley family in the late 1800s, imitate English pastoral landscaping popular at that time although Italian and Japanese influences are evident. It wasn't until 1925 that the estate became a 105-acre public park.

The Dooleys built their neo-Romanesque house here in 1890. Its 33 rooms with their ornate furnishings exemplify the Gilded Age. You can tour this old mansion and marvel at the famed swan bed, the huge tapestries, and exquisite porcelain.

Between 1907 and 1912 the Dooley family added another elegant note to the estate—the Italian Gardens. Overlooking the James River, this Italian Renaissance Garden has three tiers. The first walled terrace has a pool at one end and a fountain at the other. A wisteria-covered pergola adds a picturesque point of interest. The second level terrace is called the promenade and the third is the hidden, or secret, garden. This conceit was based on a garden that the Dooleys had enjoyed on a visit to Sorrento,

Italy. On many spring and summer weekends weddings are held in the Italian Garden. During mid-summer it is abloom with roses, gaillardias, dahlias, and candytuft.

At the time the Dooleys were adding an Italian note to the estate they were also working on the even larger Japanese Garden. Laid out over seven acres, this garden, like the Italian terrace, uses water in its design. A waterfall, streams, and stone basins add the sight and sound of water that are so much a part of the classical Japanese landscape. Here the undulating walkways, arch bridges and stone lanterns contribute to an atmosphere of serenity. The objective of the Japanese approach to gardening is to achieve a unity with nature. A quiet stroll through Maymont's Japanese Garden makes that readily apparent. In April the azaleas and Kwanzan cherries make the garden particularly appealing.

Two other specialty gardens are the Herb Garden with its boxwood hedging, best enjoyed in mid-summer, and the hillside Wildflower Collection still being developed, best seen in the spring.

Though well worth a visit for these gardens alone, Maymont offers much more. The extensive collection of 222 kinds of trees and shrubs makes it an arboretum. With the addition of native and herbaceous plants and wildflowers the total number of plants at Maymont reaches 500.

Also there is a children's farm and seven outdoor habitats presenting native American wildlife in a natural setting. Focal areas include the bear and otter habitat; the bison area; the deer and elk section; the aviary and waterfowl pond; the Thalhimer Small Animal Habitat with skunks, opossums, raccoons, foxes, beavers, and groundhogs in residence.

Because there is so much to see and do at Maymont, a visitor's information center is located in the Fountain Court area. This court is surrounded by three unusual exhibits. The Parsons Nature Center includes a variety of ecosystems in Virginia, from the mountain regions to the Atlantic coast area. Indoor habitats demonstrate how animals coexist with their environment. Another very popular area is the Carriage House with its collection of horse drawn vehicles. On Sundays, except during January and February or when the weather is bad, carriage rides are available from 1:00 P.M. to 5:00 P.M. for a fee.

Finally, the Mews Gallery and Gift Shop has a series of art exhibits and offers a selection of inexpensive and unusual gifts reflecting both the influence of nature and the Victorian-Edwardian period of the Dooley mansion.

Guided tours of Maymont Park are available at no charge Tuesday through Sunday on the half hour beginning at the Dooley mansion. One can purchase a self-guided walking tour map that outlines four walks: the Tree, Historic, Animal, and Garden walks. Allow yourself plenty of time to experience all the attractions of this special park.

Maymont is open daily at 10:00 A.M. at no charge. From April through October, it closes at 7:00 P.M., from November to March, at 5:00 P.M. The mansion, carriage house, and nature center all open at noon on weekends.

Directions: Take Beltway Exit 4, I-95 south to Richmond. Exit on Boulevard, Route 161, south to Columbus Statue. Go left at the statue and follow Maymont signs through Byrd Park to Hampton parking area.

Bryan Park Azalea Garden

The development of Richmond's Bryan Park Azalea Garden reveals three characteristics common to most gardens. The first, that "out of small beginnings greater things have been produced . . . "is so very true of this garden. What gardener hasn't faced the need for yet another flower bed? At Bryan Park officials in 1952 wanted to fill an unsightly swampy area with cuttings from azaleas planted at Forest Hill Park, another Richmond garden. Today more than 45,000 plants, encompassing more than 50 varieties, make the garden one of Richmond's major attractions in the spring.

The second characteristic is the inbred quality of gardens. Many of the east coast gardens are related to one another. The azaleas for Forest Hill Park were given to Richmond by the City of Norfolk, whose Botanical Gardens boast such a delightful array. Norfolk also contributed to the collection at Brighton Dam Azalea Garden in Maryland.

The third characteristic is that gardens are so often a labor of love. Bryan Park Azalea Garden certainly exemplifies this notion. In creating it, Robert E. Harvey, a park superintendent, and his 90-man crew worked many hours overtime. Roughly 40 percent of the work was volunteered by these enthusiasts. On their own time the men canvassed Richmond neighborhoods to acquire azalea cuttings for their new project.

Bryan Park's focal point is a small lake covering the former swamp. A spray fountain adds an appealing note, as does the rustic redwood footbridge over the small stream that meanders through the 17-acre park.

Dogwoods serve as a backdrop for the colorful azaleas. One special area has a huge cross formed by snow white azaleas and outlined by red Hinodegiri azaleas. It is particularly appropriate when the blooming coincides with the Easter holiday.

The Bryan Park Azalea Garden is best seen from mid-April to about mid-May. Normally the best display is during the last two weeks in April. There is no charge to visit this park. An advantage of this park is that automobiles can drive through it, enabling the elderly who have difficulty in walking to enjoy the beautiful flowers. Paths, of course, provide walkers with a closer look.

Directions: Take Beltway Exit 4, I-95 south, to Richmond. Use Exit 15A, Hermitage Road. Make a left at Hermitage Road and continue on Hermitage to Bellevue Street. Make a right on Bellevue, which will take you directly to Bryan Park.

Norfolk Botanical Gardens

Drifting canal boats and meandering trackless trains offer a novel way to explore the many flowering areas that are a part of Norfolk Botanical Gardens. Thirty-minute rides by either or both provide a chance for the non-walker to enjoy a garden outing. Walkways do, however, give you a chance to spend additional time in the more than 20 different areas of interest.

One of the most popular features of the garden is the extensive azalea display in April and early May. From a small 4,000 bush collection planted as a WPA project in 1936 the azalea section today includes more than 200,000 plants. It is a must for azalea lovers; and, in fact, is likely to convert all visitors to that specialty. The juxtaposition of these brilliantly colored flowers and the quiet inland water tributaries is delightful. Each year since 1954 during the third week in April Norfolk hosts the International Azalea Festival to salute the North Atlantic Treaty Organization.

Two areas at Norfolk are set aside exclusively for the azalea collections. Many familiar varieties can be recognized among the nearly 250,000 plants: Kurume hybrids, Mollis, Perricats, Satsuke, and Southern Indian hybrids, to name just a few.

Another major focus of interest at the Norfolk Botanical Gardens is the camellia display. One of the best collections in the country, it includes more than 700 varieties of camellias blooming from September through April. In mid-March there is an annual Camellia Show.

Gaining national recognition is the recently completed Bicentennial Rose Garden, a seven-year project that won an award for the most outstanding rose garden in the mid-Atlantic states. More than 4,000 rose plants representing about 250 varieties bloom from mid-May through October. Fountains, overlooks, a sculpture garden, and a pedestrian terrace all add to the charm of this garden.

Other gardens here include a Sunken Garden, Lone Pine Garden, Colonial Garden, Desert Garden, Annarino Bog Garden, Japanese Garden, and Fragrance Garden. The last two warrant further mention. The Japanese Garden was added in 1962 to honor Norfolk's sister city, Moji, Japan. Laid out in the classic Japanese hill-and-pond design, it uses water and dry lakes to highlight the traditional plantings: Japanese black pine, crape myrtle, Hankow willow, Japanese red maple, Kurume azaleas, flowering cherry, and the ginkgo plant.

The Fragrance Garden has been included so that Norfolk Botanical Gardens will be more accessible to the handicapped. Plants noted for their sensory appeal—lavender, peppermint, bayberry, osmanthus, Daphne Odora, pussy willow, witch hazel, and loquat—are all part of this special area. Ramp entrances, braille markers, and handrails accommodate the visually impaired and those confined to wheelchairs.

The Flowering Arboretum forms a 17½-acre focal point for the flowering trees donated to the garden as living memorials to deceased family and friends.

Sportsminded visitors may want to take advantage of the opportunity to fish at one of the two scenic fishing piers within Norfolk Botanical Gardens. Senior citizens and those under 16 can fish without a license; all others must get a city fishing permit.

Don't miss the chance to climb to the top of the Hill of Nations Observatory Tower, where you can get a bird's eye view of this 175-acre garden. Though not strictly a floral feature, the Statuary Vista, with its 11 large Carrara marble statues of pre-20th century sculptors, is very striking. It was originally commissioned by William Wilson Corcoran, founder of the Corcoran Art Gallery.

Norfolk Botanical Gardens is open daily from 8:30A.M. until sunset. Admission is charged. There is something in bloom year round. The Administration Building doesn't open until 10:00 A.M. on weekends. The boats and trains only operate from mid-March to October. There is an additional charge for the 30-minute rides.

Directions: From the Beltway take Exit 4 to I-95 south to the Richmond By-Pass, Route 295. Then go east on Route 64 to Norfolk. The Norfolk Botanical Gardens are off Route 170 on Azalea Garden Road.

Norfolk Botanical Garden Schedule of Flowering Dates

January–February	Sasanqua Camellias
	Witch Hazel
	Wintersweet
	Nandina
	Pyracantha
March	Camellias
	Daffodils
	Pieris Japonica
	Magnolias
April	Tulips
	Azaleas
	Dogwoods
May	Rhododendron
	Foxglove
	Roses
June	Oleander
	Hydrangea
	Day Lilies
	Roses
July	Crape Myrtles
	Annuals
August–September	Annuals
October–December	Camellias
	Wintersweet

Presby Memorial Iris Gardens

If you aren't an "Irisarian" you may become one after visiting Presby Memorial Iris Gardens in Upper Montclair, New Jersey.

Iris growers, or irisarians, from three continents have contributed to this garden that honors the founder of the American Iris Society, Frank H. Presby. Now more than 50 years old, the garden is considered unsurpassed in its presentation of the iris in its myriad varieties. It is the most complete collection of irises in the world, with varieties assembled from as early as 1500 A.D. right up to the latest hybrids of today. Public gardens in the United States and Europe have obtained iris stock from Presby.

This award-winning garden is best seen from the last two weeks of May into the first week of June. As many as 3,000 well-marked varieties bloom at this time, including the tall-bearded iris, the predominant variety in the collection. This species of iris is one of the few flowers that run the gamut from white through the color spectrum to midnight blue-black. Hostesses are on hand during this peak period to provide additional information on the more obscure varieties.

Some irises do bloom earlier, including the Remontant, which blooms in the spring and again in the fall. Also, an assortment of the original species, which was the native plant before horticulturists began cross-breeding, blooms as early as March.

In late April the dwarf iris varieties are in bloom. From this time on, irises growing in several sizes between the dwarf and the tall-bearded iris bloom in succession. The display tapers off in late June but the Louisiana, Spuria, and Japanese varieties can still be enjoyed.

No irises are sold at Presby, but during the blooming season various catalogs, supplied by iris growers, are available for those inspired by their visit to this unique display.

Although the Presby Memorial Iris Gardens are open at no charge year round, a visit should be planned for the blooming season.

Directions: The Presby Memorial Iris Gardens are located in New Jersey just north of Newark. From the Beltway take Exit 27 to I-95 north and go across the Delaware Memorial Bridge at Wilmington to the New Jersey Turnpike. At the intersection of the Garden State Parkway, take the Parkway north to the Montclair exit. The gardens are in Upper Montclair at 474 Upper Mountain Avenue.

Bible Gardens

Eleanor Roosevelt at the dedication of the Bible Gardens in Woodbridge, New Jersey, on June 2, 1957 said: "These Gardens will be of great interest to all people, of all faiths, who really care for the Bible. . . . I hope that in this country many young people, and many older people, will come here for inspiration to bring again vividly before them the history of their religious beliefs."

Thousands have come since that opening to see this unique garden established to acquaint visitors with the natural world of the Bible. In the four individual gardens—The Garden of the Promised Land, the Garden of Moses, The Garden of Jerusalem, and the Garden of the Kings—the visitor will find plants, trees, flowers, and shrubs that are mentioned in the Bible but rarely seen and certainly never before arranged in this manner.

This is not an ordinary garden with thousands of blooms; rather, here one discerns a quiet beauty that comes from sensing the enduring quality of these plants that grew in ancient days in the Holy Lands.

In the Garden of the Promised Land, the border walks are embedded with pebbles from the southernmost point of Israel. A cypress tree, such as the one from which Noah was instructed to build an ark, and an acacia, such as was used to build the Ark of the Tabernacle, are included in this section. Tamarisk, an oriental plane-tree, dates, pistachios, myrtle, cedar, olives, figs, pomegranate, and palm are all planted with the biblical reference noted. Pebbles and boulders from the Red Sea, Elath, Mt. Canaan, the Wilderness of Zen, Galatia, and the River Jordan all evoke the stories of the Bible.

Dominating the Garden of Moses is a massive wrought iron sculpture designed against a boulder from Mount Carmel. Moses is represented holding aloft the Tablets of the Law engraved with the Ten Commandments. Here you will see the plants that are mentioned in the life of this great prophet: the familiar oak, willow, and lily plus the unfamiliar almond, bullrush, manna, and a burning bush. They combine to tell the story of Moses. Water-worn stones from the Red Sea could be the very ones over which Moses walked.

The Garden of Jerusalem is also called The Garden of Peace. Plants that have been biblically and traditionally associated with peace are planted here, including the olive tree, apricot, fig, palm, and cedar. Benches carved from marble quarried in Jerusalem provide the visitor with a chance to sit and reflect on the history encompassed in these plants of ancient origin.

Finally there is the Garden of the Kings. Plants in this section suggest the stories of Israel's first kings: The tamarisk tree such as the one King Saul was buried beneath; the mulberry tree whose rustling leaves urged King David to go out into battle against the Philistines; the pomegranate used by King Solomon as a design for the Holy Temple.

Although it includes flowers found in the Holy Land like narcissus, lilies, anemones, hyacinth, irises, and the tulipa sharonicisis or "rose of sharon," the Bible Garden is noted principally for trees, shrubs, and rocks.

Towering over the garden area is a 25-foot high marble arch. The central portion is carved from rock quarried from the top of Mount Carmel and contains a Bronze Map Portrait of Ancient Israel.

The Bible Gardens of Beth Israel Memorial Park are open daily, except Saturday, from 9:00 A.M. to 4:30 P.M.. It is closed on legal and Jewish holidays.

Directions: Take Beltway Exit 27 to I-95 north to the Wilmington area. Cross the Delaware Memorial Bridge and take the New Jersey Turnpike north to Woodbridge, New Jersey. The gardens are off U.S. 1 in Woodbridge.

Fairmount Park

Fairmount Park in Philadelphia should be thoroughly explored. In its 8,000 acres, which makes it the largest city-owned park in the country, there is great diversity and appeal. Fairmount Park contains the Philadelphia Zoological Gardens, the Philadelphia Museum of Art, a number of historic homes, plus more cherry blossoms than all of Washington, D.C.

The greenhouses of the park's Horticultural Center supply the plants for the city's public areas. The center, floriferous year round, has special seasonal exhibitions: the Christmas poinsettia show, the pre-Easter spring display, and the autumn chrysanthemum spectacular.

Park land was acquired in 1873 as part of a large area planned as a zoological park. Many of the plants were planted by John

Penn in 1785, almost 90 years before the animals were added. Animals are presented in a 42-acre natural setting. It is interesting to note the substitution of local plants that bear a resemblance to vegetation found in the animals' home environments. For example, pampas grass is used in place of the African grasses and locust, for African acacia.

In addition to a variety of art in the Philadelphia Museum of Art, you'll see sculpture throughout the park. There are 200 pieces including works by such world renowned sculptors as Alexander Calder, Auguste Rodin, and Frederic Remington.

If a major zoo and art museum seem more than enough incentive to warrant a visit to Fairmount Park, wait until you see the ten historic houses within the park. The homes of noted Philadelphians of the 18th century have been restored and can be toured, including Solitude, the home of John Penn, grandson of the colony's founder. George Washington and Benjamin Franklin were guests at this architecturally and historically important house. Features to note in touring Solitude are the intricately carved moldings, the detailed ceiling plasterwork, and the craftsmanship of the handwrought railings. Other houses are Lemon Hill, Mount Pleasant, Laurel Hill, Woodford, Strawberry Mansion, Cedar Grove, Sweetbriar, Hatfield House, and the Letitia Street House. Each has its own charm and historic significance.

The Fairmount Park Trolley stops at these houses. You can get a ticket that will allow you to get on and off to visit them. Though all the houses are open, they are not all open every day. For details, call (215)568-6599.

Another very popular park feature is the Japanese House and Garden. This reconstruction of a 17th century Japanese scholar's house was given to the city in 1954 by the American-Japan Society. The gardens are designed to be viewed from the house. The landscaping represents in miniature the mountains, rivers, waterfalls, and forests of Japan.

Fairmount Park is open year round, though the Horticultural Center is closed on major holidays. Admission is charged to all the historic houses and to the Zoological Park.

Directions: Take Beltway Exit 27 to I-95 north. Follow I-95 into Philadelphia until it becomes Front Street. Continue to Route 30, Vine Street Expressway, and go left until you reach the Benjamin Franklin Parkway, where you will go left and proceed to Fairmount Park.

Gardens of Colonial Park

New Jersey's largest All-American Rose Selections (AARS) garden is the Rudolf W. van der Goot Rose Garden in Colonial Park. Named in honor of the park commission's first chief horticulturist, this one-acre garden contains more than 4,000 bushes and includes 275 different species. Award winning roses are exhibited here a year before they are available for the general public.

Dedicated to public education, the garden identifies all the roses and relates historical significance where applicable. Thousands of visitors enjoy the season, from June through October. The garden is open at no charge from 10:00 A.M. to 8:00 P.M. daily. After Labor Day the garden closes at 4:30 P.M.

At the western end of this rose garden is the Fragrance and Sensory Garden. In this oval, sunken garden 80 varieties of annuals, herbs, perennials, flowering shrubs, and vines noted for their appealing smell or unusual texture are located. This garden has been carefully arranged and is barrier free. Wide ramps make it accessible to wheel chairs. Braille labels and guide rails aid those whose vision is impaired. Redwood benches provide an opportunity to rest and enjoy the potent intermingling of fragrances. This garden is open at the same times as the rose garden.

In conjunction with the two specialty gardens, an arboretum is open year round. Featured are trees and shrubs that do well in the New Jersey area including specie roses, dwarf conifers, lilacs, flowering cherries, viburnums, forsythia, spiraea, buddleia, and numerous shade and flowering trees.

Directions: Take Beltway Exit 27 to I-95 north of Philadelphia. Take U.S. 1 north to Route 287. Exit onto Canal Road, then left again on Weston Road followed by a right on Mettlers Road, which leads into Colonial Park, just outside Millstone, New Jersey.

Arboretums

The United States National Arboretum

How fortunate residents of the Washington area are to have available so many museums, galleries, theaters, monuments, and other sites of special interest supported by federal taxes. In the field of horticulture alone there are the Botanical Gardens, the Aquatic Gardens, the White House Gardens, and probably the most splendid and diversified of all—the United States National Arboretum.

Exciting though this arboretum is year round, mid-spring is its most floriferous season. The more than 70,000 blooming azaleas create a fairyland of flowers banking the paths through wooded hillsides of Mt. Hamilton. Although no picking of flowers is allowed, visitors often pick up fallen blossoms and thread them into leis, a sight that seems to fit this floral paradise.

Combined with the azaleas are the rhododenron, many of which come into bloom at the same time. They are both of the genus rhododendron, although early classifications incorrectly grouped the deciduous, or leaf-shedding species, into the genus azalea and the evergreen species into the genus rhododendron.

Other spring blossoms to be enjoyed at the same time are the flowering dogwoods, crab apples, ornamental cherries, camellias, Japanese quince, the saucer and star magnolias, and tree peonies.

Earlier in the season you can enjoy the somewhat uncertain camellia season. Several severe winters, however, have inflicted considerable damage on this once outstanding collection. First planted in 1949, the original 100 camellia sasanqua plants did so well that the arboretum expanded to 600 varieties, providing a wide-ranging spectrum of this lovely flower. Unfortunately many did not survive.

Another popular, early spring outing is to visit the Arboretum's daffodil collection alongside Fern Valley. Each year the Washington Daffodil Society presents a show in April at the Arboretum. Call ahead and plan your visit to see both the indoor and outdoor exhibits. The Fern Valley Trail includes many native American trees, shrubs, and wildflowers that also bloom in the spring.

The Fern Valley Trail can be divided into three sections, each containing groupings called plant associations because they are found in the same type of environment. The upper valley has a wooded area typical of the northeastern part of the U.S. Here you will see hemlock, white pine, wintergreen, partridge berry, and a variety of ferns and wildflowers.

The midvalley section has plant associations common to the deciduous woodland of the Piedmont area. Chestnut trees, mountain laurel, tulip trees, native rhododendron, tupelo, and mayapples are found here.

Descending to the lower valley, you will see a collection of plants found in the mountains of North Carolina. There are rhododendron, azaleas, sandmyrtle, wandflower, Oconeebells, and blueberries.

June is a good time to enjoy the roses in the National Herb Garden. (See Herb Garden Chapter.) You can also see day lilies, water lilies, Chinese dogwood, viburnum, magnolias, and some late blooming rhododendron. Summer is the best time to see the myriad of exotic and familiar plants that make up the various collections of the herb garden as well as the collection of water lilies and other aquatic plants found adjacent to the administration building.

Truly, each season has its own specialties at the Arboretum. A winter respite can be yours if you visit two garden areas: the Holly Collection and the Gotelli Dwarf Conifer Collection. The bright red fruit and glossy leaves look particularly appealing against the austere white of a winter snowscape. Carefully labeled, this collection includes the six principal groups of holly.

Finally, the noteworthy Gotelli Collection of Dwarf and Slow-Growing Conifers is one of the most outstanding collections of its kind in the world. Donated to the Arboretum in 1962, this collection contains more than 1,500 specimens representing 30 genera. Fir, cedar, false cypress, juniper, spruce, pine, yew, arborvitae, and hemlock are just some of the species included in the display. These conifers, surrounded by a mulch of crushed blue stones, are arranged in attractive mixtures. It makes an eye-pleasing display at any time of the year.

The 444-acre National Arboretum is open daily, except Christmas, at no charge from 8:00 A.M. to 5:00 P.M. on weekdays and from 10:00 A.M. to 5:00 P.M. on weekends. The Bonsai Collection (see Japanese Garden Chapter) is open from 10:00 A.M. to 2:30 P.M.

In addition to the Daffodil Show in April, many Washington area garden clubs hold their annual shows here. Call the Arboretum for monthly calendars. Other special programs of an educational nature, as well as guided walks, are planned throughout the year. For information call (202)475-4816.

Directions: The National Arboretum is inside the Beltway at 3501 New York Avenue, N.E., Washington, D.C. There is an entrance from New York Avenue and another from Bladensburg Road.

The National Arboretum Schedule of Flowering Dates

January–February	Conifers Witch Hazel
Second Week of March	Winter Hazel
Third Week of March	Japanese Camellias Pieris Japonica Winter Jasmine
Fourth Week of March	Japanese Camellias Pussy Willows
First and Second Weeks of April	Cornus Mas Crocus Daffodils Early Magnolias Forsythia Japanese Camellias Pieris Japonica Rhododendron Mucronulatum Wildflowers
Third Week of April	Azaleas Callery Pear Daffodils Early Crab Apples Forsythia Flowering Cherries Japanese Camellias Japanese Quince Magnolias Pieris Japonica Tulips Wildflowers
Fourth Week of April	Crab Apples Daffodils Early Azaleas Early Rhododendron Japanese Quince Magnolias Violets Wildflowers

Fifth Week of April	Azaleas Crab Apples Early Rhododendron Flowering Dogwood Japanese Quince Late Camellias Late Ornamental Cherries Magnolias (Soulangiana varieties) Tree Peonies Wildflowers
First Week of May	Azaleas Doublefile Viburnum Flowering Dogwood Peonies Rhododendron Tree Peonies Wildflowers
Second Week of May	Black Locust Chinese Dogwood Late Azaleas Magnolia Virginiana Peonies Rhododendron Tulip Trees Wildflowers
Third Week of May	Chinese Dogwood Late Azaleas Magnolia Grandiflora Magnolia Macrophylla Mountain Laurel Peonies Rhododendron
Fourth Week of May	Chinese Dogwood Day Lilies Lilies Magnolia Grandiflora Magnolia Virginiana Mountain Laurel

First Week of June	Chinese Dogwood Day Lilies Fringetree Lilies Magnolia Grandiflora Pyracantha Rhododendron Southern Catalpa Viburnum Dentatum Water Lilies
Second Week of June	Day Lilies Koelreuteria Linden Viburnum Mountain Laurel Rhododendron Maximum
July	Boxwood Conifers Day Lilies Hibiscus Water Lilies
August	Boxwood Conifers Crape Myrtle Hibiscus Water Lilies
September	Boxwood Colchicum Crape Myrtle Hibiscus Pyracantha Viburnum in Fruit Water Lilies
October	Boxwood Camellia Sasanqua Colchicum Conifers Crape Myrtle Dogwood in Fruit Fall Foliage Hibiscus Pyracantha Viburnum in Fruit Water Lilies

November	Camellia Sasanqua Conifers Dogwood Fall Foliage Pine Cones Viburnum in Fruit
December	Conifers Holly in Fruit Nandina in Fruit Pine Cones

The Orland E. White Research Arboretum

Two hundred years before Christ was born, Cicero quoted an old Roman as saying, "He planted trees to benefit another generation." Such wisdom still serves as the rationale for most arboretums, but none more than the Orland E. White Research Arboretum in Boyce, Virginia.

The transition from experimental farm to a full fledged arboretum occurred when Dr. White, who directed the facility for the University of Virginia from 1927 until 1955 realized that the plants sent to the research center for genetic research needed to be systematically planted. The organized collections now cover in excess of 100 acres of the 700-acre Blandy Experimental Farm.

Fifty botanical families are represented in the collection of conifers, woody trees, and shrubs. An herb garden and a boxwood garden are highlights of the plantings which include representatives of such diverse families as the rose family, the pea family, the olive family and the magnolia family.

The gardens are open year round but late April is a good time to catch the flowering trees in bloom. During the summer months iris, day lilies, roses, and asters add color to the gardens.

Before exploring the grounds, all visitors are asked to check in at the "Quarters" to obtain information on the Blandy Experimental Farm and the Orland E. White Arboretum. A small map is available. The grounds are open from sunrise to sunset daily.

Directions: Take Beltway Exit 9 to Route I-66 west. Exit onto Route 50 west. The main entrance to the arboretum is located on Route 50 near Boyce, Virginia, 4 miles west of the Shenandoah River Bridge, in Clarke County.

The Morris Arboretum

In 1887 John Morris and his sister Lydia purchased a 175-acre section of Penn's Woods, though by the 1800s it was called Chestnut Hill. The Morrises' interest in horticulture prompted them to expand the sylvan setting with specimen trees from all over the world.

An area of particular interest to the Morrises was the Orient. During their trip in 1887 and from the subsequent collecting expeditions of E. H. White, they were able to obtain a great number of plants rarely seen in this country. The Dawn Redwoods, thought to be extinct, were brought back from China in the 1940s. On their trip the Morrises engaged a Japanese gardener and a landscape designer who returned to Philadelphia with them. With the help of these experts they created an authentic Japanese garden.

In addition to the Oriental influence the English style is evident at the Morris Arboretum. Sections of the arboretum, like the English Park, recreate the English landscape. Sweeping vistas, elaborate water displays, the Mercury Pavilion, and the Swan Arch Overlook are intriguing features of this area.

A tropical Victorian fernery, built by John Morris in 1900, is one of the first controlled-environment structures ever built. Although one of the leading greenhouse firms of the day, Lord and Burnham, said his design for an external support system wasn't feasible, John Morris believed in his concept and built the greenhouse on his own.

After her brother's death in 1915, Lydia continued the development and expansion of the family project. One of her first additions was a formal rose garden. Here roses are set in a parterre arrangement with balustrade and fountain providing a scenic backdrop. Also in this section of the arboretum is a rock wall, where colorful spring flowers can be found in profusion.

Spring is a popular time to visit the Morris Arboretum. Azalea Meadow and Magnolia Slope provide visual delights as does a stop at Love Temple with its flowering trees in the background and the reflection of this classic structure in the water of Swan

Pond. The latter has challenged more than one amateur photographer.

In 1932, when Lydia Morris died, the arboretum was bequeathed to the University of Pennsylvania for research and education as well as for public enjoyment. During the 1930s many generic collections were added to contribute to the University's botanical research program. You will see hollies, viburniums, maples, heath, and heather displays that were added during this period.

The Morris Arboretum is open daily 10:00 A.M. to 5:00 P.M., except from November through March, when it closes at 4:00 P.M. It is closed Christmas Day and New Year's Day. Admission is $2.00 for adults and $1.00 for children. On Saturday and Sunday at 2:00 P.M. tours of the arboretum are conducted.

Though the arboretum is open year round, the peak blooming period is April through July. The best time for the fall foliage is during October and November. The Morris Arboretum is located on Hillcrest Avenue between Germantown Avenue and Stenton Avenue in the Chestnut Hill section of Philadelphia.

Directions: Take Beltway Exit 27 to I-95 north to Philadelphia. From I-95 take Route 291, Broad Street. Turn left at Stenton Street and proceed to the Morris Arboretum.

The Tyler Arboretum

The enduring fascination of giant trees is an experience not limited to the West Coast where they are so abundant. They can also be seen at The Tyler Arboretum in Lima, Pennsylvania. A giant sequoia planted there between 1856 and 1860 now stands over 65 feet tall and has a circumference of nine feet.

This is just one of the thousands of fascinating trees planted by Minshall and Jacob Painter below their manor house built in 1738. Among the variety of trees planted by the two brothers between 1830 and 1875 are a multi-trunked ginkgo, a cedar-of-Lebanon, a huge tulip tree and a 100-foot-tall bald cypress.

While exploring the 20 miles of hiking trails through some 700 acres of Pennsylvania countryside, the visitor might reflect that often when man interferes or tampers with nature it is to the detriment of the natural environment. The Tyler Arboretum, however, blends the areas where nature is in a pristine state with places where nature has been enhanced. The natural beauty of the woodland streams—Rocky Run and Dismal Run—can be enjoyed as they flow for long periods alongside the hiking trails. One hillside, called Pink Hill, is so completely covered in May with mountain phlox that it almost shimmers.

Other sections reveal the subtle hand of the landscape designer. The addition of magnolias, dogwood, rhododendron, azaleas, tree peonies, crab apples, cherries, and thousands of bulbs lends a special spring charm to the arboretum.

Other areas of interest include the Pinetum and the Fragrant Garden. The 25-acre Pinetum includes a collection of dwarf conifers and other cone-bearing trees. Plants with sensory appeal create a Fragrant Garden for the visually handicapped.

More than 4,000 plants and trees make up this historic arboretum. Roughly 380 species of native southeastern Pennsylvania plants are part of the vast collection.

The Tyler Arboretum adjoins the Ridley Creek State Park, where you can picnic and also explore the Colonial Pennsylvania Plantation (see chapter on farms).

The arboretum is open at no charge from 8:00 A.M. until dusk. The bookstore and gift shop are open from 9:00 A.M. until 4:00 P.M. The historic buildings at the Tyler Arboretum are open only on Sundays from 2:00 P.M. to 5:00 P.M., April through October and by special arrangement for groups. Phone: (215) 566-5431.

Directions: Take Beltway Exit 27 to I-95 north and proceed to the Wilmington, Delaware, area. Then take the Route 452 exit, which becomes Route 352 after crossing U.S. 1. Continue to Lima, where the Arboretum is at 515 Painter Road.

Reeves Reed Arboretum

Arboretums customarily provide botanical and horticultural sights. At Reeves Reed Arboretum in Summit, New Jersey, however, there is much more, including a number of interesting geological formations, to see.

One is a glacial kettle hole called the "punch bowl," a large depression formed by the huge receding Wisconsin glacier. As chunks of ice broke off and became buried and later melted, they created depressions of various sizes. Smaller ones exist on the East Woodland Trail. In April the glacial "punch bowl" is abloom with thousands of dainty daffodils.

Another geological anomoly to notice while exploring the East Trail is a large erratic. More than 10,000 years ago when the ice mass receded, it deposited the many erratics (boulders far removed from place of origin) around Beacon Hill. The area owes its name to the fact that during the American Revolution and the War of 1812 this land was part of a farm owned by Richard Swain and was used as a signal station to alert the militia.

The arboretum has both an East and West Trail. The East Trail is a low and moist habitat while the West Trail is a high, dry woodland area. The native trees on the woodland trail are typical of the Eastern Deciduous Forest. These old trees should be appreciated as survivors from an earlier century.

In addition to the two woodland trails the 12½-acre arboretum also has a Garden Trail. Along this trail you will primarily see cultivated trees and shrubs. Represented here are varieties from all over the world including the Atlas cedar, Chinese ginkgo, the umbrella "pine" from Japan, and the Sawara cypress also of Japanese origin.

Certain special areas have also been planted: an azalea garden, a rose garden, an herb garden, and a vegetable patch. Landscaped gardens include a large planting of bulbs and perennials.

On Saturday mornings during the spring and fall, special programs involve youngsters in "hands-on" nature discovery programs. The arboretum also holds free nature programs on certain Sunday afternoons.

The grounds of the arboretum are open during daylight hours year round. The office is open on Tuesdays and Thursdays from 9:00 A.M. to 3:00 P.M.

Directions: Take Beltway Exit 27 to I-95 north across the Delaware Memorial Bridge. Stay on the New Jersey Turnpike until it intersects the Garden State Parkway. Take Exit 140, Route 24 west to Summit, New Jersey. The Reeves Reed Arboretum is in Summit off Route 24 at the Hobard Avenue exit. Turn left and watch for the Arboretum sign on the left. The address is 165 Hobart Avenue.

The Scott Horticultural Foundation

Backyard gardeners often enjoy horticultural excursions where they can get new ideas and landscaping concepts to try at home. Arthur Hoyt Scott envisioned that sort of "garden of suggestions" in developing the 350-acre Swarthmore Campus, which houses the Scott Horticultural Foundation.

The 5,000 kinds of plants in this arboretum are presented in an attractive setting. Here visitors can see the best ornamental plants recommended for this area by professional horticulturists. The carefully labeled plants here are not the unfamiliar plants indigenous to other cultures that you find in most arboretums, but rather plants that are easy to grow and readily available to the general public. It is a practical garden that anyone can grow.

The best time to visit the Scott Horticultural Foundation is April or May, when the spring blossoms highlight the collection. More than 300 varieties of azaleas, 2,000 rhododendron, flowering magnolias, cherries, lilacs, and tree peonies add their spring pastels to the arboretum. Six hundred kinds of daffodils precede this mid-spring treat.

The enjoyment of woodlands and rock gardens can be experienced in the Wister Garden. Courtyard landscaping ideas can be gained by stopping at the Harry Wood Memorial Garden. During the summer months the Dean Bond Rose Garden, beneath a lush canopy of specimen trees, presents a wide diversity of roses.

Winter's bright berries make this arboretum worth a visit even in the colder months. In the conifer collection more than 25 of the 50 known genera can be seen. Finally, the James R. Frorer Holly Collection offers an extensive assortment of these winter garden favorites. The Wester Solar Greenhouses can be visited regardless of the season.

The grounds at Swarthmore College can be explored daily at no charge from dawn to dusk. The office, however, is open only Monday through Friday, 8:30 A.M. to 4:30 P.M. If you are planning a weekend visit, write for a map of the collection. Address your request to Scott Horticultural Foundation, Swarthmore College, Swarthmore, Pennsylvania 19081.

Directions: Take Beltway Exit 27 to I-95 north to Route 320. Swarthmore College is located on Route 320, Chester Road.

Barnes Foundation Arboretum

Exploring just a few of the many gardens at the Barnes Foundation Arboretum will leave little doubt in your mind that landscaping is indeed an art. At the Barnes Foundation both horticulture and the fine arts are on display.

This arboretum in Merion, Pennsylvania, offers a number of advantages. One is that its outstanding collection of more than 290 genera of woody plants from all over the northern hemisphere is encompassed within a 12-acre setting. This makes it easy to explore.

The excellent tree notations are also especially helpful. Oriental specimens like the dove, or handkerchief tree, are rarely seen. In early May the tree appears to have a bad cold as the ground is littered with white Kleenex-like blossoms. Also from the East comes the Chinese fringe tree, the beauty bush, Korean boxwood, paperbark maple, bee-bee tree, and raisin tree.

Spring is the best time to visit, when the trees begin to leaf out and the flowering trees add their pastel hues to the countryside. Beginning in early April and extending through July, the magnolia collection is in bloom. The first to bloom are the star and yulan magnolias. In June there are the summer blooming magnolias like the Korean magnolia sieboldie; then the latest blooming magnolia, the southern evergreen magnolia, which is native to America.

Another spring blooming collection you'll want to see is the tree peonies. These fragile looking blossoms come in many shades and are bigger than the backyard varieties normally seen. The tree peonies are best seen in late May.

Though Barnes is an arboretum, a number of specialty gardens are on the grounds—the Rose Garden, Rock Garden and Vine Collection.

Also to be seen is the art collection of Dr. Albert C. Barnes, noted for its pieces of impressionistic art.

Though there is no admission charged to visit the Barnes Foundation Arboretum, you do have to make an appointment by calling (215)664-8880 or writing Director, Barnes Foundation, 57 Lapsley Road, Merion, Pennsylvania 19066.

The arboretum is open year round from 9:30 A.M. until 4:00 P.M. Monday through Thursday, from 9:30 A.M. until 4:00 P.M. Friday and Saturday, and 1:30 P.M. until 4:30 P.M. on Sunday. The art gallery is not open during July and August. Throughout the remainder of the year it is open Friday and Saturday from 9:30 A.M. until 4:30 P.M. and on Sunday from 1:00 P.M. until 4:30 P.M. You do not need advance arrangements to see the art collection.

Directions: Take Beltway Exit 27 to I-95 north to Philadelphia. Then take Route 76 west to Merion. The Barnes Foundation Arboretum is located at 57 Lapsley Lane in Merion, just 5 miles from downtown Philadelphia.

Willowwood Arboretum

Willowwood Arboretum is a 130-acre, park-like setting in north-central New Jersey. It offers pleasant informal woodland trails combined with a few small garden areas.

This shallow valley of rolling farm land has been augmented by 35 kinds of oak, 50 maple specimens, 110 willows, and a 70-foot Dawn Redwood. Attention has also been given to a noteworthy collection of conifers, hollies, magnolia, cherries, and lilacs. This makes spring an ideal time to visit the Willowwood Arboretum.

The wildflowers that bedeck both field and forest beckon in April and May. Spotting may apple, jack-in-the-pulpit, trillium, and the not-to-be-missed hillside of pink lady's-slipper adds a fillip to your arboretum hike.

About 3,500 natural and exotic plants are in this park. Before 1980 this facility was under the jurisdiction of Rutgers University and was open only by appointment; now visitors are welcome year round.

The Willowwood Farm was established as an arboretum in 1950. The farm dates from 1792 and has a house overlooking the two small formal gardens. There is a Japanese-style garden and a cottage herb garden.

This arboretum is adjacent to the Bamboo Brook Outdoor Education Center, where you will discover cultivated garden areas and trails through a picturesque natural environment. The Black River Park, where this nature center is found, also contains an 1826 grist mill, the Cooper Mill. Of considerable interest and a change of pace is the nearby Morristown National Historical Park that presents a glimpse of the struggles Washington and his men endured during the winters of the American Revolution.

Directions: Take Beltway Exit 27, I-95 north across the Delaware Memorial Bridge. Continue north on the New Jersey Turnpike to the Garden State Parkway. Exit on Route 24 west to Morristown, New Jersey. The Willowwood Arboretum is off Hacklebarney Road in the Morristown area.

Frelinghuysen Arboretum

This 127-acre arboretum preserves the warmth and charm of George Griswold Frelinghuysen's Whippany Farm while also presenting a floral display of lilacs, azaleas, rhododendron, cherries, magnolia, and roses.

Self-guiding nature trails focus on the different collections. Trails wander past the dogwood, holly, and peony collections. The Aldrich Memorial Crab Apple Trail merges with the Thyra S. Maxwell Memorial Azalea Trail. The natural setting of this arboretum adds to its appeal.

The south trail of the arboretum is a mixture of swampy terrain, open fields, and mature forested areas. It is geologically of interest because it was once covered by the Wisconsin Glacier, similar to the Reeves Reed Arboretum.

The arboretum's North Trail along the banks of the Whippany River is being developed as a horticultural demonstration area.

Other areas of special interest are a Braille nature trail, an All-American display garden, and a glossary garden.

The arboretum is open at no charge from 9:00 A.M. until sundown.

Directions: Take Beltway Exit 27 to I-95 north across the Delaware Memorial Bridge, and continue north on the New Jersey Turnpike to the Garden State Parkway. Exit on Route 24 west to Morristown, New Jersey. The Frelinghuysen Arboretum is located at 53 E. Hanover Avenue in Morristown.

Other gardens with arboretums:

Maymont Park Public Gardens
Gardens of Colonial Park
Clyburn Wildflower Preserve
Behnke Nurseries Arboretum

Colonial Gardens

London Town Publik House and Gardens

Form vs. freedom, design vs. disarray, both have their charm in garden layouts. In the Annapolis area two gardens—the London Town Publik House Gardens and the William Paca Garden (see next selection)—present these very different but appealing styles.

In London Town's natural setting, a path winds through the eight acres enabling the visitor to enjoy abundant wildflowers and masses of daffodils, azaleas, and rhododendron. The extensive planting of late blooming daffodils permits the normally sequential blooming periods to overlap.

The best time to explore the delights of London Town is spring, the season when many of its special gardens reach their peak. In fact, one part of the path is called Spring Walk, which features bleeding heart, Lenton rose, primrose, mayapple, and phlox divaricata. Branching off this semicircular walk is the native azalea area, which has blooms in mid-May. The path also leads to the winter garden area, showing an interesting variety of dwarf conifers made colorful in the spring with the random primrose and lavender.

Before you reach the next section you will smell the delightful fragrance of the viberniums that flank the path. A terrace overlook offers a good view of the South River. Along the river is the marsh garden broadwalk that provides a close look at plants rarely included in planned garden designs.

Retrace your steps along a path parallel to the one you've just come down and you will be able to enjoy the Wildflower Walk, where you will see large groupings of trillium, mayapple, jack-in-the-pulpit, Dutchman's-breeches, phlox, snakeroot, wood betony, fire pink, gentian, white baneberry, blue-eyed grass, and pachysandra. These, too, are best seen in mid-spring.

Returning to the Publik House, you will see the camellia slope. Like many area collections, it is suffering from a series of severe winters. Also to be seen are a rolling hillside of rhododendron and a grouping of irises and day lilies. The latter provides the main attraction during the summer.

A delightful touch at the London Town Publik House garden is a peaceful pond nestled in a floriferous dell. Waterfowl frequent the pond and enliven the vista. The cool breezes off the South River that laps along the northern boundary of the garden make the garden pleasant even on warm days. Picnic tables at the edge of the garden overlook the river.

Once back at the house you will see the London Town Publik House Herb Garden extending in a semicircle around an old well. Surrounded by a border of roses, the four individual herb gardens are the fragrance, medicinal, dye, and kitchen gardens.

Among the fragrant herbs you may recognize are lemon thyme, lavender, rosemary, orris root, southern wood, bergamot, lemon balm, garden heliotrope, and clove pink.

The medicinal herbs include ajuga, cowslip, yarrow, catnip, veronica, bee balm, santilina, foxglove, rue, painted daisy, camomile, and horehound.

Plants used as dyes in the 18th century are veronica, St. John's wort, tansy, lily of the valley, coreopsis, tansy, and woad.

The kitchen garden contains marjoram, parsley, winter savory, lovage, horseradish, sage, common thyme, rosemary, peppermint, curly mint, and spearmint.

Don't miss the opportunity to go inside the old Publik House. London Town was a major ferry crossing during colonial times and many historical figures availed themselves of the hospitality offered here on their travels. George Washington, Thomas Jefferson, and Francis Scott Key are just some of the well-known figures who mentioned in their diaries making the ferry crossing at London Town.

This old inn has a number of interesting architectural features. Like some of the nearby Annapolis homes it was built in the all-header brick fashion. The extra thickness provided additional insulation to offset the hillside setting.

The greater width of the bricks necessitated insetting the doors to a greater depth. The doors themselves are so enormous, you imagine they were built to accommodate giants—literally, not just the historical giants that did frequent this inn.

Another unusual feature you should notice is the way several rooms are all raised one step. It is thought that this may have been done to reduce the draft caused by the four large doors. The interior furnishings reflect the colonial period.

The basement public rooms have the original brick fireplaces and arched doorways. Again, expertise in design is apparent as the bricks curve around the openings. All exterior doors, woodwork, hardware, and many of the glass windows are original.

The London Town Publik House and Gardens is a National Historic Landmark and has been given national recognition by the Garden Clubs of America. It is open Tuesday through Saturday from 10:00 A.M. to 4:00 P.M. and on Sunday from noon to 4:00 P.M. It is closed January and February. Admission is charged.

Directions: Take Beltway Exit 19 to Route 50 east to the Edgewater-Parole exit, where you take Route 450, West Street, towards Annapolis. Turn right at Route 2 south, followed by a left on Route 253, Mayo Road, just on the other side of the South River Bridge. Proceed one mile down Mayo Road to London Town Road, make a left and follow to the end for the Publik House.

William Paca Garden

Looking out the upstairs window at the William Paca House provides a good view of a recovered colonial garden. The story of reclaiming this virtually buried treasure is inspiring.

When the William Paca House was acquired in 1965 by Historic Annapolis, Inc., the grounds were covered by a hotel, parking lot, and bus depot. This triple threat should have obliterated the lovely terraced garden that graced the Paca House in the 18th century. Archeological excavation after the hotel was demolished, however, uncovered the foundations laid for Paca's garden. They suggested the period when Annapolis was the Golden Venice of the colonies. From these foundations the contours of the original design were determined.

Reconstructing the garden was made somewhat easier because it had served as the background in a portrait that Charles Willson Peale painted of William Paca. Behind Paca you can see the trellis-patterned bridge, the two-story garden pavilion, and parts of what was called the Wilderness Garden.

From the upstairs window you can also observe the fish-shaped pond with the Chinese-style bridge, just like in the Peale portrait. Gazing down at this delightful garden, one cannot help but be impressed at what concerted effort, determination, and generously donated funds can achieve.

After exploring the beautifully decorated home of William Paca, one of Maryland's signers of the Declaration of Independence, be sure to allow time to wander through this town garden.

The first thing you will notice is that the garden is asymmetrically in line with the house. Four parterres, two on each side of the central walkway, or grand allée, lead to the wilderness area. All of the plants in the garden were known in the 18th century.

The parterres closest to the house are the Rose Parterre and the Flower Parterre. Both have constantly changing collections of plants, many rarely seen in this area. During the spring you'll see tulips, English and Shasta daisies, columbine, wallflowers, basket-of-gold, and stock. The Boxwood Parterre has tulips, periwinkle, anemones, hellebores, and fritillaria, while the Holly Parterre has waldsteinia, iberis, fritillaria, and tulips. The Wilderness Garden is abloom with spring heath, crocus, tulips, Dutchman's-breeches, American andromeda, vernal witch hazel, Virginia bluebells, Jacob's ladder plus columbine, foamflowers, scilla, phlox, narcissus, and violets.

During the summer months you will see roses, heliotrope, calendula, loosestrife, clary, lavender, coreopsis, liatris, gaillardia, snapdragon, and campanula, to name just a few of the many varieties.

Autumn presents yet another show when blooms include not only the chrysanthemum, but also asters, ageratum, zinnias, celosia, sage, statice, heliotrope, calendula, lobelia, plumbago, nicotiana, cyclamen, gazania, and New England asters.

In addition to the principal parterres there is also a kitchen garden and a garden around the Visitors' Center. At the Center you will find information on the flowers in bloom at the time of your visit plus a brochure on the history of the garden.

The William Paca Garden is open Monday through Saturday from 10:00 A.M. until 4:00 P.M. It is open on Sunday May through October from noon to 5:00 P.M. and November through April from noon to 4 P.M. Both the William Paca House and Garden are closed on Thanksgiving Day and Christmas Day.

Directions: Take Beltway Exit 19, Route 50 east, to Annapolis Exit 70 Rowe Blvd and Historic District. Turn left at State House onto College Avenue. Turn right on King George St. (light) to the William Paca Garden at King George St. and Martin St. in Annapolis, Maryland.

William Paca Garden Schedule of Flowering Seasons

Spring	
	Apple Tree
	Aurinia Saxatilis
	Banksia Rose
	Broom
	Carolina Allspice
	Cherry Laurel
	Chives
	Chokeberry
	Claytonia Virginiana
	Columbine
	Dogwood
	English Daisies
	Foamflower
	Fothergilla
	Fritillaria
	Gazania
	Geranium
	Helleborus
	Iberis
	Jack-in-the-pulpit
	Lilac
	Lungwort
	Marigold
	Marsh Marigold
	Money Plant
	Mountain Ash
	Narcissus
	Periwinkle
	Phlox Divaricata
	Pieris Floribunda
	Potentilla
	Ranunculus
	Red Horse Chestnut
	Rose du Rescht
	Sedum
	Shasta Daisy

Spring (Continued)	Silverbell
	Spring Heath
	Squill
	Star of Bethlehem
	Stock
	Trillium
	Tulip
	Vernal Iris
	Veronica
	Viburnum Lentago
	Viola
	Waldsteinia
	Wallflower
Summer	Agapanthus
	Ageratum
	Aster
	Basil
	Black Cohosh
	Black-eyed Susan*
	Border Aster
	Butterfly Weed
	Button Bush
	Calendula
	Celosia
	Clary
	Coreopsis
	Cornflower
	Day Lilies
	Dwarf Pomegranate
	Feverfew
	Field Daisy
	Gaillardia
	Gazania
	Globe Amaranth
	Golden Rain Tree
	Goldenrod
	Heliotrope
	Hollyhocks
	Hypericum
	Jasmine
	Lantana
	Larkspur
	Lavender
	Liatris

Summer (Continued)	Lily
	Loosestrife
	Marigold
	Melon
	Monarda*
	Mullein
	Nicotiana
	Oakleaf Hydrangea
	Oleander
	Periwinkle
	Pickerel Weed
	Poppy
	Pumpkins
	Raspberry Bush
	Rose de Rescht
	Safflower*
	Snapdragons
	Sourwood*
	Southern Magnolia
	Statice
	Stock
	Stokes Aster
	Strawflower
	Teucrium
	Thunbergia
	Veronica
	Vitex
	Zinnias
Fall	Ageratum*
	Aster
	Basil
	Black-eyed Susan
	Blazing Star
	Blue Sage
	Bluebeard
	Border Aster
	Butterfly Weed
	Button Bush
	Calendula
	Celosia Cristata
	Celosia Plumosa
	Chrysanthemum
	Cleome (Spider Plant)
	Closed Bottle Gentian

Fall (Continued)

Coreopsis
Crape Myrtle
Dipper Gourd
Gaillardia
Gazania
Globe Amaranth
Goldenrod
Heliotrope
Lantana
Lobelia
Mallow
Marigold
Mountain Ash
New England Aster
Nicotiana
Oleander
Periwinkle
Phlox
Physostegia
Pickerel Weed
Pineapple Lily
Plumbago
Rose de Rescht
Shasta Daisy
Sourwood
Statice
Strawflower
Turtle Head*
Zinnias

*Newly in bloom.

Mount Vernon Gardens

George Washington's meticulous stewardship was never more obvious than in the concern he showed for all aspects of his Mount Vernon estate. Despite his many responsibilities to the developing colonial cause, he managed to plan, create, and oversee the landscaping of his Potomac plantation. Shortly after he married Martha Dandridge Custis in 1759, he obtained and studied garden manuals for ideas to incorporate in his new world version of an English country estate.

With the help of the 44 volumes of Washington's writings and his voluminous weekly gardener's reports, the estate and three garden areas have been restored to their original appearance.

"Ha-haws," or sunken walls, separate the landscaped area of Mount Vernon from the surrounding field. On the river side the park wall and outer wall of the formal garden enclose the fourth side. Washington's plan was to have a bowling green dividing the flower garden from the kitchen garden. Though he devised the plan before the Revolution, work did not begin in earnest until 1785, with Washington on hand to supervise. His diary contains notations like the one for January 12, 1785, "Road to my Mill Swamp . . . and to other places in search of the sort of Trees I shall want for my Walks, groves and Wildernesses."

The principal feature of the flower garden is the boxwood hedge planted in 1798. Parterres contain flowers common to gardens in Washington's day as well as two separate rose gardens. This upper garden, as it was called, also included fruit trees as did the lower, or kitchen, garden.

Like its upper twin, this earlier garden, laid out in 1760, was shield-shaped. Vegetables were planted in geometric parterres and edged with herbs. Espaliered fruit trees were trained along the garden walls and cordoned along the walks. In a letter Washington wrote on June 5, 1796, he remarked, "Tell the Gardener I shall expect everything that a Garden ought to produce, in the most ample manner."

Expanding on the plants that he collected in 1785, Washington added a greenhouse on the north side of the upper garden. The building you see today is a reconstruction since the original was destroyed by fire in 1835.

The third garden on the estate lies closest to the house above the upper garden and was Washington's personal favorite. In his botanical garden he could experiment with cuttings not indigenous to the Virginia countryside. Like so many of his colonial compatriots he was always interested in expanding on the existing herbs, vegetables, and fruit trees that could be grown in northern Virginia.

The careful restoration given to the grounds applies to the mansion as well. More than 40 percent of the original furniture has been recovered and the additional pieces were carefully chosen to reflect the room-by-room inventory taken at the time of Washington's death on December 14, 1799. Washington, in accordance with his own wishes, is buried with Martha in a vault on the estate ground.

The mansion, grounds, and numerous dependencies can be toured daily from 9:00 A.M. to 5:00 P.M. There is an admission fee.

Directions: Take Beltway Exit 1 to the Mount Vernon Memorial Highway south directly to Mount Vernon in Virginia.

Gunston Hall

In the 1770s English garden design was dramatically influenced by the ideas of Lancelot "Capability" Brown, who received his interesting soubriquet because of his oft-repeated assurance that a particular garden had "capabilities." He would have certainly been right had he seen the grounds of George Mason's Virginia estate, where Brown's concept of natural landscaping is quite apparent. Its promising possibilities were delightfully realized to the continued pleasure of visitors today.

Though considered the largest Dutch–English-style garden in the U.S. and definitely in the Williamsburg mode of garden design, Gunston Hall still reflects Brown's landscape concepts. First, there is the size of the garden. The view from the house extends 280 feet down the main boxwood allée to the river overlook. Flanking the overlook on both sides are twin gazebos that offer a charming view of the deer park and the river half a mile away. It is obvious that the natural landscape is an important factor in this lovely garden.

The parterre garden that was planned and planted by George Mason in the late 1750s and early 1760s has deteriorated in the intervening years. When Louis Hertle deeded it to Virginia in 1949, the Garden Club of Virginia undertook to restore the garden to its 18th century appearance. No plans of the garden survived, but the boxwood George Mason had planted and the terrace did still delineate the garden's main areas.

Hertle had begun the restoration work during his tenure, propagating new bushes from the boxwood and laying out the ground in four major sections, or parterres. New research is revealing important information about the use and form of the gardens at Gunston Hall.

The parterres closest to the house have the most intricate patterns. They are laid out in geometric shapes with boxwoods forming squares, triangles, and circles. Periwinkle and creeping bugle provide a ground cover and tree peonies, crape myrtle, and fringe trees compliment the design.

Although balanced, the individual parterres are not the same, not in the design and not in the plants that are used. The garden to the left of the allée follows the English pattern approach while those to the right borrow from the Dutch, with their more crowded and overgrown look.

The Chinese influence can also be found in the garden where chinoiserie benches are placed in the upper garden. The lower garden reflects the 18th century interest in the East that was popular in England and the colonies. The matching gazebos echo the porch design and are executed in the chinoiserie style that William Buckland, Mason's indentured carpenter, was to make so popular in the colonies.

Beneath these delicate structures lie the parterres of the lower terrace. A semicircular mound divides this section in two, each containing 12 parterres separated by crushed oyster shell paths. Spring bulbs and summer and fall annuals brighten these neat beds. On the sloping bank of this lower garden quince blooms each spring. The red, pink, and white blooms are interspersed with yellow daffodils. In mid-summer day lilies bloom on the bluff.

Steps lead down to the deer park, which as the name implies, was once inhabited by Virginia white-tailed deer.

One additional area of interest is the Barn Wharf Nature Trail, which starts at the front of the house and winds down to the Potomac. This half-mile walk is particularly interesting in the spring when the wildflowers bloom. Bird fanciers enjoy this trail because efforts have been made to encourage bluebirds to nest in the area. One's chance of sighting these colorful birds is quite good. Since it is so close to Mason Neck Wildlife Refuge, a sanctuary designed to encourage nesting eagles, visitors may even sight one of our elusive national birds.

The Gunston Hall gardens are a beautiful evocation of an earlier style, which is also evident in the mansion. The interior is opulantly designed with exquisitely carved interior woodwork. The Palladian Room and Chinese Chippendale dining room are showpieces of the rooms designed by William Buckland.

A movie shown in the reception area provides highlights of the career of George Mason, who, according to Jefferson, was "the wisest man of his generation."

Gunston Hall is open daily, except Christmas from 9:30 A.M. to 5:00 P.M. Admission is charged.

Directions: Take Beltway Exit 1 in Virginia and go south on U.S. 1. Take Route 242 east to the entrance.

Morven Park

Disputes about what to plant around the house, whether it is a mansion or a bungalow, are universal. At Morven Park in Leesburg, Virginia, Mrs. Westmoreland Davis wanted a formal garden but Governor Davis wanted to grow hay. He envisioned an agricultural enterprise on the rolling grounds. Visitors to Morven Park will readily see that the victor was Mrs. Davis. The ultimate winners, though, are those who tour this Virginia estate, where the grounds enhance the appeal of this unexpectedly European mansion.

A mile-long, tree-lined drive leads to the house on this 1,200-acre estate. The trees, an integral part of the garden's distinctive appeal, include rare specimen trees collected by Governor Davis. Native varieties have also been carefully cultivated. Visitors will see the largest little-leaf Linden tree on the North American continent. An interesting illustration of their asexual propagation is apparent as you see these old trees with limbs bent to the ground beginning a new growth. It is a curious phenomenon. Other trees of interest are some fine examples of the almost extinct American chestnut, the lovely red maple, several golden raintrees, a white paper birch, and a big old catalpa or cigar tree.

The Marguerite G. Davis Boxwood Gardens in Morven Park have the largest living stand of boxwood in the United States. Augmenting these majestic boxwoods are seasonal flowers. In the spring you'll see the hillside of azaleas, rhododendron, and dogwood. Daffodils, then tulips and Virginia bluebells lend color to the garden. Blooming in the summer are roses, dahlias, and crape myrtle. A focus in this boxwood garden is the 50-foot reflecting pool surrounded by magnolias and crape myrtle. After touring the house you can picnic on the grounds at tables under the trees.

Morven Park from the outside may suggest a southern plantation, but inside it suggests Versailles. In fact, the eclectic mixture of European art and design prompts those who have visited William Randolph Hearst's San Simeon estate to equate the two. Morven Park is modest, however, when compared to Hearst's castle. Otherwise the huge rococo mirrors, six wall-size 1640 tapestries, velvet thrones from the Pitti Palace in Florence, and heavily scrolled furniture seem princely. The very mixture of styles makes exploring the house fun.

One of the secondary advantages of touring old homes is the chance to see and understand literary references to specific pieces of furniture that are no longer commonly used. Two examples are the hunt board and peer table. The hunt board, the only piece of furniture in the house that belonged to the Swann family (the 19th century owners), was used to serve "stirrup cups" before the members of the hunt began their ride. The table was built so that the seated riders could reach for the sherry or brandy without dismounting.

The peer table goes back to the crinoline era when hooped skirts made it difficult to see if one's petticoat was showing. The table had a mirror underneath so that the ladies could check their skirts.

Morven Park has much to see and do. After a house tour you should consider the guided tour of the Winmill Carriage Collection, which now includes 125 vehicles. On display are sulkies, buggies, breaks, landaus, opera coaches, phaetons, carts, sleighs, victoria class carriages, and service vehicles. Don't miss the imposing old hearse and the bright red fire engine pumper. Be sure and have the guide point out the "necessary" in the Park Drag.

If you have time there are two nature trails that meander through the estate woodlands. The circular Catoctin Trail or the Kalmia loop extension lead to lookouts that provide a panoramic view of Maryland across the Potomac River. In the spring the flowering dogwood, mountain laurel, Japanese honeysuckle, and tulip trees are all in bloom. This natural setting so beloved by Virginia Governor Westmoreland Davis and the lovely gardens planned by Mrs. Davis to enhance the estate serve to remind visitors of an earlier and more gracious era.

Morven Park is open Memorial Day weekend through Labor Day weekend on Tuesday through Saturday from 10:00 A.M. to 5:00 P.M. and on Sunday from 1:00 P.M. to 5:00 P.M. Admission is charged.

Directions: Take Beltway Exit 10 to Route 7 west to the Leesburg exit. Once in Leesburg, follow King Street (Route 15) to Morven Park.

Oatlands

Every garden has its signature, its claim to fame; and at Oatlands it is the extensive and creative use of the lovely boxwood. This is the only garden in the country that uses boxwood for the pleached, or tunnel, walk. Parterre boxwood hedges enhance the formal, terraced garden. There is also a beautiful boxwood allée.

Much of the boxwood was planted in the 1800s by George Carter, the great-grandson of King Carter who had amassed land holdings of 330,000 acres. The Oatlands estate was a modest 5,000 acres of which seven were developed into a formal, English boxwood garden and bowling green.

The garden you enjoy today is the result of the work done by Mrs. Eustis, who acquired the land, with her husband, Morton Eustis, in 1903. She restored and improved this garden which she said was noted for its "mystery, variety and the unexpected."

In mid-May the Wisteria Walk is at its very best. Lovely, fragrant lavender blossoms cascade in profusion. Color coordinated flowers add to the charm—irises, bluebells, and wild phlox. At the end of this walk, at one end of the bowling green, is a picturesque tea house that is often used for summer weddings. There is a reflecting pool at the other end of the bowling green.

At the far end of Oatlands's terraces a number of interesting areas can be explored. One is the path to the Carter mausoleum where George Carter, his widow, and a reverend who ended his own life and thus precluded burial in sanctified ground, are interred. On the lower terrace by this tomb you can see the mounds beneath which Morton Eustis buried his beloved horses. His burial of horses ran counter to the normal custom of burying only the head and heart of a horse.

On the grounds above the family tomb and to the east of the reflecting pool is a boxwood grove. Here Mrs. Eustis had a copy made of the 15th century "la Vierge D'Autun," a French Madonna. At this shrine she mourned her daughter, Edith, who died at the young age of 24.

In returning to the house be sure to notice the rosarium on the left. Planted with Dorothy Perkins roses, this garden is particularly lovely in June. Oatlands also has added an Herb Garden.

In addition to the lovely garden, the grounds at Oatlands are noted for their specimen trees. There is a gingko, European larch, and an English oak reputed to be the largest of its kind in Virginia. The osage orange is also impressive, though it is not as large as the one Patrick Henry sat beneath on his Red Hill Plantation. There is a stand of American hornbeams that you will notice as you approach the mansion.

The house itself is the focus of much attention. It has an appealing exterior with a colonnaded porch, and the interior is furnished with American, French, and English pieces that clearly represent a lifestyle in which money was never a problem. The Octagonal Drawing Room was reconstructed from a square-shaped room when the eight-sided style achieved popularity. That's redecorating on a grand scale. The ornamental plasterwork rivals that at Kenmore, reputed to be the finest example of this art in the United States. It is interesting to explore not only the formal rooms but even the 1903 bathroom.

Oatlands is open from April through November from 10:00 A.M. to 5:00 P.M. and on Sundays from 1:00 P.M. to 5:00 P.M. There is an admission fee.

Directions: Take Beltway Exit 10 to Route 7 west to Leesburg, Virginia. Oatlands is 6 miles south of Leesburg on Route 15.

Williamsburg Gardens

The concept of a planned community is really not all that new; some of our earliest colonial towns were "planned." The delightful diversity of fences and gardens in Colonial Williamsburg attest to its being a well-ordered 18th century city.

When Lieutenant Governor Francis Nicholson laid out the town each residential property was set at one-half acre in size, sufficient ground to build a house as well as provide for dependencies, service areas, paddocks and gardens. Fences were decreed by act of the General Assembly in 1705, requiring enclosure of each lot contiguous to Duke of Gloucester Street. Such enclosures were to consist of "pales" or posts and rails. "Paling" is the charming board or picket fence styles seen throughout historic Williamsburg. Brick walls were more expensive and usually were used to enclose the grounds of public buildings.

Gardens in colonial Williamsburg reflect the English style popular during the reign of William and Mary, 1689–1702. The more natural style that was gaining influence in England during the latter part of the 17th century did not manifest itself in the colonies until later. In observing the formal "parterres" at the Governor's Palace and the gardens enhancing the private properties you see elegant examples of the English garden tempered by the Dutch influence.

One of the finest formal gardens in colonial Virginia was to be found at the Governor's Palace in Williamsburg. It was partially financed from the personal purse of Royal Governor Alexander Spotswood when the original palace was constructed. Although the palace itself had burned and disappeared following the American Revolution, authentic reconstruction of the structure and its garden setting was made possible in part because of careful archeological investigation. Original paths, walls, steps, gate sites, and pieces of garden artifacts were carefully uncovered. Documentary research also revealed an 18th century engraved copperplate showing a partial view of the ballroom garden. The "Bodleian Plate," as it is called, was discovered at the Bodleian Library at Oxford University in England.

The palace grounds contain a number of separate garden enclosures beginning with a forecourt at the entrance gates. As one proceeds through the building one may glimpse through broad windows the east holly garden and portions of the upper ballroom garden. The latter contains 16 diamond-shaped beds edged with boxwoods and flanked by 12 cylindrical topiary pieces of yaupon holly. These 15-foot plant specimens called the "Twelve Apostles," were seen on many English estates. Although evergreens define the garden patterns all year long, springtime comes vividly alive with a kaleidoscope of colors; crocus, irises, jonquils, squills, anemones and grape hyacinths push up through the periwinkle groundcover.

Beyond the broad east-west walk behind the ballroom you will see the lower ballroom garden, consisting of long tulip beds with perennial borders. In April the tulips, which are usually red, are particularly striking. Later the borders are filled with colorful irises, poppies, day lilies, and phlox. During the summer annuals replace the tulips.

Pleached allées flanking each side of this garden are formed from the native American beech tree. These natural tunnels provide welcome shade during the summer and may have even provided trysting places during colonial times. Privacy was a luxury that could only be found in secluded garden retreats during the 18th century when hospitality required keeping an open house for family and friends.

Like all colonial gardens, there is much that is practical in the palace garden. The gazebos at the end corners of the ballroom garden were privies, or "necessaries." The oak tree shaded mound which could be used as a lookout post also served to insulate the icehouse, an underground barrel vault built of brick.

Eighteenth century entertainment often included games played in mazes. The palace garden includes this popular colonial garden conceit. The palace maze is made of native American holly whose prickly leaves help to discourage short cuts. This intricate design was adapted from the old maze at Hampton Court, one of the several Royal Palaces around London.

Colonists became weary of paying for the elaborate gardens at the Governor's Palace. In 1718 Governor Spotswood, in response to criticism about the ever-increasing money required to finish the mansion and grounds, offered, "if the Assembly did not care to be at the Expense of the Fish-Pond & Falling Gardens, to take them to my Self."

Pay for them he did, and we can be grateful for his generosity, as they are lovely, though uncommon, additions to this beautiful formal garden. A wooden footbridge with matching benches designed in the chinoiserie style arches gracefully over the inlet end of the canal, providing pleasant vistas towards the fish pond.

In addition to enjoying the gardens, you will want to tour the palace where a living history program involves visitors in mini-dramas of the 18th century. You might be called upon to be a relative come calling, a petitioning tradesman or an invited guest. Whatever role you play, the mood is so pervasive that you will feel you have stepped back in time and become an integral part of the colonial scene.

This feeling persists as the narrow, quiet streets of this capital city are explored. There is no automobile traffic during daylight hours on most of the streets. Old houses are enjoyed in their garden settings over white picket fences. You can marvel at the large pleasure garden at the George Wythe House, or relax in the intimate corners of the Brush-Everard Garden where you'll see a small duck pond. The Wythe House garden features a pleached allée formed from Carolina hornbeam. An extensive herb and kitchen garden on the south side balances a row of outbuildings on the north facing the side street. The entire layout recreates a plantation in miniature transplanted to this colonial city.

Though most of the restored homes are owned by Colonial Williamsburg and privately occupied by its employees, visitors may explore the surrounding gardens. A handy garden map is available with intriguing property names such as Alexander Purdie, Orland Jones, Pitt-Dixon, Ludwell-Paradise, Elkanah Deane, and Custis-Maupin. Privacy should be respected, of course, should a family activity be encountered.

Gardens should not be overlooked at the many craft shops. The Pasteur-Galt Apothecary shop has an interesting herb garden and there is also a stream garden associated with the Printing Office. You will find gardens at the taverns as well. At the King's Arm Tavern and Chowning's Tavern you can enjoy your meals alfresco in the garden. Mr. Wetherburn's and Market Square Tavern also have gardens to explore.

Obviously exploring all the gardens at Willliamsburg will take longer than a day and will offer diverse appeal as the seasons change. Colonial Williamsburg is open daily from 9:00 A.M. to 5:00 P.M. Be sure to make your first stop the Visitor Center, where you can obtain maps and tour information.

Directions: Take Beltway Exit 4 to I-95 south to the Richmond By-Pass, via I-295. Follow this to Route I-64 east, which will lead directly into Williamsburg. Use Exit 56 to Route 143 and 132 and then follow Colonial Williamsburg green shields.

Monticello

In 1767 at the age of 23 Thomas Jefferson began a garden diary that he kept until two years before his death. Jefferson's methodical record keeping made it possible to restore the grounds and gardens at Monticello with a high degree of accuracy.

The diary starts even before construction of Monticello. Jefferson began planting the land he inherited from his father two years before the building was started. A grid, made by Jefferson in 1778, gives the specific location for 300 trees. He also lists the plants for each bed.

Thomas Jefferson—President, Vice-President, Secretary of State, Minister to France, Governor of Virginia, Founding Father, educator, lawyer, and architect—once said, "I have often thought that if heaven had given me a choice of my position and calling, it should have been on a rich spot of earth . . . and near a good market . . . no occupation is so delightful to me as the culture of the earth."

In 1981, restoration work on Jefferson's vegetable garden and orchard recreated them as they would have looked following Jefferson's own 1812 revitalization of his grounds. The original 1,000-foot vegetable garden terrace was completed on the southern slope of the grounds in 1809. Together with the 8-acre orchard it provided food for Jefferson's family and guests.

But Jefferson was interested in more than putting a wide variety of food on his table. He was a great experimenter and had 19 varieties of peas, one of his favorite vegetables. Between 1769 and 1826 he grew more than 250 varieties of vegetables in his kitchen garden.

Jefferson is known to have tried cultivating both white and purple broccoli, serpentine cucumbers, reputed to grow 4 feet long, and multi-headed cabbages. He planted peas as early as February 20, which as any local gardener knows is about a month ahead of schedule. But his mountain top elevation put him above the frosts of late spring and early fall. His southeastern exposure extended his growing season by several months. Hardy vegetables like kale, spinach, and endive would often survive the Virginia winters.

Only about 15 percent of the original vegetable varieties have survived. Of the fruit trees Jefferson grew, about 45 percent still exist. The 1981 garden restoration at Monticello added 280 fruit trees to the orchard. Jefferson grew 122 varieties of 10 different kinds of fruit, including apples, peaches, pears, nectarines, quince, plums, cherries, and apricots. Monticello has one of the largest collections of pre-1820 peach and cherry varieties in the United States.

On the vegetable terrace and overlooking the orchard was a garden Pavilion where Jefferson enjoyed reading and contemplating his "little mountain". Unfortunately the Pavilion was built on land that had been filled in as Jefferson graded for his mountain top garden. The terrace on which the Pavilion rested eroded and slid down the hill. As part of the 1981 restoration the square brick Pavilion with the pyramidal roof and Chinese railings was rebuilt on a more secure foundation. Restoration will be completed in the summer of 1983. Now, like Jefferson, you can rest at this inspired location and look out over the orchard and the plains beyond.

Though agricultural plants were especially important to Jefferson, he did not overlook the ornamental beds. Around the house are oval and circular flower beds. Another unusual touch at that time was a well-stocked fish pond near the south terrace Pavilion. Bordering the southern slope is the Mulberry Row, along which there were once 19 dependencies. Today you can see only two original buildings, the weaver's cottage (now offices) and the stable.

The neoclassical house abounds with Jefferson's creative touches. Included are recessed beds in the master bedroom, a 7-day calendar clock, triple-sash windows through which James Madison once tumbled, and a room Jefferson called the "sky room" because of its domed ceiling.

Monticello is open daily except Christmas from 8:00 A.M. to 5:00 P.M. March through October, and 9:00 A.M. to 4:30 P.M., November through February. Admission is charged.

Directions: Take Beltway Exit 9 west on I-66 to Gainesville. Exit onto Route 29. Continue to Charlottesville. Take the Route 250 By-Pass to I-64 east and follow the signs to Monticello.

Pennsylvania Horticultural Society's Colonial Garden Independence National Historical Park

A "greene Country Towne," the objective of William Penn in 1682, can be seen today at Independence National Historical Park, the realization of Penn's vision. Philadelphia, a city built by Penn with the help of other colonial leaders who also realized the importance of parks and gardens, was one of America's first cities to be developed according to a plan that included plants.

Early Philadelphia, the center of American horticulture, has been rebuilt and recreated on 48 acres at Independence National Historical Park. In addition to 40 historic buildings, numerous areas have 18th century plants to help recreate a sense of those early days. The Daughters of the American Revolution in 1971 added a Rose Garden. In 1959 a Magnolia Tribute Garden was given by the Garden Club of America to honor our Founding Fathers.

Other gardens include those on the grounds of the Norris and Pemberton Houses and the Pennsylvania Horticultural Society's garden at 325 Walnut Street. Like many gardens in the 1700s, the Horticultural Society's garden has three parts: a formal garden, an orchard, and the herb and vegetable area. In the formal parterres, or sections, you can see seasonal flowers. The colorful blooms highlight the disciplined symmetry of the enclosed, rectangular designs. Both imported flowers and native varieties are used.

Fragrant blossoms for cutting were included in the herb and vegetable garden. The herbs used in cooking as well as for medicine were extremely important. Finally, most gardens, even in cities like Philadelphia, attempted to include a small orchard, not only because the different fruits could be stored but also because they could be used to make juice or wine.

While exploring the many plant varieties included in the 18th century garden, you should be aware that in many cases they are the hybrids of species actually grown in colonial times. The original plants do not provide as good a showing as the later varieties. Among the native American plants to be seen are rhododendron, clethra, bayberry, leucothoe, hawthorne, trumpet vine, winterberry, and holly.

The colonists planted not only English favorites but also those obtained by English ships as they explored the world. Consequently, you will see plants from China like the ginkgo, chrysanthemum, and roses. From South Africa the geranium was added to the English gardens, and from Central America came the ageratum, zinnia, cosmos, lantana, and salvia. Many of the fruit trees were brought from Europe, including the apple and pear trees as well as the grape vines.

These plants form a felicitous design that can be seen at no charge year round, with winter obviously being the least interesting season. A gift shop with exhibits is open Monday through Friday from 9:00 A.M. to 5:00 P.M.. The garden is open daily at the same times except during July and August when it is open 8:30 A.M. to 4:30 P.M.

Directions: Take Beltway Exit 27 to I-95 north to Philadelphia, where it becomes Front Street. Turn left on Walnut Street to Independence National Historical Park.

John Bartram's House and Gardens

Another thriving garden in Philadelphia's urban setting is John Bartram's Gardens, America's first botanic gardens, started in 1930 on a 27-acre site.

John Bartram, a Quaker farmer without formal education, was recognized as one of the world's leading botanists. A true botanical explorer, he traveled throughout North America. He brought plants, seeds, and roots to his Pennsylvania farm where they thrived, though visitors commented that they seemed "jumbled around in heaps." Through Bartram's contacts in Europe he was responsible for introducing more than 200 plants to that continent.

Bartram diligently studied botany to further his pursuit of American specimens. He taught himself Latin so that he could understand the horticultural books that Benjamin Franklin, James Logan, and others gave him. Carl Linnaius, the noted Swedish scientist, called Bartram "the greatest natural botanist in the world." His importance was also recognized by George II, who in 1765 appointed Bartram a Royal Botanist.

Following in his father's footsteps quite literally was William, who Bartram called "my little botanist." William accompanied his father on many of the plant exploration forays. In 1765 they went to Florida together. William's interest was intense and he later spent four years traveling in the deep south. He wrote of this experience in *Travels of William Bartram*, published in 1791.

Another of Bartram's 11 children, John Jr., organized the botanical garden into a nursery at his father's death. He completed the first sales catalog of American plants.

Purchased as a city park in 1891, this garden has survived. Growing here today you will see descendants of the plants that made horticultural history. One such plant now extinct in the wild is the Franklinia Alatamaha named after the Bartrams's famous friend. When you explore this garden you might consider that you follow in the footsteps of George Washington, Thomas Jefferson, and many scientists who down through the years have also visited and admired Bartram's collection.

Be sure to allow enough time to also tour the 18th century farmhouse. After buying this 102-acre farm on the Schuylkill

River, John Bartram enlarged the existing stone house. Bartram, a skilled stone worker, added a pillared stone porch and carved stone window frames. One in the attic says "John–Ann Bartram 1731." His stone work can also be observed on a water trough and on the cider mill at the river's edge.

The Bartram Gardens are open daily during daylight hours year round. There is no charge to explore the gardens. A nominal admission is charged to tour the house, open April through October on Tuesday through Saturday from 10:00 A.M. to 4:00 P.M. The house is open Tuesday through Friday from November to March.

Directions: Take Beltway Exit 27, I-95 north, to Philadelphia. Exit from I-95 at Island Avenue. Go west on Island Avenue to Lindbergh Blvd. Travel north on Lindbergh to 54th Street. The John Bartram House and Gardens is at 54th Street and Lindbergh Blvd. in Philadelphia.

Schuyler-Hamilton House Colonial Garden

When you begin visiting colonial gardens, you can focus on the large well-known estates like Mount Vernon, Monticello, or Gunston Hall, or you can discover the smaller, less developed colonial gardens.

In the second category is the colonial garden of Dr. Jabez Campfield at the Schuyler-Hamilton House in Morristown, New Jersey. Though the Campfield garden was totally destroyed, the Home Garden Club of Morristown in 1964 presented the Schuyler-Hamilton House with a colonial garden in which the old flowers as well as the culinary and medicinal herbs grown 200 years ago by Dr. Campfield can be found.

You may wonder why the garden isn't named after Dr. Campfield? Dr. Campfield, who served in Colonel Oliver Spencer's regiment, offered his home to officers serving with Washington as they wintered over in Morristown in 1779–80. Dr. John Cochran, a member of Washington's staff and the Chief Physician and Surgeon of the Continental Army, stayed at the Campfield house with his wife and her niece, Miss Elizabeth Schuyler.

This lively young lady renewed her acquaintance with one of Washington's promising secretaries, Alexander Hamilton. By spring, when the flowers in Dr. Campfield's garden began blooming, their romance blossomed into a formal engagement. They were married in December 1780 in Albany, New York. Thus the house has come to be called the Schuyler-Hamilton House.

The house at 5 Olyphant Place now serves as the headquarters of the Morristown Chapter of the Daughters of the American Revolution. You can tour the house Tuesday through Sunday from 1:00 P.M. to 5:00 P.M. and also on George Washington's Birthday.

Directions: Take Beltway Exit 27 to I-95 north across the Delware Memorial Bridge. Continue north on the New Jersey Turnpike to the Garden State Parkway. Exit on Route 24 west to Morristown, New Jersey. In Morristown follow signs to the garden on Olyphant Place.

Herb Gardens

The National Herb Garden

From man's first experiments with plants to their analysis in today's science laboratories, herbs have been grown, collected, and used for a variety of purposes. Herbs also have often figured in music, legends, and folklore.

The world's largest designed herb garden is located in Washington, D.C. at the National Arboretum. This two-acre garden, directly opposite the Arboretum's Administration Building, is arranged according to three major areas of interest. Spacious walks and benches provide easy access and numerous opportunities to contemplate the felicitous mixture of smells and sights.

After passing the reception area you will see the first focal point of the collection, the Knot Garden. Your initial view will be from the fountain terrace overlooking this sunken garden. The terrace is surrounded by osmanthus and boxwood hedges and a collection of thymes in semicircular beds.

Knot gardens, popular in 16th century England, with their intricate, geometric patterns, decorated many of the old manor homes. This Knot Garden is larger than most of the older gardens of this type; and because of its larger size, it uses dwarf evergreens rather than the more traditional herb plants. Interwoven chains are created by the massed dwarf evergreens. In keeping with the nature of the garden the three varieties of evergreens that make up this classic knot design are used for medicinal and industrial purposes. The resins, barks, and needles of the arborvitae, cypress, and holly may all be used.

Proceeding down the walkway to the second special area, you will come to the Historic Rose Garden. A trellis-covered, benched overlook enables you to enjoy this fragrant garden, which features species roses that bloom in June and early July. These roses have long been used as medicines, perfumes, food, and the pleasure that comes from the aromatic blossoms. Other fragrant plants in this garden are rosemary, lemon verbena, and heliotrope.

As part of the Historic Rose Garden you will also see the armillary, a series of circles used as an ancient astronomical instrument to tell the "sun time."

The third section of the National Herb Garden is actually 10 specialty gardens surrounded by a boxwood hedge. In the center is a grassy oval planted with small herbal trees.

The first grouping is the Dioscorides' Garden. Dioscorides was a Greek physician, who practiced in 60 A.D. Modern pharmacology started with his systematic listing of medicinal plants. The herbs in this garden are from the list *De Materia Medica,* which Dioscorides wrote in 60 A.D. Plants include marsh mallow, anise, coriander, oregano, garlic, and chamomile.

Other specialty gardens include the Dye Garden, Early American Garden, Indian Garden, Herbs Around the World, Plants in Medicine, the Culinary Garden, Industrial Garden, Fragrance Garden, and the Beverage Garden.

These gardens are not only interesting for their plants but also for the historical and cultural information that can be gleaned from a careful noting of the various herbs.

The National Herb Garden is a joint project of the National Arboretum and the National Herb Society of America. The Herb Society provided the funds necessary to begin this project as a Bicentennial gift to the nation. As information on herbs is continually growing, these gardens are not a static finished product but a changing display reflecting new knowledge and the availability of new plants. Each visit can provide new insights.

The variety of plants presented in this Herb Garden far exceed any listing in the most complete garden catalog. It provides a fascinating chance to see plants that, heretofore, you may have only encountered in old cookbooks, historical studies or on the pharmacist's shelf.

This garden alone is certainly worth a trip to the National Arboretum (see listing in Arboretums), but combined with the annual flower shows held here and the seasonal variety to be enjoyed the Arboretum should be a repeated garden excursion.

The National Arboretum is open daily at no charge from 8:00 A.M. to 5:00 P.M. on weekdays and from 10:00 A.M. to 5:00 P.M. on weekends. It is closed Christmas Day.

Directions: The National Arboretum is within the Beltway at 3501 New York Avenue, N.E. There are entrances from New York Avenue and Bladensburg Road.

Rosamonde Bierne Herb Garden at the National Colonial Farm

Some gardens should not be visited alone, not because they have romantic appeal but because the visitor alone cannot fully experience them unless accompanied by a guide.

This is particularly true of the Rosamonde Bierne Herb Garden. Its many delights become apparent only when viewed with the help of a costumed staff member of the National Colonial Farm. Those who work there not only have planted and tended these herbs, they have also used the herbs as they were in the 18th century. As the colonists in their day experimented with the different spices and herbs so do their 20th century counterparts. Many rashes and allergies, of course, resulted from the initial efforts of those in both eras.

The story of how the herbs can be used is only one benefit of an escorted foray into the herb garden. The second advantage is that with a trained guide you can smell, touch, and even taste the various herbs. This is something you should never try on your own because many herbs were grown for medicinal use and have to be taken carefully; others are not meant to be tasted.

At the National Colonial Farm herb garden you will see herbs that might have been grown on a Maryland farm from 1750 to 1775. These herbs were very important to colonial families; not only did they give the colonists a chance to vary their diets by adding herbs, they also served a very important medicinal function. A third, cosmetic use should also be mentioned.

Some herbs actually could be used for all three purposes. For example, marjoram, introduced into the colonies in 1631, has leaves that were mixed with mint for a tea believed to cure nervous headaches. The leaves, either fresh or dried, were also used to flavor soups, meats, vegetables, and poultry dishes. When home-brewed beer became popular the fresh tops of the marjoram plant were added for a little extra "snap." Sprigs of the fresh herb were used to scent linens and to repel moths. The oil from this plant could also be used as a furniture polish.

Costmary can also be used for all three purposes; bundles of leaves were put on the bed to scent the linen and to protect against moths. Leaves were also used for antiseptics and astringents; and they were added to ale, salads, soups, sausage, and teas for fragrance. Another use demonstrates how clever colonists were in adapting this multifaceted herb. The custom of placing a leaf of costmary in the family Bible enabled colonists during long church services to sniff the aromatic herb and to stay awake through extended sermons. From this practice the herb came to be called "Bible leaf."

Many herbs have interesting footnotes to their usage. Of sage it was said, "Why should a man die when sage flourishes in his garden?" Sage was believed to ensure long life. In New England early Americans chilled lemon balm in a bucket down a well to make "New England lemonade." The Indians introduced the colonists to iris versicolor, or blue flag, which they used as a laxative. This is not recommended today as side effects include nausea and severe prostration.

These are some of the more than 50 different herbs that can be seen at the National Colonial Farm. Other colonial favorites include bugle, burnet, clary, feverfew, Good King Henry, hyssop, rue, Saint Johnswort, santolina, soapwort, wormwood, and yarrow. If you get inspired by the smell or taste of these herbs you can purchase a number of varieties of dried herbs and herbal products at the farm's Herb Shop.

One departure from the 18th century that this farm does concede 20th century visitors is that today the animals are penned. In colonial days the gardens were fenced and the livestock wandered. All the livestock and crops at this farm, however, were common in the 1700s. It is interesting to watch the farmers till the fields and prepare the home-grown produce in the out-kitchen.

In addition to the herb garden and fields of tobacco, corn, and wheat you can see the orchard and grape arbors. Water was rarely consumed in colonial times so they made fruit juice and wine.

A nature trail winds through the woods. You will have several good views of Mount Vernon looking like a doll house across the river. This is a good place to reflect on America's past. It was here in 1608 that Captain John Smith encountered the Piscataway Indians at a town he called Moyaone. Before the Indians settled in this area five prehistoric groups are known to have used this land. As you walk the trail you can indeed feel that you are walking the path back to the beginnings of man's time on this continent.

The National Colonial Farm is open Tuesday through Sunday from 10:00 A.M. to 5:00 P.M.. A nominal admission is charged. On many summer weekends there are craft and cooking demonstrations. Many of these programs deal with the growing, drying, and cooking of the herbs grown here.

Directions: From the Beltway take Exit 3 in Maryland to Indian Head Highway south for 10 miles. At the traffic light for Bryan Point Road, turn right and continue 4 miles to the end of the road.

Clearwater Nature Center Herb Garden

A small but new herb garden can be seen at the Clearwater Nature Center, part of the Louise F. Cosca Regional Park in Clinton, Maryland.

Encompassed within a shield-shaped, 48-by-15-foot area, this combination herb and wildflower garden was begun from seeds and small plants in 1978. It includes both domestic plants that were considered "edible wild plants" and those used for herbal tea. You'll see motherwort, anise hyssop, woad, mountain mint, beebalm, beefsteak plant, santolina, costmary, comfry, orange mint, fennel, sage horseradish, lemon balm, borage, lavender, European horsemint, wormwood, catnip, chives, soapwort, ajuga, and others.

This is not a garden with large showy flowers. Rather, it is planned to illustrate herbs once commonly used in this area. Herbs are also featured in the Clearwater Nature Center's Sensory Garden, which was established as a trail accessible to the handicapped. A wide asphalt path permits wheelchairs to negotiate this garden walk. The forest canopy limits the plants that can be included in this garden. Plants chosen were picked for their visual appeal as well as their appeal to touch and smell.

Plants in the Sensory Garden include goldenrod, lamb's ears, spearmint, mullein, paulownia, yarrow, raspberries, burdock, teasel, violet, fern, pinxter flower, mistflower, lemon balm, wild strawberry, and Jerusalem artichoke.

Visitors should check to see what nature-oriented programs are planned at the Clearwater Nature Center. They have a year-round schedule of interesting activities. Along the wooded trails at this 500-acre park you can see 67 different species of trees.

Naturalists conduct many different hikes throughout the year: bird watching hikes, creek hikes, wildflower hikes, night hikes, insect hikes, and others. There are five miles of hiking and bridle trails at Cosca.

The lovely Lake Louise is a focal spot in the park. Boats are available to rent during the summer. On the banks of the lake is an innovative children's playground area. Fort Clinton provides an impetus to youthful imaginations and many a recreated battle has been fought here. A pumpkin coach, rocket slides, wagons, and Indian teepees all add to the fun.

The park is open at no charge to county residents year-round during daylight hours. To obtain information on special programs you can call (301)297-4575.

Directions: Take Beltway Exit 7A to Route 5 south. Continue south on Route 5, then turn right on Route 223 and then left on Brandywine Road, Route 381. Continue on Brandywine Road, then make a right turn onto Thrift Road, which leads directly into the park.

Stillridge Herb Farm

Have you ever heard of a "tussie mussie?" After a visit to the Stillridge Herb Farm, these delightful 17th century nosegays may well become a must on your gift-giving list.

At Stillridge these floral messages that were so popular during the colonial period express a myriad of sentiments. A bouquet with rosemary and sweet marjoram amid the pretty dried flowers will offer wishes for rememberance and happiness. The uncertain giver can choose basil, which symbolizes both love and hate. Other herbs and their meanings include: thyme, courage and bravery; mint, wisdom; sage, long life; strawberry leaves, foresight; and pansy, immortality. These long-lasting bouquets wrapped in lace and tied with ribbons are just one of many special herbal gifts created by Mary Lou Riddle with the more than 350 herbs grown at the Stillridge Herb Farm.

Stillridge is a perfect example of an avocational interest that grew into a thriving business. Mary Lou Riddle in 1972 planted orange mint, lavender, lemon balm, and oregano in the garden of her newly remodeled farm. All but the orange mint died, but her reading about herbs and her fascination with their multiple uses encouraged her to try again. Visitors to her nine-acre farm can readily see how successful she has been.

You can arrange to attend a tour of the herb gardens, a delightful herbal lunch, and an informative talk by Mary Lou Riddle on the intricacies of growing and using herbs. If you don't want to bother with advance reservations you are welcome to drop in to see the herb garden, greenhouses, drying rooms, and the Herb Shop. Should the many aromatic smells and charming herbal arrangements inspire you to plant herbs in your own garden you may want to heed Mrs. Riddle's advice to start with small plants since seeds take a long time to germinate and to become established.

You can buy more than 100 different herb plants at the farm, from the common ones to the hard-to-find. Interested persons unable to schedule a trip to the farm can send 75¢ to Stillridge Herb Farm, 10370 Route 99, Woodstock, Maryland 21163 to obtain a catalog. It includes a listing of plants plus an array of unusual gifts and decorative herbal arrangements. The Stillridge Herb Wreath was featured in *House and Gardens* magazine in the December issues of 1978 and 1979. This special wreath uses more than 30 different fragrant herbs, herbal flowers, and cinnamon sticks. It is just one of the wreaths created at the farm.

If you visit the farm you may also want to stop at the nearby Stillridge Herb Shop in Ellicott City. Hours for the shop are 10:30 A.M. to 5:00P.M. daily, excluding holidays. The Stillridge Herb Farm is open 9:00 A.M. until 4:00 P.M., Monday through Saturday. To arrange an herbal luncheon, lecture, and tour, call (301)465-8348.

Directions: Take Beltway Exit 30 to Route 29 north past Columbia, Maryland. Make a left on Route 99. The farm is located at 10370 Route 99 in Woodstock. The Stillridge Herb Shop is located at 8129 Main Street in Ellicott City, Maryland.

Rising Sun Tavern Garden

An award-winning re-creation of an 18th century tavern garden can be enjoyed today in Fredericksburg, Virginia, at the Rising Sun Tavern. Structurally unaltered, the story-and-a-half frame building has been fully restored to its colonial appearance. Suggestive of the original garden is an oyster shell path leading to the grounds from the brick-paved courtyard.

A small vegetable garden and an herb planter in colonial days produced enough to augment the tavern fare. Herbs grown at the Rising Sun Tavern are rosemary, lemon balm, tarragon, lavender, tansy, wormwood, santolina, rue, sage, and mint. Herbs were also used in the colonal period for medicinal purposes and housekeeping.

Also in the yard area are three small dependencies: the meat house, well house, and dovecote. A grape arbor and fruit trees provide the necessary ingredients for making juice and wine.

This tavern has an interesting history. It was owned during the colonial period by George Washington's younger brother, Charles. Many well-known figures of that era enjoyed the hospitality of this tavern, including Thomas Jefferson, Patrick Henry, George Mason, Hugh Mercer, Richard Henry Lee, Francis Lightfoot Lee, and of course George Washington and General Lafayette.

Spring and fall are the best seasons to enjoy the tavern garden but the Rising Sun Tavern is open daily year round. Hours are 10:00 A.M. to 4:00 P.M. in January and February; 9:00 A.M. to 5:00 P.M. in April through October; and 9:00 A.M. to 4:00 P.M. in November and December. Admission is charged.

Directions: Take Beltway Exit 4 to I-95 south to Fredericksburg, Virginia. The Rising Sun Tavern is at 1306 Caroline Street.

Agecroft Hall

Many exquisite copies of English and European estates have been built on this side of the Atlantic. Few, however, have been moved here stone by stone and beam by beam. But that is, in fact, what Mr. and Mrs. Thomas C. Williams, Jr. did with Agecroft Hall.

This ancient Tudor house was built in the 1400s before Columbus began his voyage of discovery. John Langley built Agecroft near a 12th century village in Lancashire, England. The name was derived from a combination of ache, meaning wild celery, and croft, meaning field.

This sturdily built home was a combination of Gothic and Renaissance styles, in the half-timbered manner. The house was built to endure and it did, into the 1920s. By that time industrialization of nearby Manchester threatened the foundations of the house. It was then that the Williamses stepped in and had the house carefully taken apart, shipped to Richmond, Virginia, and faithfully re-created on the banks of the James River. You see it today as it would have looked in 16th century England.

The interior is not extensively furnished; but it, too, gives an idea of the lifestyle of an English family of substance. It is the craftsmanship of the house that impresses visitors—the grandeur of the two-story Great Hall, the delicacy of the mullion windows and carved oak panels.

But all this is just an added bonus to garden fanciers who will enjoy exploring Agecroft Hall in order to see the English gardens. One of the most exciting gardens was recently added and contains herbs known in Elizabethan England. This garden is wheel-shaped, with roses forming the center and rosemary the long spokes. Between these spokes you will see a variety of early English herbs, many of which found their way into Shakespeare's plays—he spoke of rosemary for rememberance; rue symbolized repentence; thyme and heartsease were mentioned in *A Midsummer's Night's Dream.* In the Shakespearean Garden in Stratford-on-Avon one can see the same small marigolds. Other herbs include lavender, which was Elizabeth I's favorite, gillyflowers, sage, savory, burnet, horehound, scented geraniums, yarrow, artemisia, hyssop, lemon balm, tansy, lovage, larkspur, and wallflowers.

This is just the beginning. Another popular attraction at Agecroft Hall is the sunken garden copied from Hampton Court.

This rectangular garden appears more open than most formal English gardens because it is not arranged with parterres.

Below the sunken garden is the formal garden which does have parterres. In early spring the garden features daffodils and tulips. In fact, the peak blooming period is in April when both the tulip and azalea, with bordering candytuft, are in bloom. The pink and white hues are particularly attractive.

Throughout the summer the authentic 15th century cutting garden has flowers in bloom. The plantings go back to those suggested in John Parkinson's 1629 edition of *Paradise in Sole-Paradisus Terrestris*. Along the river side of the garden is a lovely crape myrtle allée best seen in late summer.

Like the Elizabethan Garden in North Carolina, Agecroft Hall has created a little bit of old England on our shores. Agecroft is open year round. The hours are 10:00 A.M. to 4:00 P.M., Tuesday through Friday, and 2:00 P.M. to 5:00 P.M. on weekends. Admission is charged.

Directions: Take Beltway Exit 4 to I-95 south to Richmond. In Richmond pick up the Powhite Parkway. Take a right on Cary Street, a left on Locke Lane, and another left on Sulgrave Road. Agecroft Hall is at 4305 Sulgrave Road on the James River in Richmond, Virginia.

Other gardens with herb gardens:

The Bishop's Garden
Hershey Gardens
Reeves Reed Arboretum
Willowwood Arboretum
London Town Gardens
William Paca Garden
Oatlands
Swiss Pines

Wildflowers

Cylburn Arboretum

There is a natural harmony to the 12 trails that criss-cross the 70 acres of the Cylburn Wildlife Preserve, part of the larger 176-acre Cylburn Arboretum in Baltimore.

Along the trails, flowers and trees are labeled. There is even a special Bird Walk. At least 150 species of birds have been sighted at Cylburn, which is designated as a bird sanctuary. Bird feeders are randomly placed; in the wooded areas, trees and bushes that fall are left to be used as homes by the birds and small animals.

The major thrust at Cylburn is the informal areas, but Cylburn does contain a Formal Garden with beds of flowering perennials that are particularly appealing during May and June.

Another formal area has been selected as one of 105 All-American Display Gardens. Here flower and vegetable annuals not yet available for sale to the public can be seen.

Cylburn has special attractions for special people. The visually impaired and wheelchair visitors can enjoy the Garden of the Senses. Plants in this garden appeal through their scent and texture. They are labeled and all information is repeated in Braille. Youngsters can also benefit by exploring the Educational or Children's Trail, which has learning appeal to others as well. An arboretum also enables visitors to identify and study trees and shrubs.

All this natural beauty is arranged on the grounds of the Cylburn Mansion, which was started in 1863 by Jesse Tyson. Construction was interrupted by the Civil War, but the house was completely ready in 1888 for Tyson's new bride. It was not until 1942 that the mansion and grounds were purchased by the city of Baltimore to be used as a park. Garden exhibits are often held in the mansion.

Today this city arboretum provides a great deal of country to explore. It is open daily year round during daylight hours. Cylburn is not a park for picnicking or ball playing; rather it is an open-air classroom that makes learning a pleasurable experience. As at all public grounds, there is no picking or collecting the delightful blossoms.

Directions: Take Beltway Exit 27, I-95 north, to the Baltimore Beltway. Turn left towards Catonsville. Then take the Greenspring Avenue exit south from the Baltimore Beltway and follow that to 4915 Greenspring Avenue and the well-marked arboretum entrance on the left.

Woodend

Though not technically an arboretum, Woodend—the headquarters of the Audubon Naturalist Society in Chevy Chase, Maryland—is noted for its magnificent specimens of native and ornamental trees.

This 40-acre estate bordering Rock Creek Park is a wildlife sanctuary where along the trail you will see a variety of fruit and flowering trees as well as many of the more than 30 resident species of birds. By walking quietly you may even see a squirrel, rabbit, or woodchuck. Their different habitats can also be seen: wooded areas, including a hemlock and pine grove, an open meadow, and a pond. This permits a greater diversity in both plant and animal life.

Around the Georgian revival mansion built in 1928 are a number of specimen trees and a sunken garden. The estate has been naturalized and little else remains from earlier formal garden arrangements. By late winter the snowdrop and winter aconite add their delicate blossoms to the rock garden that is part of the sunken area. Springtime flowers include chionodoxa, spring beauty, columbine, phlox, primrose, and Greek valerian. The grounds are also brightened with wildflowers along the nature trail and with bluebells, trout lily, and foamflowers on the stream bank.

Flowering trees join the spring show—magnolia, dogwood, redbud, cherry, horse chestnut, crab apple, and pears. Each April Woodend hosts an annual spring plant sale. Visitors can enjoy the peak garden display and also purchase some of the lovely day lilies that bloom in late June and early July. The day lily is the featured plant, but many others are also on sale.

After the flowers of spring and summer, the foliage of fall provides yet another inducement for an afternoon's excursion. Colors range from the yellow of the gingkos, the vibrant gold of the sassafras to the red of the Japanese maples and the purple and blue of the porcelain berries.

One tree that actually blooms in the fall is the rare Franklinia Altamaha you can see behind the greenhouse. Discovered in 1790 by William Bartram, son of the famous colonial botanical collector John Bartram, this tree is a member of the camellia and tea family along the Altamaha River in Georgia. William Bartram sent specimens back to his father's garden in Philadelphia, where the tree was grown and propagated. Return trips to this part of Georgia failed to reveal other trees of this type so the only ones to be seen today are descendents of the specimens preserved by William Bartram and named for his father's good friend Benjamin Franklin.

The grounds of Woodend, which with the house are listed in the National Register of Historic Places, are open daily dawn to dusk and are free to the public. The mansion, designed in the 1920s by John Russell Pope, architect for the Jefferson Memorial and the National Gallery of Art, is open Monday through Friday, 9:00 A.M. to 5:00 P.M.

The Audubon Naturalist Society operates a bookshop that offers a particularly fine selection of books related to plants, animals, and bird life. The shop is open Monday through Friday, 10:00 A.M. to 5:00 P.M., and on Sundays from mid-March through mid-April, except Easter, from 1:00 P.M. to 5:00 P.M. For information on the annual spring plant sale call (301)652-9188.

Directions: Take Beltway Exit 33 south on Connecticut Avenue towards Chevy Chase. Turn left on Manor Road, then right on Jones Bridge Road. Turn left on Jones Mill Road to entrance on left at 8940 Jones Mill Road.

Chancellor's Point Natural History Center

Chancellor's Point Natural History Center is a new attraction recently added to what has long been one of the best family summer outings available, a day at St. Mary's City, Maryland. Opened in 1981, this 66-acre natural history park allows you to see how man has interacted here with the land and the water from the earliest times to the present.

At this beautiful park on the St. Mary's River, a 40-foot long mural depicts the history of this site. It shows how the native population before 1634 practiced a "slash and burn" approach to clearing the underbrush and hunting the wild deer. The first settlers are shown in the years 1634 to 1700 clearing the land, raising livestock, and cultivating the soil. Although hopes that St. Mary's would become an important city died when the capital of the colony was moved to Annapolis in the 1690s, St. Mary's has continued as a successful farming area. The mural ends with the present and you will recognize the very building that houses the center, complete with resident dog and cat.

Fossils and other natural "finds" from the site are set out for the visitor to handle. The park naturalist will tell you about these and other exhibits. A popular activity with the young is doing a rubbing from available carved wooden patterns. There is a wooden rubbing on native wildlife and another on introduced species such as dandelions and housecats.

An excellent pamphlet will help you explore the park. The map of the woodland trails points out some of the indigenous vegetation you will observe. The pamphlet also includes information on recovered fossils, dating to a period 12 million years ago when a shallow sea extended as far inland as Washington, D.C. Drawings in the pamphlet will help you identify shells in the Miocene Marineland, a stop on your walk around the grounds.

Just outside the center is a lovely garden, where many of the plants used in the nature programs are grown. Proceeding to the water's edge you can enjoy the striking panoramic view of the St. Mary's River. The pamphlet will tell you about the historical points of interest that existed along this river hundreds of years ago. You can see Priest Point, the location in 1637 of the first Catholic Mission in British North America. Another interesting spot is the place where a 1645 sea battle took place between an English ship under the command of Captain Richard Ingle and the Dutch merchant ship *Spyglass*. Looking north you will see where the King of the Yeocomico Indians had his home in prehistoric times.

Throughout the year there are many special programs hosted by the Chancellor's Point Natural History Center, which is open daily, except Christmas, from dawn to dusk. In mid-October, the annual Aboriginal Life Day offers a chance to try hunting bows, scraping out a canoe, a sauna-like sweet lodge, flintknapping, and Indian foods such as persimmons, eels, and racoon stew. There is a program on edible plants, beekeeping, birdwatching, stargazing, and many other topics of interest. To obtain additional information you can call (301)994-0808. Picnic tables, charcoal grills, and even a beach for swimming or wading make this a great place to enjoy a leisurely lunch after exploring the nature center and the woodland loop trail. After June, however, swimmers should be on the alert for jellyfish.

No visit to this part of southern Maryland during the summer months is complete without a stop to see the Living History Theatre, which is performed at St. Mary's City on weekends. Stop at the Reconstructed State House of 1676 for directions to the day's activities. These may include a lively vignette at the Godiah Spray Plantation or a spirited treason trial at the Old State House. Annual events that are popular include the Children's Festival, Philip Calvert Crab Feast, and Militia Day.

Directions: Take Beltway Exit 7 to Route 5 and go all the way to St. Mary's City. Signs will direct you to the State House and the Chancellor's Point Natural History Center.

The Henry Foundation for Botanical Research

We all know one gardener who can grow anything, who often achieves the impossible—fruits that wither on your vines thrive on his; bugs, moles, and killing frosts also seem to make fewer dents in his garden.

Though inspiring a bit of envy, gardens nurtured by these uncanny horticulturists can offer a glimpse of rarely seen and hard to grow plants. One very special connoisseur's garden is in Gladwyne, Pennsylvania—the Henry Foundation for Botanical Research.

Don't be put off by the name, the foundation is a lot less formal than it sounds. In fact, the grounds are maintained in a natural state even to the extent of having no paths to follow. It is surprising how much of a difference this makes. The wild, uncultivated effect is achieved even though the plants are labeled and carefully nurtured. It is important to keep in mind that the foundation is primarily a research facility. Gardens are laid out to facilitate the plants' growth and survival. Visitors must do some real walking to see the collection.

The terrain is steep and rocky, offering protection for some of the fragile plants. The rock garden is planted amid a large outcrop of Baltimore gneiss boulders. It is the perfect backdrop for the phlox, hesperales of Mexico, artemisia of British Columbia and penstemon from the Rocky Mountains, to name just a few of the varieties to be discovered here.

It was in 1926 that Dr. J. Norman Henry and his wife, Mary, purchased 90 acres outside of Philadelphia. In 1948 a section of that land was set aside as The Henry Foundation for Botanical Research. Today, this is a 40-acre sanctuary for many rare and endangered plants.

One of the first plants that Mary Henry attempted to find for her collection in the late 1920s was the scarce deciduous rhododendron. A trip to Georgia enabled her to obtain some of these flowering spring bushes. On the lower slopes of the foundation's southern garden these deciduous rhododendron can be seen with other plants. Of particular interest to Mrs. Henry was the genus Lilium, one of which bears her name, L. Mary Henryae. Following in her mother's footsteps, Josephine de N. Henry, has since described three new lily species and continues to direct and add to the collection. Other native American plants grown and propagated at the foundation include styrax, halesias, magnolia, and trillium.

A visit to the Henry Foundation is a very unique garden excursion that allows visitors to see plants as they would appear in the wild. The peak periods are in April and May for the azaleas, rhododendron, trilliums, and wildflowers and in September and October for the perennials and fall foliage. The Henry Foundation for Botanical Research is open at no charge April through October on Tuesday and Thursday from 10:00 A.M. to 4:00 P.M. and at other times by appointment. Call (215)525-2037 or write the Henry Foundation for Botanical Research, Box 7, Gladwyne, Pennsylvania 19035.

Directions: Take Beltway Exit 27 to I-95 north to Philadelphia. Pick up I-76 (Route 13, Chester Pike, serves as a link between I-95 and I-76) and continue westbound to the Gladwyne exit. Turn left from ramp and drive to Conshohocken State Road, Route 23. Turn right and go west 2 miles to Henry Road. Turn right on Henry Road and left on Stony Lane; the entrance to the foundation is on the right.

Bowman's Hill Wildflower Preserve

The names of the 26 trails and habitat areas at Bowman's Hill Wildflower Preserve reveal the scope of this 100-acre park—Audubon, Azalea, Azaleas-at-the-Bridge, Bluebell, Bucks County Nature, Cornus Bend-Aster Walk, Evergreen, Fern, Foresters' Forest, Gentian, Little Meadow, Marshmarigold, Medicinal, Poconos Laurel, Pond, Sphagnum Bog, and Wayside and Violet trails.

This preserve has been maintained since 1934 as a "living memorial to the valiant patriots of Washington's Army." When Washington Crossing Historic Park was established it called for the preservation of the adjoining land. In pursuing this objective more than 1,000 different kinds of native trees, shrubs, vines, and wildflowers have been protected. Although most grow here naturally some were added in appropriate habitats.

April and May are the best months for spotting wildflowers in bloom along the trails, with the greatest concentration occurring in early May. Monthly blooming lists and self-guiding trail maps can be picked up at the Headquarters Building. Outside this information center is the Headquarters Garden, which demonstrates the native plants best suitable for the ordinary garden.

Also adjacent to this building and visible from the windows of the auditorium is the Sinkler Observation Area. A natural habitat has been carefully created to attract birds and other wildlife. Those interested in spotting various birds should see the bird collection, with its well-marked specimens, eggs, and nests, in the Charles Platt Museum on the lower level of the Headquarters Building.

Both the Audubon Trail for bird watchers and the Little Meadow Trail are good for summer hikes. The spring blooming wildflowers are followed by the meadow flowers and you can see marsh mallow, Turk's-cap lily, and lizard's-tail in bloom. Later in the fall, the Cardinal-Flower and goldenrod bloom along the pond banks. Around the restful pond you will also see other water-loving plants.

Other water sensitive plants can be seen at Sphagnum Bog, where the cranberry, climbing ferns, and swamp hyacinths prosper.

At any time of the year it is interesting to explore two other areas of Washington Crossing State Park, Foresters' Forest and Penn's Woods. The former is a heavily wooded area along Pidcock Creek. A trail follows an old logging road to this special ecology study area. In Penn's Woods 400 trees have been dedicated in memorium as part of a major reforestation effort.

The park is open at no charge Monday through Saturday 10:00 A.M. until 4:30 P.M. and from 9:00 A.M. to 5:00 P.M. during Daylight Saving Time. Sunday hours are noon to 5:00 P.M.

While in this area two other points of interest are worth visiting. The first is Washington Crossing Historic Park. Many of the historic buildings of 1776 have been restored. You can tour the Thompson-Neely House, which was used as headquarters for various Continental army officers. From here Washington planned his surprise attack on the Hessian soldiers. At the Memorial Building is a copy of the over-size painting by Emanuel Leutze of *Washington Crossing the Delaware*. These historic reminders are open Tuesday through Saturday from 10:00 A.M. to 4:30P.M. and on Sunday from noon to 4:30 P.M.

Just two and a half miles north in New Hope, Pennsylvania, is another "must" stop. Here are quaint craft shops, interesting restaurants, barge rides on the Delaware Canal, and a 14-mile steam train ride through rural Pennsylvania on the New Hope and Ivyland Railroad. This town is also noted for its artists and galleries that can be found throughout the community. It makes for a full day's excursion but one with great diversity.

Directions: Take Beltway Exit 27 to I-95 north to Pennsylvania. Exit at New Hope just before crossing the Delaware River into New Jersey. Go north to Pa. 532 and then east to Pa. 32. Signs will direct visitors to the various attractions in the park including Bowman's Hill Wildflower Preserve.

Conservatories

U.S. Botanic Garden Conservatory

The first U.S. Botanic Garden greenhouse was built in 1842 to accommodate the collection that Captain Charles Wilkes of the U.S. Exploring Expedition to the South Seas brought back to Washington, D.C. The objectives of the new conservatory were " . . . to collect, cultivate and grow the various vegetable production of this and other countries for exhibition and display. . . ."

This is certainly being done at the U.S. Botanic Garden Conservatory's six houses. These houses aren't separate buildings but rather a series of interconnecting rooms under 29,000 square feet of glass. A self-guiding tour map enables you to locate groups of plants of botanic, esthetic, or economic interest.

Upon entering you will be in the Subtropical House, where you will see the world famous Orchid Collection. Orchids are found in every continent except Antarctica, and there are 30,000 species. The Botanic Garden raises more than 11,000 plants and at any given time 200 flowering orchids are on display. Behind the orchids is one of the oldest plants in the conservatory, a vessel fern believed to be part of the garden's original collection in 1842.

Children are always interested in the next specimen, the sapodilla, because it is also called the chewing gum tree. Sapodillas are tapped for chicle, a milky latex substance used in making gum. The tree also bears a fruit popular in the tropics that looks like an Irish potato and tastes like a pear.

Two plants in the same family are the banana and the traveler's tree. One of the staple plants in tropical areas, the banana has one of the highest yields per acre of any crop. The fan-like traveler's tree, as the name suggests, provides a drink to the thirsty. Tropical travelers discovered that water accumulates at the base of its leaves which spread like a fan from the trunk.

The botanical collection also has vanilla and coffee plants as well as the interesting banyan and breadfruit trees. The banyan's unusual asexual propagation sometimes results in one plant producing a dense forested area through which light cannot penetrate. Fables claim that in 330 B.C. Alexander the Great was able to shelter an entire 7,000 man force under a banyon tree.

Breadfruit also has a place in history. Captain William Bligh's ill-fated mission to bring breadfruit from Tahiti to the British West Indies was immortalized in *Mutiny on the Bounty*. Breadfruit did ultimately make the transition to the Caribbean and is now common there, providing a fruit that can be fried, boiled, or baked.

The second house at the Botanic Garden contains the Cycad Collection. The cone-producing trees bear one to three large cones weighing up to 50 pounds each. Considered fossil trees because of their great age, cycads predate the dinosaurs. The garden's collection of 12 varieties of this ancient plant is considered the finest in the world.

You will next explore the Fern, Palm, Cactus, and Bromelian Collections. Each displays a wide selection of plants. The Botanic Garden also includes some 90 varieties of the American-developed azalea group in its 400-plant collection. The three hundred chrysanthemums are particularly enjoyable in the fall.

Seasonal emphasis is noted in the four annual plant and flower displays. The first of the yearly shows is at Easter time and features masses of spring flowering plants. From late May through early September the Summer Terrace Display is on view. There are hundreds of hanging baskets of fuchsias, lantanas, impatiens, ivies, coleus, and petunias. Around the terrace are beds with more than 500 annuals.

The third show is held from mid-November through Thanksgiving weekend and spotlights the garden's chrysanthemum collection. The last show of the year is the Christmas poinsettias.

A public park on Independence Avenue across from the conservatory features blooming annuals and perennials. The U.S. Botanic Garden Park has marigolds, begonias, geraniums, and verbenas, as well as many other varieties. One of the garden areas that delights the young is the butterfly-shaped bed.

The U.S. Botanic Garden Conservatory is open 9:00 A.M. to 5:00 P.M. There is no charge to visit and meter parking is available in front of the building.

Directions: The U.S. Botanic Garden Conservatory is inside the Washington, D.C. Beltway at 245 First Street, S.W., near the base of Capitol Hill at the eastern end of the Mall.

Brookside Gardens at Wheaton Regional Park

It's worth remembering in mid-winter that a world of colorful plants is waiting for you at the Brookside Gardens in Wheaton, Maryland.

The Brookside conservatories, part of a 50-acre free public garden complex, has flowers blooming year round. Within this greenhouse environment you'll see tree ferns and ficus benjamina along side a meandering stream. Permanent plants include bird of paradise, hibiscus, pittosporum and azaleas. Children enjoy crossing the stream on the stepping stone path while older visitors use the footbridge.

In addition to the regular exhibits that can be enjoyed all year, the Brookside Gardens hosts three seasonal displays—the Chrysanthemum, Christmas, and Spring Flower Displays. In November chrysanthemums decorate the conservatories. You'll see multiple varieties growing in cascades, upright columns, and even miniature tree-shaped chrysanthemums.

The annual Christmas Display at Brookside Gardens not only includes 12-foot poinsettia trees but also flowering cyclamen and Jerusalem cherry.

Fuchsias, hydrangeas, azaleas, lilies and many other spring flowering plants are regular favorites at the spring flower showcase. Of course, depending on when this annual event occurs, you may also be able to explore the outdoor display area for flowering spring bulbs. In late April the outdoor azaleas begin blooming; they reach their peak during the month of May.

Next to bloom in June at Brookside Gardens is the Rose Garden. This garden, which includes approximately 60 varieties, is one of the All-American Rose demonstration gardens. Rose fanciers will be able to get a preview of each year's All-American Rose selections a full year before they become available. Another area where you may get a glimpse of things to come is the Trial Garden, where annuals are tested and evaluated.

In 1974 a Fragrance Garden was added to Brookside Gardens. This is a representative collection of herbs chosen with emphasis on their aroma rather than their visual appeal. Be sure to sample the smells—the delicate lavender, spicy oregano, and tangy peppermint. You can also experience this garden by touch. The texture of the lamb's ear plant leaves little doubt as to how it got the name.

The disciplined Formal Gardens feature bulbs in March and April, annuals and perennials bloom from May until frost, and chrysanthemums in September and October. A series of ponds in the Aquatic Garden feature flowering water plants.

Another pond complex creates an island for the Japanese Gazebo, which is set amid the trees and plants of the Gude Garden. To increase your appreciation of this and other garden areas you can check out a free self-guided recorded tour of the entire garden. The grounds at Brookside Gardens include collections of cherry and crab apple trees, azaleas, viburnums, rhododendron, and winter blooming plants.

Two other features at Wheaton Regional Park, where Brookside Gardens is located, should also appeal to nature lovers. The Brookside Nature Center has exhibits, guided hikes, and appropriate study programs and films. Trails connect the nature center and the conservatory. The other is Old MacDonald's Farm, a typical Maryland farm re-created on a small scale. Children like to see the cattle, sheep, pigs, and chickens. Behind the farm is Pine Lake, where youngsters can fish for bass, bluegill, crappie, and catfish. The five-acre lake is open to fishermen of all ages.

One way to explore the park is by renting a bike or a horse. There are trails for both through Wheaton Regional Park.

For the very young there are pony rides during the summer and on some pleasant spring and fall weekends. Another ride for the young is on the Wheaton Lines Railroad, a 24-gauge reproduction of an 1865 steam train. Two miles of winding track lead over a bridge, through a tunnel, and into the woods and meadows of the park.

The park is open year round from 9:00 A.M. to 5:00 P.M. Brookside Gardens is closed on Christmas Day. For special features like the train ride, pony rides, and horseback riding call (301)622-0056.

Directions: Take Beltway Exit 31 to Georgia Avenue north. Turn right at Arcola Avenue and then left on Kemp Mill Road to the park entrance.

Baltimore City Conservatory

Though not large, the Baltimore City Conservatory, built in 1888, is well worth exploring, particularly during the winter when the delights of gardening seem months away.

In the conservatory, called the Palm House, three major exhibits are held each year: the Christmas, the fall, and the spring displays. December adds the bright reds, brilliant pinks, and pristine whites of the poinsettia to the tropical plants seen year round. Three small greenhouses at the rear of the conservatory also have tropical plants on view. One room is devoted to orchids.

The annual fall display in November features chrysanthemums.

In the spring during March and April you can see tulips, hyacinths, lilies, cinerarias, primroses, and other seasonal flowers. Also in the adjacent one-acre garden outside the conservatory flowering bulbs can be seen in April and May. Annuals bloom outdoors in Druid Hill Park from June until October. The garden overlooks Druid Lake.

The conservatory has recently been renovated and is now open daily from 10:00 A.M. until 4:00 P.M. at no charge.

Directions: Take Beltway Exit 27 to I-95 north to the Baltimore Beltway, I-695. Go towards Towson and exit south on the Jones Falls Expressway, I-83, toward town. Go right at Druid Park Lake Drive to the conservatory.

Duke Gardens Foundation

One of Walt Disney's most charming conceits in Disneyland and Disney World is the ride "It's a Small World." It could well serve as the theme of the Duke Gardens Foundation, which presents, in miniature and under glass, gardens from around the world.

A brief look at this wide range of garden styles is provided during a one-hour walking tour along the half-mile conservatory path. The overall effect is more important than any individual plant. Specimens are not labeled nor is plant identification stressed; knowledgeable guides, of course, can satisfy the curious.

All but two of the 11 permanent display gardens, the Tropical Jungles and American Desert, present garden designs reflecting various cultures: Japanese, Chinese, French, English, Edwardian, Elizabethan, Italian, Indo-Persian, and Colonial. Each one is delightfully evocative of distant shores. These displays can really be appreciated in mid-winter. The Duke Gardens are open only from October through May. Be sure to visit this garden escape during the winter season when a glimpse of flowers can provide a real lift to one's spirits.

One garden is called a paradise garden, taken from the Persian word *pairidaeser*, which meant walled garden. Here you can see the components of gardens created for the Mughal emperors of India in the 16th and 17th centuries. The brick-patterned tiles duplicate those found in the Shalimar Gardens at Lahore, India. Water is an intrinsic element of this garden design, with both the water canals and fountains having symbolic meaning. This dimension of the garden as art, including the art of other cultures, is carefully presented at Duke Gardens.

At Duke you will also see the garden concepts of André Le Nôtre, French garden architect of Louis XIV, done on a small scale. The traditional parterres, shaped in fleur-de-lis patterns with seasonal flowers, make this particularly appealing. In fact, the one real regret you may have with Duke Gardens is that photography is not allowed. Cameras, like high heeled shoes, are forbidden.

Each garden is a small area of charm—the Elizabethan knot garden, the topiary garden, the lush foliage of the tropics, the Chinese grotto, and the stylized simplicity of the Japanese arrangement. Many of the plants are exotic: the orchids, jacarandas, camellias, gardenias, tree ferns, delphiniums, passion flowers, gloriosa lilies, and cypress, for example.

Special exhibits also include spring bulbs, chrysanthemums, and poinsettias.

The gardens are open daily Monday through Sunday from noon until 7:00 P.M. On Wednesday and Thursday evenings from 8:30 until 10:30, the greenhouses are illuminated for special evening tours. Duke Gardens is closed on New Year's, Christmas, and Thanksgiving as well as from June through September. An appointment is necessary to see this garden but it is worth the effort. To make reservations call (201)722-3700 or write Duke Gardens Foundation, Inc., Route 206 South, P.O. Box 2030, Somerville, New Jersey, 08876. There is an admission fee.

Directions: Take Beltway Exit 27 to I-95 north to the New Jersey Turnpike. At Perth Amboy connect with Route 287 going west to Somerville, New Jersey. At Route 22 go north to Route 206. Take Route 206 west and look for signs to Duke Gardens.

Other gardens with conservatories:

Longwood Gardens

Japanese Gardens

The Japanese Embassy Ceremonial Tea House and Garden

One can feel like an international traveler, yet never leave the Washington area, by experiencing the cultural richness, for example, at the Museum of African Art or the Islamic Mosque. One can do the same by also experiencing the delights of certain gardens. The Franciscan Monastery gardens recreate shrines from the Holy Lands and Lourdes. At the Japanese Embassy on Massachusetts Avenue in Washington, D.C. you can see an authentic ceremonial tea house, which serves as the focal point to the Japanese traditional garden. Together, the tea house and the garden are named "Ippakutei".

The name means both "virtue" and "one hundredth anniversary," reflecting the dual nature of this Japanese gift to America. The tea house and garden were added to the Japanese Embassy as a commemorative gift in 1960, a century after Japan's first ambassadors came to ratify a Treaty of Amity and Commerce.

The tea house and garden were designed by Nahiko Emori, an outstanding architect and author of several books on the art of the Japanese tea house and garden. Ippakutei was built in Japan and then transported to Washington, including the decorative stone lanterns and even the fine gravel that makes up the austere stone garden.

The tea house was designed to present the architectural style of traditional Japanese homes and the ceremonial tea house. In its two rooms a number of representative forms have been combined to achieve this goal.

The smaller room, *koma*, is the tea ceremony room. Floor space in Japan is measured by tatami mats, which are each 3-by-6-feet. The tea ceremony room measures 3½ mats. It resembles the Jo-an, a 17th century tea house at the Mitsi Villa in Oiso, Japan. Before guests enter the room, they are supposed to clean their hands in the nearby stream. By passing through a narrow entrance barely 2 feet square, each guest symbolically humbles his spirit upon entering.

The ceremony designed to put the mind and soul in harmony is conducted with no conversation. All the senses are involved; appreciation of the total experience includes the sound of the silk kimono against the tatami mats and the aroma of the straw, cedar, and green tea. For the ceremony powdered green tea is brewed. It should be consumed in four swallows. Guests are served one at a time; after one finishes the tea he returns the cup. The cup is carefully cleaned before being given to the next guest. A Japanese pastry is served with the tea. Unfortunately the tours of the garden do not include the charm of this special ceremony although it is described in detail.

The *hiroma*, or larger room, has a 12-mat floor area which would be about the size of the living room in a Japanese home. It is meant to suggest the Kagetsudoko, an 18th century structure in Kyoto.

One of the three garden styles at the Embassy is also copied from a Kyoto garden. Even the bamboo fence that surrounds the tea house and garden can be seen in Kyoto at the Kinkakuji garden. From that city's Ryoanji garden comes the sand garden and masonry wall design. There are no plants or flowers in this part of the garden, just fine gravel and stone. It is designed to encourage meditation. As in the Rorschach test, you are not supposed to see any particular image since the stones suggest different things to different people.

A second stylistic garden resembles a 19th century garden in Matsue. This garden area, which uses gravel, grass, and shrubbery, is graced with two stone lanterns. The taller lantern is like those of the Matsuo Shrine, while the smaller one is a Sanko lantern. Three openings represent the sun, moon, and stars.

The third garden area surrounds the granite water basin where guests clean their hands before partaking of the tea ceremony. The stone walk is deliberately irregular to ensure that guests walk more slowly in preparation for this ceremony.

It would be misleading to suggest that this is an elaborate garden. It is not; but it is a garden of serenity and beauty for those who look carefully. It also provides a glimpse of another cultural approach to gardening.

Tours of the Japanese Embassy Tea House and Garden are held on Tuesdays and Thursdays from April through November. There is no charge but reservations must be made. Individuals and families who wish to tour are added to scheduled group tours. No one under 11, however, can be scheduled. To add your name to the list call (202)234-2266.

Directions: The Japanese Embassy is at 2520 Massachusetts Avenue, N.W., Washington, D.C., between Sheridan Circle and Rock Creek Park.

The National Bonsai Collection

Man and nature in close harmony. That's the objective of the National Bonsai Collection in Washington, D.C. at the National Arboretum. This Japanese-style arrangement borrows the classical combination of plants, bonsai, and stones to create a harmonious and pleasing effect.

A narrow stone path encourages you to walk single file, thus intensifying your relationship with this natural environment. A stone lantern indicates a turn in the path. Like the Japanese Ikebana flower arrangements, graceful tree branches overhang the daintier blossoms of small plants.

Many of the plants along the path are presented in miniature in the bonsai collection. The gardens and adjacent pavilion were designed to accommodate and set off the 53 bonsai given to the U.S. as a Bicentennial gift from Japan. This special collection was assembled by the Nippon Bonsai Association. Many of the bonsai are astonishingly old. One specimen has lived almost 375 years. How interesting to ponder that this very tree was hand-shaped before the first colonists landed in Jamestown in 1607. In fact, it was probably being nurtured in its pot while Shakespeare was nurturing his verse in England. Bonsai provide a truly living link with the past. Gardeners will marvel at their endurance.

The 180-year-old Japanese Red Pine, a magnificent specimen, is worth noting because it was the first bonsai from the Imperial Household ever permitted to leave Japan.

Bonsai is the Japanese term for dwarf trees that are planted in shallow pots. Those in deeper pots, as some in this collection are, should be called *hachi-uye*, or pot-planted; but here all are referred to as bonsai.

Specimens in this collection include several varieties of pine, spruce, cypress, cedar, beech, elm, and maple. Flowering plants include an assortment of azaleas, camellias, crab apples, and quince. It is interesting to note the contrast between the bonsai and a single trunk in the cluster of trunks that create an effect of wooded tranquility.

Another related, but less well-known, Japanese collection is displayed in the adjacent Administration Building. These are the viewing stones, or *suiseki*. Again you can see the Japanese love for nature in its unique untampered state. The nine stones on display reveal by their very names why they are prized: Chrysanthemum Stone; Saji River; Puddle Stone; Ibi River; Mountain Shaped Stone; Noble Boat Stone; Stream Stone; Quiet Mountain Stone; Mt. Hakkai. The natural landscape they suggest speaks to the contemplative mind.

This Japanese garden complex is still growing. Plans include adding a walkway over a pool in which brilliantly colored Japanese *koi* (carp) swim, a reception court with a bubbling fountain, and a pavilion suitable for a bonsai display and conducting Japanese tea ceremonies.

The National Bonsai Collection may be visited from 10:00 A.M. to 2:30 P.M. daily at no charge.

Directions: The National Arboretum is inside the Beltway at 3501 New York Avenue, N.E., Washington, D.C. Visitors' entrances are located on New York Avenue and R Street. To reach the R Street entrance turn off Bladensburg Road and follow signs. The Japanese garden complex is located adjacent to the Arboretum's Administration Building.

Swiss Pines

A curious geographical confusion at first glance appears to be operating at Swiss Pines in Malvern, Pennsylvania. The gardens reflect not European but Eastern ambience. Both its name and the Japanese influence derive from elements Mr. and Mrs. Arnold Bartschi found when they bought the land in 1957. The stand of 42 Swiss Stone Pine, of which now only a few remain, and the fact that the Bartschis are from Switzerland, inspired the name.

A number of Japanese lanterns scattered on the grounds prompted the development of the "Garden of Japan." One of the most famous of Japan's contemporary landscape architects, Katsuo Saito, designed the gardens surrounding the "Chosho-Tei," Japanese tea house, which is a copy of one of the oldest tea houses in Japan.

Not surprisingly, the lanterns which prompted the garden have increased to more than 100. These ornamental Ishi-Toros come in two styles: the tall and slim lanterns are called Kasuge-doro; the low, broader ones are Yukimi-doro.

The music of the waterfalls suggests another aspect that is important to the harmony of the Japanese garden. Water is used in a myriad of ways, including water basins, streams, and ponds. The effect is enhanced by tropical fish and a picturesque foot bridge. Water is also suggested in the Karesansui, or stone garden, where a carpet of white sand represents flowing water.

Though Swiss Pines is noted primarily for its "Garden of Japan," another focus is a country far removed from Japan. As you explore this unique display of about 200 varieties of heath and heather, you may indeed feel you have found Brigadoon and Scotland.

A geometrically laid out Herb Garden includes both culinary and aromatic herbs. Most of the 62 different cooking herbs are arranged in circular beds while the 52 varieties of aromatic herbs can be found in rectangular sections. A ground cover garden of 28 varieties has been added.

Rhododendron, azaleas, a crab apple grove, wild flower trail, and a dwarf pinetum of 200 varieties complete the major garden areas at Swiss Pines.

The peak visiting time is May. Swiss Pines is open at no charge Monday through Friday from 10:00 A.M. to 4:00 P.M. and Saturday from 9:00 A.M. to noon. The gardens are closed from

December 15 to March 15 as well as on Sundays and major holidays.

Directions: Take Beltway Exit 27 to I-95 north to Wilmington. Then take Route 202 north to Route 30 and make a left to Malvern, Pennsylvania. At the traffic light make a right on Morehall Road, pass under the Pennsylvania Turnpike overpass and continue straight on Charlestown Road to Swiss Pines.

Other gardens with Japanese gardens:

Fairmount Park
Maymont Park Public Gardens
Norfolk Botanical Gardens
Hillwood Museum Gardens
Hershey Gardens
Morris Arboretum
Willowwood Arboretum

Commercial Gardens

Kensington Orchids

The setting may not be grand but it is curious, with hanging pots and long roots dangling down to obstruct your passage through the narrow rows of the greenhouse. But wait until you see the blossoms. The uninitiated will marvel that this fragile beauty can be combined with such a lackluster, even ugly plant.

Kensington Orchid's large collection of about 100,000 plants in eight greenhouses assures visitors that numerous varieties are always in bloom.

Many people may not be aware that orchids, like purebred dogs or prize-winning horses, are listed in a Royal Horticultural Society "stud" book. This connoisseur's guide provides the parentage of noted hybrid orchids. Orchids were first deliberately cross-pollinated in 1856 by enterprising collectors. Since that time 75,000 hybrids have been registered by the prestigious Royal Horticultural Society.

One of the orchids in the Kensington collection can be traced to a 1913 hybrid. Many others go back to the 1920s. Special orchids may cost from $2,000 to $4,000; but a more likely choice would be about $25.00. Beginners can pick up a common variety for less than $10.00. Supplies needed to pursue this hobby can also be purchased at Kensington.

Sensory confusion usually ensues when you visit the warm, moist greenhouses of Kensington Orchids in mid-winter. It is from the moisture in the air that the jungle-like roots nourish the orchid plant. In their natural habitats orchids grow in rain forests of the Amazon, Congo, Central America, and Southeast Asia.

The variety of colors will surprise those not familiar with

the multiplicity of hybrids. In addition to the expected purple hues and pristine whites, you will see pink, yellow, salmon, deep rust red, and bronze. Some are so unusual that you have to resist the urge to feel the flower to see if it is real. You also may be amazed to learn that these beautiful flowers that are so short-lived when cut will last a month on the plant.

Kensington Orchids grew out of the gift of a single orchid to Dr. Edgar McPeak. He was so enchanted with this lovely flower that he began collecting orchids and built his first greenhouse in 1948. The following year he began selling orchids. In 1964 the current manager and owner, Merritt Huntington, took over operation.

Whether you are an orchid fancier, an interested beginner, or a lover of beauty you will want to see this gorgeous collection of orchids, unequaled in this area. There is no charge to visit Kensington Orchids, which is open daily 8:00 A.M. to noon and from 1:00 P.M. until 5:00 P.M.

Directions: Take Beltway Exit 33 to Route 185 north (Connecticut Avenue) to Plyers Mill Road. Turn right and watch for sign for Kensington Orchids.

Lilypons Water Gardens

"Down on the farm" takes on a different meaning when your destination is Lilypons, Maryland. Here the fields are undulating ponds where ornamental fish, tropical water lilies, and lotus are grown rather than cattle, corn, and tobacco.

Actually this fascinating 275-acre farm dates from 1917, when George Leicester Thomas grew water lilies in a goldfish pool alongside the road. Passersby frequently would stop to ask about his water lilies or to buy flowers and fish to stock their own pools. These recurring requests prompted Mr. Thomas to begin the Lilypons Water Gardens.

His original pond expanded to 500 ponds covering 200 acres along the Monocacy River. By 1936 so much business was being done by mail that a post office was needed to handle the increasing volume. Leiscester Thomas, an avid opera fan, felt that using the name of Lily Pons not only would suggest the nature of his growing enterprise but would also honor his favorite so-

piano. Miss Pons was there in June of 1936 with the Governor of Maryland and her fiancé conductor André Kostelanetz to dedicate the post office in Lilypons, Maryland.

Lilypons boasts dual distinctions. It is both the largest enterprise featuring the sale of ornamental fish and aquatic plants and also the smallest town in Maryland. Lilypons is not a one-horse town, it's a one-family town.

The casual visitor may enjoy the variety of migrant birds that are here. Fish fanciers, however, will realize that the intriguing osprey that delights ornithologists may consume as much as $300 worth of ornamental fish in a day's foray. Goldfish are bred in these seemingly endless ponds. More expensive Japanese Koi, as well as Black Chinese Moor, Japanese Fantail, Shubunkin, Calico Fantail, and many other ornamental fish are also raised here.

Much of the business, both fish and exotic aquatic plants, is done by mail. A visit, however, will give you a chance to see the many unusual fish and plants. The best months are June, July, and August, with July being the peak period. In July the hardy lilies, tropical lilies, and lotus are all in bloom, a combination not to be missed.

The gardens are open 51 weeks a year, closed only during Christmas week. As early as mid-May the white and pink hardy water lilies begin blooming. At the other end of the spectrum tropical lilies can still be seen until a killing frost, usually mid to late October. Each year on the second weekend in July there is a Lotus Blossom Festival at Lilypons and on Labor Day Weekend there is a Koi Festival. The hours of operation are 9:00 A.M. to 4:00 P.M., Monday through Saturday, and noon to 4:00 P.M. on Sunday (except Easter) March through October. November through February hours are 10:00 A.M. to 3:00 P.M., closed holidays and weekends.

Directions: Take Beltway Exit 35 to I-270 north 25 miles to Exit 7 at Urbana, Maryland. Turn right on Route 80 west for 1½ miles. Turn right on Park Mills Road south for 3 miles. Turn right on Lilypons Road for 1½ to entrance on right.

The Daffodil Mart

Hundreds of acres of daffodils once carpeted Gloucester County, Virginia, but don't lament their loss. Rather, be sure to see the 150 acres that still bloom each March through early April. The Daffodil Mart may no longer have a display garden, but the fields themselves are a sight to behold.

English settlers in the 1600s brought these daffadowndillies with them to remind them of the home they would never see again. Now throughout this part of Virginia you can see the delicate spring harbingers blooming along the road.

The Daffodil Mart is a family business that is managed by Brent Heath, the family's third generation to work in the daffodil business. Over the years the acreage has decreased from 350 to five, still a considerable number of bulbs and a show well-worth seeing. Unlike some growers in Gloucester County the Heaths grow bulbs for small gardeners who order by mail. Other fields sell cut flowers. Each spring workers take to the fields to harvest this fragile crop.

You can make arrangements to order bulbs or to visit the Daffodil Mart by appointment from mid-March into April. Call (804)693-3966.

Directions: Take Beltway Exit 4, I-95 south, to Fredericksburg. Exit on Route 17 (By-Pass) south. Continue to Gloucester. The Daffodil Mart is off Route 3 and 14 in Gloucester, Virginia.

The Behnke Nurseries and the Behnke Nurseries Arboretum

A Christmas visit to see the thousands of poinsettias at Behnke Nurseries is a tradition for many Washington families. Tradition is important to the Behnke family.

Albert Behnke at the age of 26 started the business in Beltsville, Maryland, in 1930. From a family in Germany that had a successful nursery business, the young Behnke, shortly after arriving in the United States, investigated nurseries and greenhouses throughout the country before opening his own business where he combined old world lore with new world know-how.

The combination certainly succeeded. Behnke Nurseries is without a doubt one of the finest on the East Coast, having more than 150,000 square feet of greenhouse space plus substantial outside space. The bulk of the stock for this retail outlet is grown at the 80-acre Largo site, which opened a small retain center at 700 Watkins Park Drive in the spring of 1983.

At the Behnke Nurseries of Beltsville or Largo you can see thousands of poinsettias in bloom during November and December. It's fun to bring a camera and frame younger family members amid the brilliant red blossoms—it also makes a great photograph to use on next year's Christmas card. A Santa Claus is present on selected December weekends in the Christmas shop. In addition to the traditional red, white, and pink poinsettias you will also find Christmas cactus and other seasonal house plants.

House plants are another major thrust at the Behnke Nurseries. In addition to splendid examples of all the major varieties, you can find orchids, cactuses, bonsai, and terrarium plants. Another special area of interest at this nursey is African violets. Since 1945, when they became popular under Rose Behnke's management, Behnke has hybridized and introduced many lovely varieties, including My Maryland, the Washington Star, and the Fantasy strain. Behnke grows and sells 250 varieties at the nursery. These are reviewed and updated yearly.

Another area in which Behnke specializes is pansies. Behnke sells over half a million annually. These are not just average pansies; the seed is purchased from all over Europe, and some are specially grown for Behnke.

A relatively recent emphasis is being placed on perennials. A fenced display area contains many of the 40 "can't miss" varieties that anyone can grow with ease and confidence. In another section you'll see roses, peonies, camellias, evergreens, azaleas, and rhododendron. In addition, the annuals production runs over two million plants yearly. A complete garden shop as well as a pottery and basket outlet provides what most gardeners need to enjoy their hobby.

A stop at Behnke Nurseries during the spring, summer, or early fall should include a side trip just down the road to the Behnke home in Burtonsville, Maryland, to see Mr. Behnke's backyard arboretum. Here, as the sign states, "responsible visitors" are invited to browse through the Behnke's private gardens. Outside Mr. and Mrs. Behnke's home on seven acres the nursery founder has set up appealing informal gardens. These gardens are strictly private and no plant material is for sale.

If you have ever wondered as you visited a nursery what the owner's garden looked like, this is your chance to find out. In the spring Mr. Behnke has 20,000 tulips, 3,000 to 4,000 daffodils, and a delightful assortment of spring bulbs. There are also 75 varieties of peonies, including some fancy new specimens. For iris fanciers there are 95 varieties of this lovely flower on display.

Roses are a particular interest of Mr. Behnke. He has an extensive collection of 800 rose bushes, including 200 varieties. You'll see roses here that are unavailable even to avid collectors. One example is the Evangeline Bruce, a rose Mr. Behnke feels is the finest rose ever produced. If you're lucky Mr. Behnke may be out in his garden when you visit and he can give you some hints on growing roses as large as the ones in his beds. Each variety is carefully labeled, as are most of the plants in his yard.

As you walk along the pebbled paths you will also see a day lily collection with 125 varieties, some very rare. Burtonsville is also a test garden for the Beltsville Nursery. Here all new plants, shrubs, and trees are tried out before they go to market. Annuals and Mr. Behnke's current project of assorted perennials grace the beds. He often suggests to visitors that they plant blueberries as a shrub in their yards as he did because they provide both a useful fruit and a colorful fall bush. He gets six to ten quarts from each of his bushes.

The Behnke Nurseries at Beltsville is open seven days a week and visitors are always welcome to drive through Mr. Behnke's arboretum in Burtonsville.

Directions: Take Beltway Exit 25 to Route 1 north and the Behnke Nurseries on the left. To go to Mr. Behnke's private garden, stay on U.S. 1 into Laurel. Go left on Route 198, past I-95, and turn left on McKnew Road. A sign marks the garden at 15201 McKnew Road.

Star Rose Garden

You don't have to travel to Holland to see fields of flowers in bloom. A short drive to West Grove, Pennsylvania, will give you a chance to see 30 acres of hybrid roses. Stretching out along these rolling hills and verdant farm land from mid-June through September are roses of every imaginable hue.

After an overview of the fields you'll want to stop at the Robert Pyle Memorial Garden to look more closely at these lovely flowers. Here the Conard-Pyle Company has planted 3,500 selected roses, many of them All-American Award winners. More than 80 varieties of old favorites and interesting additions are included in this collection.

During the work week, there are group tours of the research and developmental fields. These conducted tours provide additional insight into the business of growing roses. If you're interested in this more personal view, write to make arrangements for joining a group: Star Rose Garden, The Conard-Pyle Company, West Grove, Pennsylvania 19390.

In West Grove there is a delightful spot to enjoy a lunch break, appropriately named the Red Rose Inn. It dates back to 1704 when this colonial inn was situated on a primitive westward trail. Colonists heading north and south would exchange news with the Delaware Indians, who used this trail to reach the western hunting territory.

The now apt name reflects the Pennsylvanian tradition of paying William Penn a red rose as the ceremonial "rent" for the land. Each year on the first Saturday after Labor Day this tradition is still observed and a single red rose is given to a descendant of William Penn's.

The Star Rose fields are located just south of West Grove, Pennsylvania. The Red Rose Inn is on Route 1 just past West Grove. The Robert Pyle Memorial Garden is at the intersection of Route 1 and 796 in Jennersville, Pennsylvania.

Directions: Take Beltway Exit 27 to I-95 north to the Wilmington area. Exit at Route 48 and go to Route 41. Proceed on Route 41 until it intersects with U.S. 1 at West Grove, where you will find the Star Rose fields.

Farther Afield for Flowers

Biltmore House and Gardens

To see splendor anything like the great chateau George Vanderbilt erected in Asheville, North Carolina, you would have to travel to France's Loire Valley. The 11,000-acre Biltmore estate may not be in Europe, but it has all the grandeur of the older European homes on which it is patterned.

The scope and beauty of the gardens can easily overwhelm most visitors. After driving through the lodge gates, you wind your way up the drive past a forested area banked with rhododendron and mountain laurel that is best seen in the spring.

Another set of massive iron gates introduces the Esplanade. Here you see the Rampe Douce, a series of six steep inclines providing a gradual approach up the embankment. A stone-retaining wall, niches, balustrade, and shallow steps make the steady climb on foot easy and pleasant.

Above this another grassy rise leads to a pergola. This picturesque spot is a great place from which to get an overview of the chateau. Within the pergola is a statue of Diane the Huntress, a seemingly perpetual threat as she looks out over the deer park. Now a new restaurant, appropriately called Deerpark Restaurant, also overlooks the former preserve.

Once you arrive at the house the gardens will be on your right. From the wisteria-covered library terrace you'll look out over the old bowling green where a swimming pool is now ensconced.

Moving down to the left of the boxwood enclosed pool area you'll find the Italian Gardens. The water motif so apparent in European-style gardens is represented here by three pools. In the first pool you'll see lotus, the second unusual aquatic plants, and in the third lilies.

To the lower left of this garden is another pergola. This, too, is wisteria covered and particularly lovely in the spring. Below it is the Shrub Garden, which leads to the four-acre Walled Garden.

Annuals and perennials make the Walled Garden a year-round garden. The floral show begins in early spring with daffodils and tulips, followed by irises and peonies. Flowering trees and espaliered trees and shrubs add to the display. Summer bedding plants are followed by chrysanthemums. One specialty garden in this section is the Rose Garden, where thousands of roses bloom through the spring, summer, and fall.

Below the conservatory and greenhouse is the less formal Azalea Garden.

All of the garden areas were laid out according to a plan by Frederick Law Olmsted, who designed Central Park in New York City. Only part of Vanderbilt's vast 125,000-acre holding in the Blue Ridge Mountains was utilized to form this grand garden. A large block of it was deeded to the government and now forms a major part of Pisgah National Forest, where the nation's first school of forestry was established in 1898. Work was inaugurated under the direction of Gifford Pinchot, America's first trained forester, to arrest erosion and begin reforestation.

The chateau house itself is filled with works of art, with the rooms evoking an elegant age. The house remains as it was when George Vanderbilt enjoyed it as his "country home." The 20th century dawned here in style.

Biltmore House and Gardens is open year round, except Thanksgiving, Christmas and New Year's Days, from 9:00 A.M. until 5:00 P.M. The Deerpark Restaurant is open from mid-March through December. Admission is charged.

Directions: From the Washington Beltway take Exit 4, I-95 south, to Petersburg, Virginia. Then continue south on I-85 to Greensboro, North Carolina. At Greensboro pick up Route I-40 to Asheville. Biltmore House and Gardens is located on U.S. 25, three blocks north of Exit 50 or 50B on I-40 in Asheville, North Carolina.

Orton Plantation

Offering hospitality to both friendly folks and feathered fowl, Orton Plantation outside of Wilmington, North Carolina, is a garden well worth discovering. Like so many of the Carolina gardens, water is an integral part of the landscape at Orton.

The garden encompasses 20 acres of water-edged land, peninsulas jut out into the river lagoon, and flooded rice fields with Cape Fear River in the background are visible. Over the lakes that intrude into the garden area are chinoiserie bridges.

Dr. James Sprunt, the grandfather of one of the present Orton owners, was deeply interested in the Orient and one of his philanthropies was the establishment of a missionary school in China. Many years after his death an eye-catching, zig-zag bridge at Orton was constructed. It has a sign reading, "The Ancient Chinese . . . believed that evil spirits followed them but could not turn. The crooked bridges forced the evil spirits to fall overboard and drown."

The garden's most unique feature and only real formal area is the Scroll Garden. The Sprunts's landscaper envisioned the design when he saw Mrs. Sprunt resting one day beneath a paisley shawl. Idly tracing its design, he envisioned it duplicated on the lawn.

Following the irregular terrain, the Scroll Garden features curving evergreen Podocarpus hedges. Within the curves and arabesques are colorful bedding plants. From March until May 10,000 pansies add a cheerful note. They are followed by summer annuals. To retain the lush green lawn that contrasts so nicely with the dark hedges, visitors view the Scroll Garden from terraced overlooks. Distance is an advantage in viewing the Scroll Garden since it is difficult to perceive the charming design from up close. Again the Chinese style can be observed in the white lateral fence.

On the edge of the lagoon are cypress, palms, and palmettos. Bordering most of the garden paths are avenues of live oaks. An avenue of camellias makes a February visit brighter. Camellias usually can be seen as late as April.

The most spectacular time to visit Orton is in the spring. In March and April you can enjoy the camellias, azaleas, rhododendron, wisteria, dogwood, Indian hawthorne, and flowering fruit trees. A tree house covered with banksia roses is also a colorful sight.

In May and June the pansy show continues, along with the day lilies, oleander, hydrangea, irises, magnolias, gardenias and water lilies that are in bloom.

At one end of the garden are the colonial burying grounds where you can see the impressive tomb of Orton's original owner, "King" Roger Moore. He obtained the land from his brother in the late 1720s and built this great plantation a mile upriver from Brunswick Town.

In 1776 the town and several nearby plantations were burned by the British, but Orton was not damaged. It escaped damage again during the Civil War when Orton was used by federal troops as a hospital. Later restored by three generations of Sprunts, the house itself is still inhabited by the Sprunt family and is not open to the public. It is centrally located and may be viewed from the garden paths.

Orton Plantation Gardens are open March through November. Hours are 8:00 A.M. to 6:00 P.M. March through Labor Day and 8:00 A.M. to 5:00 P.M. after Labor Day through November. Admission is charged.

Directions: Take Beltway Exit 4, I-95 south, to Lumberton, North Carolina. Then take Route 211 to Bolton. From there take Route 74-76 to Wilmington. At Wilmington continue south on Route 17 for 18 miles to Orton Plantation.

Elizabethan Gardens

In 1587 settlers under the leadership of Governor John White established the first English settlement in America on Roanoke Island. War with Spain diverted England from regular contact with these brave adventurers and a relief ship in 1590 found no trace of them. Indeed, none was ever found, and the settlement became known as "The Lost Colony."

In memory of these settlers a pleasure garden was established, one that might have been planted by the settlers had the colony survived and prospered. It is an unusual combination of Elizabethan design and indigenous plants.

Because Sir Walter Raleigh sent the colonists to the new world, the garden planners copied the gatehouse at Raleigh's

English home as the entrance to the Elizabethan Gardens. The gatehouse has a 1590 painting of Elizabeth I as well as period furniture.

A pleasure garden appeals to the senses—all the senses, not just the visual. As you come into the garden the fragrance of the herbs leaves no doubt that these criteria will be well met. A feature is Queen Elizabeth's favorite, rosemary, an herb she carried with her throughout the day. The 32 others are medicinal, culinary, and aromatic herbs.

From the gatehouse, flower-bordered paths lead to a natural hill, the Octagonal Mount, where you will have a commanding view of the garden and the waters of Roanoke Sound. You can also see the dunes of Nags Head across the water.

The poignant statue of Virginia Dare is at the edge of the garden. Depicted as an adult, though it is unlikely she lived past childhood, this first child of English parentage born in America is seen draped in fishnet and adorned with Indian beads. The statue was carved in 1859 but was lost at sea for a time before it was salvaged and ended up at this site where Virginia Dare may once have played.

From the mount you can proceed in several directions, although most visitors head for the sunken garden, a copy of a Shakespearean garden and one of the most popular features at Elizabethan Gardens. The parterre is decorated with statues of Apollo, Diana, Venus, and Zeus. Bordered by a hedge of Herrer's holly, the beds are changed seasonally with pansies, petunias, ageratum, and begonias. The beautiful statue in the center of the fountain is from the Farnese Palace outside Rome and is attributed to Michelangelo. Enclosing this garden area is a low brick wall and a pleached allée of native yaupon. Clipped "windows" or openings in the yaupon provide interesting vistas and make great photographs.

Other areas of interest are the Great Lawn, which is an open, game lawn so much a part of English estates, and the terrace overlooking Roanoke Sound. A walkway along the water abounds with wildflowers in the spring. The sensory appeal of the lapping water is strongest here but it accompanies you throughout the garden.

A visit to the Elizabethan Gardens is enhanced in the summer by a visit to The Lost Colony and the Fort Raleigh National Historic Park Site. The Elizabethan Gardens is open daily from 9:00 A.M. to 5:00 P.M. During the summer months when The Lost Colony Drama is running, the garden hours are extended. Admission is charged.

Directions: Take Beltway Exit 4, I-95 south, to the Richmond By-Pass, Route 295. Follow this to Route 64 east past Virginia Beach to Route 168 south to North Carolina. Take Route 158 south and continue past Nags Head to Route 64-264 across Roanoke Sound to Manteo. The Elizabethan Gardens is located on Roanoke Island near Manteo, North Carolina.

Tryon Palace

Far less familiar than Williamsburg but no less exciting is the Tryon Palace restoration complex in New Bern, North Carolina. This capital of colonial North Carolina has many historic buildings that can be enjoyed during a walking tour, but the crown of the complex is Tryon Palace, which had the dual function of serving as both colonial capitol and governor's residence. Built in 1770 for William Tryon for a princely sum of 15,000 pounds, roughly the equivalent of $75,000, the palace was considered one of the most magnificent buildings in colonial America.

Though it was destroyed by fire in 1798, careful restoration work in the 1950s restored the complex to its colonial glory. Within walls of handmade brick and fronted by a striking wrought iron gate brought to America from a 1741 London house are six acres that garden enthusiasts will want to explore.

The gardens, designed in the 18th century English manner, have plantings that are consistent with those grown in colonial times. The restorers of the six acres had no original plans of the Tryon grounds to follow. Rather, the gardens are appropriate to the period, 1760–1770, and provide a beautiful setting for this handsome Georgian mansion.

Fashionable in Tryon's day was to have a garden that reflected nature, rather than to have symmetrical formality. Gardens were no longer rigidly designed in straight lines although straight lines were still used in the approach avenues and in the kitchen and work gardens.

All artificial plantings, including the formal areas, had to be hidden by shrubs and trees because they were not "natural." It was popular at this time to have a wilderness area, an example of which you can see on a smaller scale in the town garden of the William Paca house in Annapolis.

As in England the gardens at Tryon Palace were designed to be enjoyed by the residents of the palace, not by the public.

High brick walls provided privacy as well as supported the espaliered fruit trees. From the windows of the house you can see two privacy or privy gardens—the Green Garden and the Kellenberger Gardens.

In the Green Garden all the plants, with the exception of the crape myrtle, are green. The trim evergreen pattern is accented by statuary. An intricate design is formed from low dwarf yaupon. The form is highlighted by the contrast with the surrounding gravel walks. In the corner curlicues are four clipped cherry laurels.

The Kellenberger Garden, on the other hand, has a series of small beds with colorful blossoms that change with the seasons. Tulips, portulacas, and chrysanthemums are just a few of the principal plantings. Along the walls are trellised yellow jessamine, Confederate jessamine, cruel vine, and pyracantha. Statuary, an intrinsic part of an English garden, serves as a focal point for the beds.

Moving farther from the palace you'll come to the most elaborate garden in the complex, the Maude Moore Latham Memorial Garden, named in honor of the benefactress of this impressive restoration. In the English landscape tradition, this garden has a delightful scroll of small beds that bloom brightly during the growing season. In the spring you'll see tulips, crocus, and violas. Summer brings colorful annuals. Chrysanthemums highlight the fall bloom.

Closer to the Trent River are both Hawk's Allée and the Pleached Allée. Five antique Italian statues are the center of attention at Hawk's Allée. Low flowering plants frame the greensward while white Cherokee roses climb the brick wall. The second allée has a double row of yaupon trained to form a covered walkway like the ones so popular in the 18th century. The view through this lofty arch of the river is an example of the sweeping vistas so important to gardens of this period.

Ornamental and economic plants were not carefully separated in this period and you can see lovely flowering plants mingled with the vegetables and herbs in the kitchen garden. You will also notice herbs included in the elaborate formal flower gardens.

The kitchen garden is east of the kitchen wing and is noted for its extensive planting of espaliered pear, apple, quince, and fig trees. The orchard effect is increased by an assortment of flowering crab apple, cherry, peach, and apple trees. The vegetables, flowers, and herbs grow in profusion. The beds are bordered with herbs and French strawberries. Also of interest historically is the Indian corn grown from seed provided by the Tuscora Indians, descendants of those who lived in North Carolina during the early colonial period.

A work garden contains planting beds, hot beds, and slat houses. This is where plants used within the complex are raised. In addition to the palace gardens, other smaller gardens are associated with the Stevenson, Stanly, and Jones Houses.

At the Visitor Center you can obtain a map that shows you the walking tour route of the Tryon Palace complex gardens and grounds. While at the center you should see the 18-minute orientation film.

The Tryon Palace complex is open 9:30 A.M. to 4:00 P.M. Tuesday through Saturday and 1:30 P.M. to 4:00 P.M. on Sunday. The last tour is at 4:00 P.M. The complex is closed Mondays, except Easter Monday, Memorial Day Monday, and Labor Day Monday. It is also closed on Thanksgiving Day, December 24–26, and January 1. From mid-May to late August historical dramas add to the fun. Special events are also held during the Christmas season.

Directions: Take Beltway Exit 4, I-95 south, to Smithfield, North Carolina. Turn left on Route 70 to New Bern and the Tryon Palace complex. It is an hour and a half from I-95.

Sarah P. Duke Gardens

Renaissance terraces, a wisteria pergola, a Grass and Sky Garden, Azalea Court, and an iris collection are just some of the special areas you'll see at the Sarah P. Duke Gardens in Durham, North Carolina.

Located on the west campus of Duke University, this pleasure garden truly gives pleasure. Open expanses are offset by areas of quiet charm like the rock garden and fern glade.

You enter the garden through wrought iron gates designed to suggest stained glass. The metal was chemically treated to achieve a multi-hued effect. To the left of these gates is the informal Blomquist Garden. Small signs identify the wildflowers growing among a fine stand of loblolly pine. Here, too, is the fern glade best seen in early May when the leafy ferns gracefully unroll.

Continuing along the garden walkway you will pass a circular rose garden, then reach the hexagonal wisteria-covered pergola, which is transformed into a riot of cascading lavender sprays each year in late April.

Descending dramatically from this is a series of terraces conceived in the Italianate manner, though flowers are used to grace the terraces rather than greenery alone as is the case normally. In the spring thousands of tulips and other bulbs put on a show, while the fall display is highlighted by massive chrysanthemum plantings.

Even more striking than the view down the terraces from the pergola is the one you get from the Rock Garden across the water lily pool with the terraces ascending gracefully up the slope.

Another popular area is the Grass and Sky Garden, an informal open area around a central pool. Finally, if you visit in the spring, don't miss the April display in the Azalea Court or the May bloom in Hanes Iris Garden, the first flowers planted at the Sarah P. Duke Gardens.

The gardens are open at no charge daily from 8:00 A.M. until dark.

Directions: Take Beltway Exit 4, I-95 south, to Petersburg. From there take I-85 to Durham. The Sarah P. Duke Gardens are on the west campus of Duke University at Anderson Street in Durham, North Carolina.

Magnolia Plantation and Gardens

Charleston, South Carolina, has a triumvirate of gracious gardens for you to visit, each one with its own charm and appeal. Plan to visit all three: Middleton Place, Cypress Gardens, and the lovely Magnolia Plantation and Gardens. Middleton is called the oldest landscape garden in America, but Magnolia Gardens is considered the oldest major garden, as well as the oldest man-made attraction, in America. It dates back to the 1670s.

Magnolia Plantation is a remarkable saga of one family's perseverance. The estate has been in the Drayton family for 10 generations, spanning over 300 years. As early as 1867 Rev. Drayton, who had worked to restore the garden to its pre-Civil War appearance, opened his garden to visitors each spring. Enthusiastic throngs flocked up the Ashley River by paddle steamer. So popular was this garden that in 1900 Baedecker's guidebook to America recommended it as one of three major attractions. The other two were Niagara Falls and the Grand Canyon.

Although it began as a seasonal garden, this 500-acre estate, with 50 acres of lawn and gardens, is now a year-round attraction. Spring, however, is still the best time to visit. The trio of South Carolina's gardens are all water-enhanced. Magnolia Plantation, like Cypress Gardens, relies upon the natural vegetation of the low country. Thus you'll see Spanish moss-draped bald cypress trees along the lakes. Color is added by the 250 varieties of azalea Indica and 900 varieties of camellia Japonica that make spring such an ideal time to visit.

Another garden in the Middle Atlantic area that similarly combines the colorful azalea with natural vegetation is Winterthur Gardens in Delaware. This one provides an interesting contrast with Magnolia Gardens.

The various varieties of camellias offer an assortment of blossoms over a long span. The camellia Japonica, of course, starts in early October and blooms through mid-April. One unusual touch is a maze formed with camellia bushes. At Magnolia Gardens you can also see the camellia Sasanqua that blooms from September through January.

The blooming calendar begins with the last of the camellia Sasanqua in January along with holly and firethorn. In February you will see some early blooming crocuses and narcissuses. But the show really begins in March; even the admission fee is raised from mid-March to mid-April to reflect the added interest the garden provides during high spring. In addition to the world famous collection of camellias and azaleas there are massed jonquils and violets as well as flowering fruit trees.

Early April is the height of the azalea flowering. Some trees are so heavily laden that it is impossible to see the leaves; all you see is a solid bank of blossoms. Wisteria, roses, and lilies add their own appeal to the garden.

At Magnolia Gardens the summer season starts in May. You will see a continuous showing of roses until December. Other summer flowers include the oleander, gardenia, pomegranate, hydrangea, and crape myrtle.

The garden is certainly the primary attraction here but there are other sights as well. You will want to take time to visit the plantation house. Guided tours through the Drayton family home reveal plantation life in the Carolinas since the Civil War.

Much of the estate's 125 acres is devoted to a wildlife refuge. After exploring the garden you can enjoy canoeing through this protected enclave or hiking to get a good view of the diverse bird population. A Wildlife Observation Tower gives a view of the sanctuary for those who do not have time for a more intensive look.

Nature can also be enjoyed at the petting zoo where children seem particularly captivated by the rare mini-horses.

Magnolia Gardens charges a garden admission plus an additional fee to tour the house. The estate is open daily from 8:00 A.M. until 6:00 P.M.

Directions: Take Beltway Exit 4, I-95 south, to South Carolina. Exit on Route 26 east towards Charleston. Take Alt. 17 south through Summerville, then left on Route 61. Magnolia Gardens is located on Route 61.

Middleton Place

Middleton Place near Charleston, South Carolina, has the oldest landscaped gardens in America. Started in 1741, the gardens at this lovely southern rice plantation were conceived on a grand scale. The "grand design" of André le Nôtre was employed as it was at Nemours in Delaware. Here you will see the long central path and greensward leading unobstructed into near infinity. The visitor can see across the Ashley River into the mist-enshrouded woods on the opposite shore.

The gardens extend from the house down to the river since most 18th century guests came from Charleston by boat. Such an arrangement is more suggestive of an English country manor than a southern plantation house.

Looking down the long terraced greensward to the Ashley River, one can see the lovely butterfly wing lakes. A grassy bridge forms the body. It took more than 100 of Middleton's 800 slaves working for 10 years to create the rippling effects of the terraced lawn.

To the right but not obstructing the clear lines of the greensward is the formal garden area. Here again water is an integral part of the design, with the formal garden bordered on the western side by a reflection pool. True to 18th century custom, swans grace this pool, adding a further picturesque note to the scene.

Flanking the pool is a camellia allée. These bushes are so lush that they are now flower-strewn tunnels in the spring. Though there is a dispute about just how old some of the camellias actually are, none can argue that they are not indeed long standing. One story, disclaimed by the American Camellia Society, has it that three of the bushes were given to Middleton by the French botanist André Michaux and were the first such plants in America.

Also of ancient lineage are the giant crape myrtle to be seen directly in front of the reflection pool. Again Michaux is believed to have introduced this smooth-barked Oriental tree to America at this South Carolina plantation in about 1787. Middleton has one of the largest known crape myrtle trees. Also in the formal area are the sunken Octagonal Garden, the geometric Sundial Garden, and the Secret Garden used for family games and tête-á-têtes.

Beside the formal garden is the mid-19th century addition of an informal azalea pool garden. Narrow paths wind through azalea banks, providing a contrast to the form of the adjacent area. Azaleas can also be found on the low hills surrounding the rice-mill pond to the right of the butterfly lake. Swans can be seen on the pond.

One other newly created area of interest is the cypress lake. It was added to form a barrier between the garden and the swampy ground beyond. You'll enjoy the numerous southern bald cypress with their spiky, cone-like protrusions called knees. Interestingly, when cypress grow on firm ground as they do at Longwood Gardens they do not have these protrusions. It seems as though the protrusions serve the purpose of supporting the tree in the unstable mud.

The logo of Middleton Place is the statue "Wood Nymph," the only one of many garden statues to survive the destruction of the Civil War period. The statue was buried in 1865 before Union troops arrived in Middleton. After enjoying the hospitality of Middleton the northern troops of General Sherman burned the plantation house. Only the southern wing, though gutted, could be salvaged.

Middleton Place has a history that goes back to America's earliest days. In 1741, when Henry Middleton married Mary Williams, he acquired this South Carolina plantation. He added wings on both sides of the house and began work on the estate's splendid gardens. Important to the political scene in South Carolina, he was chosen as a delegate to the First Continental Congress. He served that illustrious body as President of the Congress. His son, Arthur, was a member of the Second Continental Congress and was a signer of the Declaration of Independence.

The third generation at Middleton, Henry's grandson and namesake, was Governor of South Carolina and the U.S. Minister to Russia. His son, William Middleton, was a committed Confederate supporter and signed the Ordinance of Secession. It was no surprise that the Union troops dealt harshly with Middleton Place. A further disaster occurred in 1886 when an earthquake leveled the charred buildings, sparing only the south wing.

In the 20th century a member of the Middleton family, J. J. Pringle Smith, began restoration of the estate and garden. The south wing, added in 1755 as a gentlemen's guest room, was converted to the main house and was carefully decorated to reflect the scope of the Middleton family history. Portraits of the four pre-Civil War generations grace the walls. The rooms contain treasures collected by Henry Middleton while he served in St. Petersburg. Both a winter and a summer bedroom reveal the two different aspects of the lifestyle of a South Carolina rice plantation.

In the 1970s another aspect of life on this estate was revealed in the outdoor museum at the plantation's stableyards. You will see blacksmiths, carpenters, coopers who make the barrels used on the grounds, shinglemakers, tanners, potters, spinners, candlemakers, and weavers. All were part of the extended community that made up a large southern plantation.

Animals commonly found in the Low-Country area include horses, cows, mules, ducks, chickens, geese, guineas, peacocks, sheep, pigs, and goats. Spring is a good season to explore the grounds as well as to see the new baby livestock.

While in the Stableyard Museum you can help with the milking, feed the peacocks, enjoy a mule-drawn wagon ride, grind corn, or help with other farm "chores."

The 110 acres of Middleton Place are a National Historic Landmark. The gardens and stableyard are open daily 9:00 A.M. to 5:00 P.M. and admission is charged. The house is open 10:00 A.M. to 4:30 P.M. except Monday and during mid-December. There is an additional charge for touring the house. Allow at least two hours to tour the house and grounds.

Directions: Take Beltway Exit 4, I-95 south, to South Carolina. Exit on Route 26 east toward Charleston. Take Alt. 17 south past Summerville and turn left on Route 61. Middleton Place is on Route 61 just 14 miles northwest of Charleston, South Carolina.

Cypress Gardens

Many of South Carolina's verdant gardens are former rice plantations. One such plantation which failed and lapsed into its natural state, replete with giant swamp cypress and an overgrown tangle of weeds and vines, was reclaimed in the 1920s.

Benjamin Kittredge, who purchased the old Dean Hall rice plantation, was hunting wild turkey within its watery junglelike habitat when it occurred to him that the area would be particularly interesting if it could be cleared and arranged in a natural garden. His concept became Cypress Gardens and is now billed as "one of the seven Great Gardens of the Western World."

Cypress Gardens is primarily a seasonal attraction; however, the gardens are open most of the year. During the main blooming season, between mid-February and May, you can see a profusion of flowers among the ancient cypress trees as you float under rose-draped bridges along the meandering water trails.

February begins the show with hundreds of camellias, daffodils, and magnolias. Then March and April bring the azaleas, wisteria, roses, and jessamine.

In addition to enjoying the garden by boat, you may take advantage of miles of foot paths that weave through this water wonderland. Even after you take a tour by boat, try to spend a little extra time on foot to see the flowers up close. Native wildflowers can be found in abundance as can many different species of birds.

Although the water in its inky depth seems fathomless, it is actually only two feet deep in most places.

During its season Cypress Gardens is open daily from 8:00 A.M. to 5:00 P.M. There is an admission charged and boat rides cost extra.

Directions: Take Beltway Exit 4, I-95 south, to South Carolina. Exit on Route 26 east. Then take Route 52 north toward Oakley. Cypress Gardens is located off Route 52 just 24 miles north of Charleston, South Carolina.

Brookgreen Gardens

A single statue often serves as the focal point of a garden design, but seldom does a garden center around an entire collection of statues as it does at Brookgreen Gardens, South Carolina.

The sculpture is framed naturally by boxwood, azalea, yaupon, and other native plants. Though classical renditions of the hunt and the taming of wild animals abound here, this garden really is designed to preserve nature—wild plants, animals, and birds.

Brookgreen was originally conceived as a permanent exhibition of the sculpture work of Mrs. Anna Hyatt Huntington. When the Huntingtons acquired this old South Carolina rice and indigo plantation, they restored the garden as a setting for her work. Mrs. Huntington planned the garden in the form of a butterfly with a lovely avenue of oaks gently draped with Spanish moss serving as the frame from which the two great wings spread.

More than 1,000 varieties of native plants and wildflowers are augmented by over 450 works of art. American sculpture from many artists from the mid-19th century to the present are represented. It is, to quote Mr. Huntington, "a quiet joining of hands between science and art."

At this unusual outdoor museum, art is just one attraction. There is an aviary, the Cypress Bird Sanctuary, created by a huge net, 180 feet across and 90 feet high, which allows visitors to observe birds and plants indigenous to this South Carolina cypress swamp forest. Bald cypress, red maple, swamp black gum, and Canadian ash create an unusual forest background for the colorful birds within its confines.

As you walk along a special boardwalk you may see a white ibis, great egret, snowy egret, great blue heron, Louisiana heron, little blue heron, yellow-crowned night heron, fulvous whistling duck, wood duck, green heron, black-crowned night heron, and glossy ibis.

At a second natural area called the White-Tailed Deer Savannah you can see deer.

A wildlife preserve attempts to display native animals in their natural setting and children particularly like the addition of alligators, otters and deer to the garden setting. It's certain to interest the whole family.

Of particular interest artistically is the Gallery of Small Sculpture. Here you will see 170 small pieces displayed on pedestals in a loggia surrounding an interior pool. Other small pieces are scattered throughout the garden in wall niches. Many pieces of sculpture, however, are in fact quite large. Mrs. Huntington's *Fighting Stallions,* the symbol of Brookgreen Gardens, is one of the largest aluminum sculptures ever cast. Another, carved from a 125-ton granite rock, was done in place by Laura Garden Fraser. Her *Pegasus* took four years to complete.

While a visit here is interesting at any time of the year, garden lovers may want to schedule a trip for late March or April, when the spring blossoms reach their peak. The wild azalea and dogwood make a lovely backdrop for the sculpture.

Brookgreen Gardens is open 9:30 A.M. until 4:45 P.M. daily except Christmas. There is an admission to the gardens.

Directions: Take Beltway Exit 4, I-95 south, into South Carolina. Take Route 38 east until it intersects with Route 501, then go east on Route 501 to Myrtle Beach. From there go south on Route 17. Brookgreen Gardens is 18 miles south of Myrtle Beach, South Carolina, on U.S. 17.

The Cloisters

It is normally on trips to the south that one begins to think of exploring the local garden attractions, but there is one northern garden that should not be missed. It is the garden associated with the Cloisters in Fort Tryon Park in upper Manhattan, New York City.

The Cloisters, like the Hortulus of the Bishop's Garden at the Washington Cathedral, recreates medieval times. A visit to the Cloisters transports you to the medieval monasteries of France. Five of the medieval cloisters that are part of this complex were originally found in southern France. A typical cloister consists of a covered arcade that surrounds a courtyard. Within the courtyard, open to the sky, a garden of fragrant plants grows. Water flows from the fountain at its center.

The Cloisters incorporates sections from Gothic and Romanesque chapels and a 12th century Spanish apse. The world famous 15th century tapestry series "The Hunt of the Unicorn" is included in the medieval works of art.

Three cloister gardens have particular interest. The Cuxa Cloister uses stonework originally found at the monastery of

Sant-Michel-de-Cuxa in the eastern Pyrenees. Here you will see an earth garden planted with grass, fruit trees, and fragrant flowers. Not all of the plants are native to western Europe. In order to achieve a full display of color throughout the growing season, some modern species have been included.

A second cloister garden, Trie Cloister, brings to life the flora of the tapestries, "The Hunt of the Unicorn." You'll want to study the tapestries carefully before exploring the garden. It is interesting to see the detailed manner in which the tapestries capture familiar plants like violets and strawberries. Those fruits which were known in France but grew elsewhere, such as the pomegranate on Mediterranean shores, were correctly depicted, while the form of the plant itself was guessed at by the medieval designers. The floral backgrounds of the first and seventh tapestries show a millefleur design. Literally, "a thousand flowers" are woven throughout, many faithfully represented.

The Bonnefont Cloisters contains an herb garden with more than 250 species of plants cultivated in western Europe during the Middle Ages. All plants are labeled, and they are grouped in beds according to their uses. You will see those herbs used for medicinal purposes, aromatic herbs, those that could be used as dyes, and those added to foods for seasonings or leafy varieties that served as fresh vegetables.

The Cloisters is a medieval museum, and the collection of sculpture, paintings, stained glass, tapestries, and religious objects is beautifully complemented by the authentic setting. The museum is owned and operated by the Metropolitan Museum of Art and was a gift of John D. Rockefeller. It is open Tuesday through Saturday from 10:00 A.M. to 4:45 P.M. and Sunday and holidays from 1:00 P.M. to 4:45 P.M. May through September it opens an hour earlier at noon. The gardens are open year round.

Directions: Take Beltway Exit 27, I-95 north, to New York. Once in New York City, the Cloisters can be reached from the Henry Hudson Parkway. Take the first exit off the George Washington Bridge, following signs for the Henry Hudson Parkway north. Follow signs to Fort Tryon Park and the Cloisters.

Farms

Beltsville Agricultural Research Center

Ever wondered where your tax dollars go? At Beltsville Agricultural Research Center you can actually see where some of that money has gone, and how well it has been spent. A guided tour will make it clear why Beltsville enjoys a worldwide reputation in the field of agricultural research. Its projects have tangible benefits for everyone.

This 7,250-acre establishment begun in 1910 is the largest and most complex agricultural center in the world. The 2,700 employees at Beltsville are involved in a wide range of projects. They monitor test crops from the Landsat satellite, conduct research on heavy metals in the human body, grow apple tree clones, and do extensive work with ruminant animals. These are a few of the more than 3,000 ongoing projects at this fascinating facility.

You can visit Beltsville alone or as part of a guided group. Without a knowledgeable tour leader, however, the individual can miss a great deal. The audiovisual shows and exhibit boards cannot provide the myriad of interesting data and amusing sidelights a conducted tour provides. Such free, guided visits can be planned only during the week and must be arranged by calling (301)344-2483. Driving on your own through Beltsville will probably take an hour but the tour runs about 2½ hours. The Visitor Center is open 8:00 A.M. to 4:30 P.M. Monday through Friday.

A tour of Beltsville provides a veritable smorgasbord of trivia and little-known facts. For instance, did you know that cattle can eat newsprint as 12 percent of their diet with no ill effect providing it's not the Sunday comics? Do you know the origin of the expression "getting a cold shoulder"? Or the four indigenous plants in the U.S. that are harvested in any quantity? While you won't leave this agricultural center an instant expert you will leave knowing more than when you arrived.

On either type of tour at Beltsville you will see the sheep and swine area. It is important to remember if you are on your own not to touch the animals. They are all under preventive quarantine, which means they are disease free and should not be handled.

Spring is a good time to visit the farm when the offspring of the animals—the ewes, calves, and piglets—are out in the field. The maternal instinct in pigs is very strong and persons who work with the sows have to be careful when they handle the piglets. The pig, claimed to be the smartest animal on a farm, learns faster and retains more than any other domesticated animal. Pigs also metabolize food very much like man. For this reason research for human diseases often is done with pigs.

Animals are just part of the story at Beltsville. Across Route 1 is the section dealing with plant research. Here on the last three stops of the self-guided route you'll find out that Uncle Sam has a green thumb. At Stop 10, the conservatory offers a short audiovisual program. From June through September much of the plant work is done in the fields, some of which have research turf grasses that are part of a study—now in its 30th year. Other fields have machine harvestable tomatoes, the National Collections of strawberries, blueberries, and thornless blackberries. Fields of soybeans, alfalfa, sunflowers, and day lilies are also important. In addition, major research is being done with fruit trees, such as tissue-propagated apple trees as well as dwarf apples and peaches.

After September the work moves into the greenhouses, which are divided into four sections: fruits and vegetables, ornamental flowers and shrubs, major economic crops, and one dealing with national problems like pesticide degradation. At Beltsville they have an outstanding collection of 85,000 varieties of small grains and one containing 18,000 varieties of rice.

Also on the grounds is the National Agricultural Library containing 1.7 million volumes that can be used by those interested in doing agricultural research.

As Beltsville proudly points out, "Agriculture Makes Tomorrow Better." Why not visit and find out how?

Directions: Take Beltway Exit 25, U.S. 1 north, to Powder Mill Road, Route 212, in Beltsville, Maryland. Turn right and go to the Visitor Center at the Beltsville Agricultural Research Center.

Oxon Hill Farm

If the words to *Old MacDonald's Farm* have little meaning to your children, take them to Oxon Hill Farm to see what life was like on a turn-of-the century farm. It's certainly easy to get them "down on the farm" as it's right off the Beltway in Oxon Hill, Maryland.

It's fun to watch children who have never seen a cow help park personnel milk one during one of the milking demonstrations at the farm. Many youngsters are flabbergasted that milk actually comes from a cow.

Watching a sheep get a haircut in May is another marvel to the young. After the shearing, the farm hosts demonstrations of carding, spinning, weaving, and dyeing.

The emphasis, however, is not entirely on farm animals. You can also observe the planting of corn and then check its progress throughout the summer. Another spot you may want to keep your eye on is the vegetable patch where a well-marked assortment including lettuce, tomatoes, squash, onion, green beans, corn, peas, and beets is grown.

Horse teams are used to plow the fields and in mid-summer the grain is harvested with a binder and an old-fashioned steam-powered threshing machine. In the fall workers go to the fields to pick the corn by hand. No other ways were possible in the early 1900s.

At Oxon Hill they also grow sorghum cane which is cut and hauled to the farm's mill. Here it is stripped and mashed. The extracted juice is then boiled down, ultimately to form sorghum molasses.

Those who work at the farm wear bib overalls or long dresses. As they go about their work they explain to visitors what they are doing and why it was done by the old-fashioned methods they use.

During the spring and fall months you can take a naturalist-led hike on the trail that winds through the orchard, fields, and surrounding forest. Many special programs are also possible. Call (301)839-1176 to get information on them.

The farm is open daily at no charge from 8:30 A.M. to 5:00 P.M.

Directions: Take Beltway Exit 3A and follow signs to the farm, which is off Oxon Hill Road in Oxon Hill, Maryland.

Frying Pan Farm Park

Though few would like seriously to turn back the clock, many urban and suburban dwellers are fascinated by country life. This accounts in part for the popularity of farms that recreate early times. In Herndon, Virginia, the Frying Pan Farm Park brings to life a working farm of the 1920s.

This is a small family farm, like so many that could be found in rural Virginia well into the 20th century. Farmers utilized horse-drawn machinery to harvest the corn, oats, and hay. Mechanization was limited and the family would milk their own cows, feed the sheep, pigs, goats, rabbits, geese, and turkeys as well as collect the eggs from the chicken coop each morning.

Sequential visits will allow you to watch the fields being prepared for planting and the crops sown. During a mid-summer visit you can see the fields in full growth and then a final visit in the fall to see the harvest.

In addition to seeing early farming techniques you will also be able to observe the working blacksmith at the Moffett Blacksmith Shop on summer weekends. Horse and livestock judging are planned for summer at the park's Equestrian Center. An Indoor Activities Center enables the park to host musical groups, flea markets, and auto shows. The park is open daily from 10:00 A.M. to 6:00 P.M. There is no charge.

Directions: Take Beltway Exit 9, Route 66 west, to Chantilly. Turn right at Centreville Road, and right again at West Ox Road. Frying Pan Farm Park is at 2709 West Ox Road in Herndon, Virginia.

The Claude Moore Colonial Farm at Turkey Run

The Claude Moore Colonial Farm, formerly Turkey Run Farm, is a living history park that recreates the life of a low-income family living in northern Virginia before the Revolutionary War.

Costumed interpreters, who emulate the poor tenant farmers of the 1700s, plant crops, cook meals, tend the livestock, and make all the necessities essential for survival. After you visit this colonial farm, which illustrates how a meagre existence was eked out from a few worn-out acres, you will have a better understanding of the women and children who followed the Revolutionary soldiers during the war.

"Camp follower" was not a term of opprobrium but a literal expression. The women had to follow their husbands; for many of them it was the only way to receive rations. There was no provision for the women to receive part of their husbands's pay. Consequently, they followed the troops, receiving half rations in return for their work as cooks, laundresses, and nurses.

The Claude Moore Colonial Farm is closed in the winter months but when it opens in April the larder (pantry) reflects the "six weeks of want" before the early greens of spring appear. In the 18th century people did not have our modern means of preserving food so they were left with the few rotting potatoes left from the late fall harvest plus dried beans, rice, corn meal, and hard cheese.

At this farm, as at all colonial farms, clothes were washed in the spring after the very cold winter. Cleanliness was not a strong enough motive for the farmers to risk a winter chill by bathing in frigid weather. Colds, like all illnesses in the 18th century, were treated at home and often led to death.

Spring was also the time for planting so you'll see the fields being prepared, the fences mended, and the corn and tobacco being planted. Then in the summer a visit will show the plants being tended in the field. Stop by for one of the Sunday afternoon craft programs, or on warm summer evenings you can join the staff in a musicale.

By the fall the crops are harvested for the most part, though late greens are still plentiful. The tobacco is drying in the barn and it's time to butcher some of the full grown chickens and turkeys. The large animals are not butchered until the very cold weather to prevent the meat from spoiling.

Apples are also plentiful at this time of year. The expression "American as apple pie" comes from the 18th century practice of using apples as a substitute for meat in their pies. The colonial poor did not have enough meat for traditional English pies and so they used the abundant apples instead.

The Claude Moore Colonial Farm at Turkey Run is open Wednesday through Sunday from 10:00 A.M. until 4:30 P.M. from April through November. Admission is $1.00 for adults and 50¢ for children.

Directions: From the Beltway take Exit 13 to Old Georgetown Pike, Route 123. Travel east towards Langley for 2½ miles. Turn left at Farm sign. From the George Washington Memorial Parkway, take the McLean exit, Route 123, and follow the signs to the Farm.

Chippokes Plantation State Park

Although 350 years of American history are encompassed at Chippokes Plantation near Jamestown, Virginia, the most interesting aspect for garden enthusiasts is the model farm which demonstrates agricultural changes from the 17th century to the present.

This land was patented in 1612 by Captain William Powell, who named the holding after a friendly Indian, Choupouke, who had been helpful to the early settlers. The land passed from Powell to his heirs and then to Royal Governor Sir William Berkeley.

The plantation's main house, an antebellum mansion that dates from 1854, is on the site of an earlier homestead. Laid out behind the mansion is the gracious six-acre garden planned to provide blossoms from early spring through fall. Magnolias and dogwood provide a lovely background for the azaleas and spring flowering bulbs. Visitors will see daffodils, narcissuses, primroses, irises, forget-me-knots, metensias, and wood hyacinths. The garden has no formal pattern; rather it is a felicitous blending with the natural setting. Massed plantings of crape myrtle provide vivid color to the garden in late summer.

The scope of the Chippokes model farm can be enhanced by a stop at the Visitor Center, where you will see Virginia's agricultural expansion traced from 1619 to the present. The changing agricultural methods and crops are also noted. Then you can proceed to the fields where samples of all the principal crops can be seen.

In the 17th and 18th century grain crops and tobacco were grown. From the Chippokes's apple orchards a fine brandy was distilled. In the 19th century peanuts became the primary cash crop even though tobacco was still grown. Figs, cotton, sorghum, tobacco, peanuts, corn, soybeans, rye, and barley are all grown here.

In the pasture beef cattle graze and the loblolly pine on the plantation suggest the lumber industry, which also is an economic reality of this area.

Chippokes Plantation State Park has a network of trails ideal both for hiking and biking. A lovely trail that you may want to explore if you have the time skirts the James River. On many weekends park rangers lead tours that describe not only the natural environment but also cover the historic background of various plantation buildings. These include slave quarters, barns, a carriage house, the brick kitchen, tobacco house, and a second large home, called "River House," built in the 1700s. Of these only the kitchen is open to the public.

Chippokes Plantation State Park is open year round during daylight. The Visitor Center is open from Memorial Day weekend until Labor Day weekend.

Directions: Take Beltway Exit 4, I-95 south, to Route 295, the Richmond By-Pass. Then take Route 64 to Williamsburg and the toll ferry at Jamestown across the James River. Continue on Route 31 to Surry. Chippokes Plantation is 3½ miles east of Surry on Route 634.

Peter Wentz Farmstead

Everything old is new again at the Peter Wentz Farmstead in Worcester, Pennsylvania, an 18th century farm restored to look the way it did in 1777. The furnishings and the fields are all "as it was," which is the theme at this interesting rural Pennsylvania farmstead.

Demonstration crops, an orchard, plus a well-designed kitchen garden make this a meaningful excursion for garden fanciers. In the fields you'll see crops that were grown in this area during colonial times. The orchard contains old varieties of apples, peaches, and pears. Plants in the kitchen garden serve a variety of purposes: culinary, medicinal, fragrance, and landscape.

The trim garden border is itself formed from a number of useful plants, including: houseleeks, chives, parsley, creeping boys and girls or sedums, Johnny-jump-ups, Jacob's ladders, bugles, portulacas, nasturtiums, mountain pinks and sweet alyssums.

The garden contains almost 100 different seasonal vegetables, herbs, and flowers. A traditional German kitchen garden, it is laid out with a crossed path forming four raised beds.

The farm's barn was built in 1744, 14 years before the main house. The barn was taken down to its original foundation then carefully restored with rough stones and freshly painted planks to look the way it would have in 1777.

This farmstead opened in 1976 and like so much that occurred during that much celebrated Bicentennial year it has made a lasting contribution to an understanding of the everyday life in the colonies.

The farm house was built in 1758 by Peter Wentz, Jr., whose German background influenced the design of both house and garden. The bright colors in the house are indicative of the German influence. It is the interior painting which surprises most visitors; in fact, many cannot believe that the spots, stripes, and squiggled decorations were really there in 1777. The walls of the kitchen are brightened by splotchy black dots on a white background. The dados of the living room and one of the bedrooms have a red background with white dots. Other variations include diamond-shaped striping and painted tadpole-like designs. The "pièce de résistance" is an upstairs bedroom that not only has dados covered with black polka dots, but also red diamond striping and red tadpoles.

This farmstead is one place that can boast with truth that Washington slept here. He enjoyed the Wentz hospitality several times during the American Revolution. He spent the night before the Battle of Germantown at the Wentz farmstead planning the Continental army strategy. During a later stop at this farm Washington is reported to have heard that Burgoyne surrendered to General Gates at Saratoga. So promising was this news that Washington ordered a victory salute be fired and the resulting concussion broke several of Peter Wentz's windows.

An audiovisual presentation at the farm's Reception Center provides additional background on the farm house, with costumed hostesses on hand to answer your questions. On most Saturday afternoons a craft of the period is demonstrated for you to see such diverse arts as block printing, scissor cutting, theorem and fraktur painting. Also, popular favorites like quilting, candlemaking, spinning, and old-fashioned cooking techniques are frequently spotlighted.

The Peter Wentz Farmstead is open year round Tuesday through Saturday from 10:00 A.M. until 4:00 P.M. and Sunday from 1:00 P.M. to 4:00 P.M. The farm is closed on Mondays and on Christmas and Thanksgiving days.

Directions: Take Beltway Exit 27, I-95 north, to Wilmington. Exit north on U.S. 202, Concord Pike, to Route 363 at Valley Forge. Go north on Rt. 363 to Route 73, Skipjack Pike. Turn east one block on Route 73 to the first intersection, then left to the Peter Wentz Farmstead.

The Colonial Pennsylvania Plantation

Life on a family farm in southeast Pennsylvania during the 1770s is re-created at The Colonial Pennsylvania Plantation. Unlike visits to the restored plantations in Maryland and Virginia, a visit to this working farm in Ridley Creek State Park will reveal how different farming was farther north.

The agricultural methods of the 18th century are used to work this farm. You will see that tobacco is not grown here, unlike the southern farms you may have explored. In this part of Pennsylvania the major crops were wheat, corn, buckwheat, potatoes, rye, oats, and even flax in the damp areas. Because farms in this area practiced crop rotation, you are likely to see a field of clover or grass.

In the kitchen garden you will find an assortment of vegetables and herbs for the family. Research of the records for Edgemont, where the farm is located, indicates that the typical household consisted of a husband and wife, a grandmother, three children over 16, and three under 16. Records also show that the average farm had two or three horses, three or four cows, five or six sheep, a sow and boar, and a number of fowl. These animals can be found in the barns of the farm today.

In addition to the old farm house, which has been standing since the 18th century, there is also a stillroom, root cellar, and springhouse. Colonial stillrooms were generally attached to the kitchen and served to store spices and herbs as well as soap, flour, molasses, and even firewood. They also were used as drying sheds for flowers and herbs.

The root cellar was very important as it was hard to preserve food during the long winters. To aid in preservation certain vegetables were buried beneath sandy soil in the cellar. Others were placed in bins beneath leaves or straw. Vegetables like onions, carrots, potatoes, and turnips were stored in the root cellar. Also beverages like cider, beer, and wine were kept here.

Lastly, the 18th century equivalent of our refrigerator, the springhouse, was built over a spring to cool the food during the warm summer months and to reduce spoilage. During the cold months the same flow of water kept food from freezing. Cheese, butter, and soap were often made in the springhouse.

Actually these and many more necessities of colonial life are still made at the farm. You are encouraged to join in the work when you visit this Colonial Pennsylvania Plantation. You may be able to help cut the curd for cheese, card wool, prepare candles for dripping, or help with meal preparation. Since the farm is a working one there are both daily and seasonal activities.

This farm is in Ridley Creek State Park in Edgemont, Pennsylvania. Hours of operation are 10:00 A.M. to 4:00 P.M. on weekends from April through October. While in the area you can also visit the John J. Tyler Arboretum, which is next to Ridley Creek State Park. (See Arboretum chapter.)

Directions: Take Beltway Exit 27, I-95 north, to the Wilmington area and exit on Route 202. At the intersection with Route 1 go right and continue to Route 352 just past the Franklin Mint. Make a left on Route 352 and then right at the sign for Ridley

Garden Plots for Rent

If you're an apartment or condo dweller and are frustrated every spring at not having a garden, read on. There is help even for homeowners who have yards but are unable to give full rein to their horticultural bent. What do you do, for example, if you have a small formal garden and also want to grow corn and watermelon? Try renting a garden plot from your city or county.

A 1,000-square-foot plot, which is standard in the area, can provide enough vegetables to feed not only your family during the summer but also enough for freezing, canning, preserving, pickling, and drying. Gardening is a good way to beat rising food costs and also enjoy produce guaranteed to be fresh. But you don't have to grow just vegetables. You may want to try your hand at planting some of the larger flowers not suitable for most backyard gardens, such as large dahlias, gladioluses, and sunflowers.

Renting a plot is surprisingly easy to do, and it is inexpensive, too. Prices range from $15 to $25 per plot for the season. It is also convenient since all area counties offer residents a choice of plots dispersed around each county to provide easy access to as many as possible.

Speedy action is required for those interested in the idea. Keeping in touch by telephone with the county office handling the program is essential to learning when the plots become available.

Fairfax County in Virginia has a first-come, first-served program that customarily begins in early March. A phone call to the Fairfax County Park Authority (703)941-5000 will provide updated information on its program. They charge a modest fee for a plot that is plowed, rototilled, and staked by the county. From there on it's up to the gardener.

Alexandria, Virginia, also has a Garden Plot Program that fills up rapidly. For information call (703)838-4838. It is only fair to warn you that these plots are not plowed; you have to do that yourself.

In Arlington County, Virginia, registration for garden plots begins on January 1 and the lots go quickly. Arlington County residents can obtain information by calling (703)558-2475.

In Maryland, the Montgomery County Recreation Department has a number of sites throughout the county. To check the availability of garden plots call (301)468-4203.

Two separate organizations rent garden plots in Prince George's County, Maryland. The county's Rent-a-Garden Plot Program usually begins registration in March for 1,000-square-foot lots that are plowed, disked, and staked. For more information on this program call (301)952-4230. The Maryland National Capital Park and Planning Commission also has several garden plot sites within Prince George's County. To learn about this program call (301)699-2415.

In the District of Columbia space is at a premium so the few available lots go very quickly. Information about a few plots offered by the Regional Community Garden Coordinator for the National Park Service can be obtained by calling (202)282-7080. The park service has reduced the size of the lots to try to accommodate the increased demand.

A church affiliated group has begun the Garden Resources of Washington, a project of the Hunger Task Force of the Interfaith Conference. This group is compiling a list of available land for rent and other information helpful to those who want to try farming on a small scale. They keep records of available space in the District, Maryland, and Virginia. To find out more about GROW call (202)234-6300.

With real estate prices soaring, renting garden plots may be the best land deal available. Who says everyone can't afford his own plot of land?

Estimated Planting Dates for the Washington Area

When to Plant	What to Plant
May 15–August 5	Beans
May 1–August 1	Beets
May 15–June 15	Broccoli
May 15–June 15	Brussels Sprouts
May 1–July 1	Cabbage
May 15–August 1	Carrots
May 15–July 1	Cantaloupe
May 15–July 1	Cauliflower
July 1–September 1	Collards
May 15–July 1	Corn
May 15–July 1	Cucumber
May 15–June 1	Eggplant
April 15–August 15	Kale
April 15–May 1	
July 15–September 1	Lettuce
June 1–June 15	Okra
April 15–June 1	Onions
May 15–June 1	Parsley
June 1–July 1	Parsnips
April 1–April 15	
July 25–August 5	Peas
May 15–June 10	Peppers
June 1–June 15	Pumpkins
April 1–September 15	
July 20–September 15	Radishes
May 1–June 1	
August 1–September 5	Spinach
May 15–July 15	Squash
May 15–July 25	Swiss Chard
May 15–July 1	Tomatoes
June 15–September 1	Turnips
May 15–June 15	Watermelon (icebox type)

Vicinity of Beltway—Last frost May 15 and first frost October 15.

Inside Beltway—You can plant 1–2 weeks earlier and frost usually 1–2 weeks later.

For individual varieties consult Burpee's Catalog and Park's Catalog to order seeds.

Pick-Your-Own Fruits and Vegetables

Pick-Your-Own Produce

How are you going to get them back on the farm? That question now has a new answer for many urban dwellers—let them P-Y-O. The popularity of "picking your own" fruits and vegetables has grown almost as much as the fancy new hybrids now available to be picked.

Why do so many confirmed suburbanites enjoy following the fields of ripening fruits and vegetables? For two reasons: finance and freshness.

It's no secret that P-Y-O produce costs less than store fare. This is particularly true if you have a group that can car pool to the farm. This way you have have someone to commiserate with as you make your way up and down the rows, plus somebody to share the cost of driving.

The second major benefit is that the produce is "just picked." Almost all varieties taste better when they are picked at their peak of ripeness. In fact, sometimes they barely resemble what's in the grocery store. The best example is tree-ripened peaches, as opposed to the grocery store variety that is picked and shipped green to save on spoilage. People just can't believe the difference in sweetness and flavor.

Corn, strawberries, tomatoes, sugar peas, and blueberries all have a special taste that can only be enjoyed during the first few hours off the plant.

Most pick-your-own farms weigh your container before you fill it to determine how much you pay. But you won't be weighed, so enjoy nibbling while you work. One note of caution about this practice, however: many fields are sprayed to protect the fruit and vegetables from insect damage. It is not a good idea to eat unwashed produce.

A genuine advantage of the Washington, D.C. area is the wide variety of farm produce that is grown locally. One will not have any trouble in locating a variety of fruits: strawberries, blueberries, raspberries, blackberries, peaches, nectarines, cherries both sweet and sour, pears, plums, grapes, apples, cantaloupes and watermelons. In the vegetable category you can readily find asparagas, beans, beets, broccoli, cabbage, carrots, corn, cucumbers, eggplant, gourds, okra, peas, peppers, potatoes, pumpkins, spinach, squash, tomatoes, and turnips.

Knowing where and when to go are two important considerations.

In Maryland a brochure, compiled by the Maryland Roadside Marketing Association in cooperation with the Cooperative Extension Service and the Division of Marketing and entitled *Pick Your Own and Direct Farm Markets in Maryland,* provides a county-by-county guide to picking fruits and vegetables with a handy chart on harvest dates. To get this brochure, send a self-addressed, stamped envelope with your request to the Division of Marketing, Maryland Department of Agriculture, Parole Plaza Office Building, Annapolis, Maryland 21401.

To obtain a copy of the *Virginia Berry and Vegetable Guide* with its listing of farms, directions, hours of operation, and harvest information, send a self-addressed, stamped envelope to the Virginia Department of Agriculture and Consumer Services, Division of Markets, Room 810, Direct Marketing Agent, P.O. Box 1163, Richmond, Virginia 23209.

After each pick-your-own section in this book is included a list of farms where the produce discussed in that section can be picked. Check these lists also to find out what additional vegetables or fruits are available at each farm.

Estimated Harvest Dates for the Washington Area

	Fruits
August 15–November 5	Apples
July 5–August 1	Blackberries
August 1–September 10	Blackberries (thornless)
June 20–August 1	Blueberries
June 15–July 15	Cherries (sour)
June 10–July 10	Cherries (sweet)
July 21–September 20	Cider
August 15–September 20	Grapes
July 25–August 25	Nectarines
July 5–September 20	Peaches
July 15–September 15	Plums
May 15–June 20	Strawberries
June 15–July 10	Raspberries (black)
June 15–July 10	Raspberries (red)
	Vegetables
April 25–June 15	Asparagas
June 10–September 15	Beans (green)
July 20–September 1	Beans (lima)
June 24–August 30	Beans (pole)
July 4–September 1	Beets
July 10–September 1	Broccoli
June 1–September 15	Cabbage
July 15–September 15	Cantaloupes
July 10–September 15	Carrots
October–November	Corn (Indian)
July 4–September 15	Corn (sweet)
July 1–September 1	Cucumbers
July 1–August 1	Cucumbers (Pickles)
July 25–September 10	Eggplant
August 15–October 30	Gourds
July 15–August 30	Okra
June 10–July 1	Peas (green)
July 20–August 30	Peas (black-eyed)
July 25–September 15	Peppers
July 1–September 30	Potatoes
September 5–December 15	Potatoes (sweet)
September 10–November 30	Pumpkins
May 1–30 and October 1–30	Spinach (spring and fall)

June 25–September 1	Squash (summer)
August 1–September 30	Squash (winter)
July 4–September 15	Tomatoes
August 15–November 1	Turnips
August 1–October 1	Watermelon
July 21–October 1	Watermelon (sugar baby)

Information on approximate harvest dates is from the *Pick Your Own and Direct Farm Markets in Maryland* brochure, compiled and edited by the Maryland Roadside Marketing Association.

Strawberry Picking

Have you ever wondered how a lush and juicy berry came to be called the strawberry? The association came from the French practice of placing straw around the plants to prevent the berries from rotting in the mud.

The practical French who have given us the etymology of the word could also offer practical tips to strawberry pickers. Because the fields are often damp and muddy, pickers should wear old clothes, and even boots if it has just rained. Strawberry stains are hard to remove and difficult to avoid when picking in the field.

Kids and stains always seem to go together. Consequently, unless you're taking the youngsters along for the experience, it's probably best to leave them at home. Some fields, in fact, do not allow anyone under 12 to pick. It is a good idea to check before you head for the farm with a carload of children.

Another good idea is to go with a friend. It's more fun and more economical. You need to exclaim to someone about the size, smell, and taste of the luscious berries. Pickers have a tendency to be friendly, though, and it's perfectly normal to get into a conversation with someone harvesting the next row. Field managers usually assign pickers to a row in order to cover the field methodically. The rows provide such a lush amount that the berries don't even look bigger on the other side.

Pickers often find it impossible to quit. The temptation is strong to add just one more berry to an already overloaded colander or dish. The result is likely to be a veritable avalanche of red berries.

Whether you pick a bowl full or a bucket full depends on how you plan to use the berries. This is not only an important consideration in the quantity you pick, it is also important in selecting the variety. Some berries can be frozen without losing flavor, others are better eaten fresh.

Before going to the fields, call to ask what varieties are available. Earligrow, a small, sweet berry frequently grown in this area, is the only variety considered to be very good both fresh and frozen, according to the Cooperative Extension Service of the University of Maryland. Two varieties that are especially good for freezing are Red Chief, a tart berry that is also good in pies and preserves, and Midway. They are also very good fresh. While Guardian and Delite are good fresh, they are judged only fair when frozen. Darrow, Surecrop, and Red Star are ranked good for both uses.

The Cooperative Extension Service publishes Fact Sheet 223 on "Growing Strawberries in Your Garden." One can obtain a copy or get additional information on strawberry varieties by calling (301)952-3226.

Because the berry-picking season coincides with finding well-stocked fruit bins in the grocery stores, the question arises whether it is really worth the time to pick your own. One advantage is that you know they are fresh when you pick them off the vine. Even at roadside stands, they may be a day or two old. Strawberries do taste sweeter if they are eaten the day they are picked. Few can resist sampling the berries as they pick them, but do inquire first if they have been sprayed.

In addition, you can pick strawberries for a price less than you pay at the market. You also get the largest, most luscious berries you can find for that price. The result is you have a better product than what is found in a pre-packaged grocery container.

Strawberry season in the Washington area extends from mid-May through mid-June. Call for a day-to-day update before heading out to any of the pick-your-own fields listed below. Take your own containers. A shallow container works best to prevent the berries from being bruised on the way home.

Once you've enjoyed fresh-picked, vine-ripened strawberries, you'll repeat the outing every spring. Seasoned pickers are usually there the day the fields open. They know the berries tend to get smaller later in the picking season.

For more information on picking strawberries in Maryland and Virginia, send for the two guides mentioned in the pick-your-own produce section.

Strawberry Picking in Maryland

Anne Arundel County

Belvoir Berry Farm
Linda Brown
1489 Generals Highway
Crownsville, MD 21032
(301)923-2107

Open: May through November.
P-Y-O Selections: Strawberries, Thornless Blackberries, Pumpkins.
Special Comments: You can arrange farm tours and hayrides for birthdays.

Watts Farm
Thomas V. Watts
948 St. Stephens Church Road
Gambrills, MD 21054
(301)858-1393

Open: May through summer months.
P-Y-O Selections: Strawberries and Snap Beans.

Howard County

Dunteachin Farm
John H. Nicolai, Jr.
5377 Kerger Road
Ellicott City, MD 21043
(301)465-8310, (301)465-0503

Open: Spring, summer and fall.
P-Y-O Selections: Strawberries and Cauliflower.
Special Comments: Hayrides can be arranged and eggs are available.

Larriland Farm
G. Lawrence Moore
2525 Florence Road
Woodbine, MD 21797
(301)854-6110

Open: Late May through October and in December.
P-Y-O Selections: Strawberries, Apples, Blackberries, Red Raspberries, Peaches, plus a complete selection of vegetables.
Special Comments: There is a farm festival the first weekend in October; tours and hayrides can be arranged; farm also has Christmas trees.

Sharp Farm Produce
Denise Doerer-Sharp
3779 Sharp Road
Glenwood, MD 21738
(301)489-4630

Open: Spring, summer and fall.
P-Y-O Selections: Strawberries and a complete selection of vegetables.
Special Comments: Tours and hayrides can be arranged.

Montgomery County

Butler's Orchard
George H. Butler, Jr.
22200 Davis Mill Road
Germantown, MD 20874
(301)972-3299

Open: Spring, summer and fall.
P-Y-O Selections: Strawberries, Thornless Blackberries, Red Raspberries, and a complete selection of vegetables.
Special Comments: Free hayrides on October weekends.

Farmer Fulks Greenhouses
Charles B. Fulks
18849 Laytonsville Road
Gaithersburg, MD 20879
(301)926-0772

Open: Spring, summer and fall.
P-Y-O Selections: Strawberries and Tomatoes.
Special Comments: Nursery stock and poinsettias are available.

Homestead Farm
Benoni Allnutt
15600 Sugarland Road
Poolesville, MD 20837
(301)977-3761

Open: June through November.
P-Y-O Selections: Strawberries, Thornless Blackberries, Red Raspberries, Table Grapes, and a complete selection of vegetables.
Special Comments: You can arrange tours, wagonrides and hayrides.

Rock Hill Orchard
Richard A. Biggs
28600 Ridge Road
Mt. Airy, MD 21771
(301)831-7427

Open: June through November.
P-Y-O Selections: Strawberries, Red Raspberries, Snap Beans, Broccoli, Green Peas, Pumpkins, Spinach, Tomatoes, Snap Peas, Cauliflower, and Lettuce.
Special Comments: Farm has fall pumpkin tours; you can also purchase grapevine wreaths and herbal products.

Schaefer Innstead Farm
Ed and Kathy Schaefer
18020 Edwards Ferry Road
Poolesville, MD 20837
(301)972-7247, (301)972-8091

Open: June through October.
P-Y-O Selections: Strawberries, Thornless Blackberries, Broccoli, and Green Peas.
Special Comments: Annual Strawberry Festival is held in early June.

Prince George's County

Cherry Hill Farm
William A. Gallahan & Sons
12300 Gallahan Road
Clinton, MD 20735
(301)292-4642, (301)292-1928

Open: April through November.
P-Y-O Selections: Strawberries, Apples, Blueberries, Peaches, and a complete selection of vegetables.
Special Comments: There are wagonrides to and from the fields as well as children's wagonrides in October.

Darrow Brothers
John Richard Kurtz
6000 Glenn Dale Road
Glenn Dale, MD 20769
(301)390-6611, (301)390-6612

Open: Spring and summer.
P-Y-O Selections: Strawberries, Thornless Blackberries, Snap Beans, and White Corn.
Special Comments: Playground equipment for young children is provided.

E. A. Parker & Sons
Rod and Chris Parker
12720 Parker Lane
Clinton, MD 20735
(301)292-3940

Open: Spring, summer and fall.
P-Y-O Selections: Strawberries, Thornless Blackberries, Table Grapes, and a complete selection of vegetables.
Special Comments: You can arrange hayrides in the fall.

Hare's Berry Farm
Dwight M. Hare
7806 Colonial Lane
Clinton, MD 20735
(301)868-4755, (301)868-7704

Open: Late spring and early summer.
P-Y-O Selection: Strawberries

Johnson's Berry Farm
Rene M. Johnson
17000 Swanson Road
Upper Marlboro, MD 20772
(301)627-8316

Open: Spring and summer.
P-Y-O Selections: Strawberries, Thornless Blackberries, Red Raspberries, and Blueberries.
Special Comments: You can arrange hayrides.

Miller Farms
Henry P. Miller and Charles P. Miller
10200 Piscataway Road
Clinton, MD 20735
(301)297-5878, (301)297-4562

Open: May through December.
P-Y-O Selections: Strawberries, and a complete selection of vegetables.

Walzel Farm
Franz Walzel
11108 Ft. Washington Road
Fort Washington, MD 20477
(301)292-1647

Open: June.
P-Y-O Selection: Strawberries.

Strawberry Picking in Virginia

Fauquier County

Manor Lane Berry Farm
Jack and Louise Vinis
Rt. 2, Box 103
Warrenton, VA 22186
(703)347-4883 (May–Oct.) or
(703)347-7267 (pre-season only)

Open: May through October.
P-Y-O Selections: Strawberries, and Pumpkins.
Special Comments: Autumn pumpkin outings begin in mid-October.

Loudoun County

Chantilly Farm Market
Tim Hutchinson or Claire Crockett
Rt. 2, Box 238-B
Leesburg, VA 22075
(703)777-4041

Open: Late May through October.
P-Y-O Selections: Strawberries, Pumpkins, Sugar Snap Peas, Eggplant, Corn, and Tomatoes.

Cochran's Vegetable Farm
George B. and Emily Cochran
P. O. Box 3
Lincoln, VA 22078
(703)338-7248, (301)338-7002

Open: May through October.
P-Y-O Selections: Strawberries, Pumpkins, Peas, Sugar Snap Peas, Beans, Beets, Summer Squash, Tomatoes, Okra, Winter Squash, and Spaghetti Squash.

Hill High Orchards
John Sleeter
Rt. 1, Box 14
Round Hill, VA 22141
(703)338-7997, 471-1448 (toll free/dial direct)

Open: May through November.
P-Y-O Selection: Strawberries.
Special Comments: A country store features fresh-baked pies, jelly, honey, and cider.

Wheatland Vegetable Farms
Charles and Susan Planck
Rt. 1, Box 78
Purcellville, VA 22132
(703)882-3996

Open: May through September.
P-Y-O Selections: Strawberries, Peas, and Beans.

NOTE: A complete selection of vegetables means that the farm offers at least seven vegetables. These usually include green beans, sweet corn, tomatoes, cucumbers, peppers, squash, and pumpkins, as well as cantaloupes and watermelon.

Raspberry, Blueberry, and Blackberry Picking

If you have memories of picking wild blueberries years ago, you're in for a big surprise. When you go berrying today, you will find cultivated berries that are more than twice the size they once were. An added bonus with blackberries is that the thorns have been bred out. The new hybrid varieties eliminate the wear and tear of scratches.

An important point to keep in mind is that today's berry bushes have been sprayed. It is not really a good idea to sample the berries before they've been washed. Also, use some form of insect repellent on yourself before you start to pick or you may end up with more bites than berries. Even when the weather is warm, long pants and long sleeves are suggested.

Harvesting dates for berries in the Washington area range from mid-June for black and red raspberries until the second week in July. For blueberries, picking usually begins around June 20 and continues until August. Blackberries mature a little later, with picking beginning about the 4th of July for regular berries and in early August for the hybrid thornless blackberries.

Why not just go to your neighborhood grocery store or roadside stand when the berries are in season and save yourself both time and trouble? The answer is you will get large, select, bush-ripened fruit when you pick your own. The difference can be quite noticeable when berries are allowed to reach their full sugar content on the bush. Picking your own is also more economical if you are picking more than a quart.

If you want to pick blueberries keep in mind that the blue color is not a good indication of ripeness. They reach full color several days before they have full sugar content. When fully ripe they separate easily from the stem with no scar tearing.

Blueberry varieties that do well in this area include: for early picking Earliblue; for mid-season, Blueray, which has an excellent flavor and large berries; and for late picking, Herbert, also a large, luscious type of berry. More information on cultivars popular in the Maryland–Virginia area for backyard cultivation can be obtained by contacting the Cooperative Extension Service at (301)952-3312.

If you're interested in planting raspberries, an excellent red berry for this area is Southland. Cumberland is considered a very good black raspberry and Brandywine is a good bet for a purple berry.

When planting blackberries you can choose Darrow or Cherokee. However, both have thorns. For excellent thornless blackberries, Dirksen is the best.

Listed below are local farms that permit you to pick your own berries. Call first to see if they're picking on the day you want. Ask about the conditions of the field—after summer storms the ground can be muddy and boots may be needed. Also check whether children are permitted in the field and remember to use plenty of insect repellent on young kids, who may become more entangled in the bushes than the more cautious adults.

If you wish to bring your own container, a bucket or colander will be adequate. Some farms, however, supply the containers.

For more information on picking berries in Maryland and Virginia, send for the two guides mentioned in the pick-your-own produce section.

Berry Picking in Maryland

Allegany County

Stegmaier Orchards, Inc.
Jack Stegmaier
R.F.D. 9, Box 355
Cumberland, MD 21502
(301)722-5266

Open: June through February.
P-Y-O Selections: Black Raspberries, Red Raspberries, Strawberries, Peaches, and Apples.

Baltimore County

Arrowhead Farm
Howard W. Kerr, Jr.
South Offutt Road
Randallstown, MD 21133
(301)922-5465

Open: Late spring and summer.
P-Y-O Selections: Thornless Blackberries, Strawberries, and Peaches.

Calvert County

Josef & Donann Seidel
Box 233A, SR #2
Plum Point Road
Huntington, MD 20639
(301)535-2128

Open: Summer and fall.
P-Y-O Selections: Thornless Blackberries, Red Raspberries, Wine Grapes, Table Grapes, and Blueberries.

Carroll County

Baugher's Farm Market
Allan Baugher and
Stan Dabkowski
1236 Baugher Road
Westminster, MD 21157
(301)848-5541

Open: Summer and fall.
P-Y-O Selections: Black Raspberries, Red Raspberries, Strawberries, Sweet and Sour Cherries, Snap Beans, and Green Peas.

Charles County

Murray's Farm
Patrick & Barbara Murray
Rt. 232, Box 277
Bryantown, MD 20617
(301)932-1429, (301)725-6660

Open: May through July.
P-Y-O Selections: Red Raspberries, Blueberries, and Strawberries.

Frederick County

Catoctin Mt. Orchard
Harry Black
15307 Kelbaugh Road
Thurmont, MD 21788
(301)271-2737

Open: July through March.
P-Y-O Selections: Thornless Blackberries, Black Raspberries, Blueberries, Sweet and Sour Cherries, Peaches, and Strawberries.

Howard County

Larriland Farm
G. Lawrence Moore
2525 Florence Road
Woodbine, MD 21797
(301)854-6110

Open: Late May through October and again in December.
P-Y-O Selections: Blackberries, Red Raspberries, Strawberries, Peaches, Apples, and a complete selection of vegetables.
Special Comments: There is a farm festival the first weekend in October; you can arrange farm tours and hayrides, and Christmas trees are available.

Montgomery County

Butler's Orchard
George H. Butler, Jr.
22200 Davis Mill Road
Germantown, MD 20874
(301)972-3299

Open: Spring, summer and fall.
P-Y-O Selections: Thornless Blackberries, Red Raspberries, Strawberries, and a complete selection of vegetables.
Special Comments: There are free hayrides on October weekends.

Homestead Farm
Benoni Allnutt
15600 Sugarloaf Road
Poolesville, MD 20837
(301)977-3761

Open: June through November.
P-Y-O Selections: Thornless Blackberries, Red Raspberries, Strawberries, Table Grapes, and a complete selection of vegetables as well as flowers.
Special Comments: You can arrange tours, wagonrides, and hayrides.

Schaefer Innstead Farm
Ed and Kathy Schaefer
18020 Edwards Ferry Road
Poolesville, MD 20837
(301)972-7247, (301)972-8091

Open: June through October.
P-Y-O Selections: Thornless Blackberries, Strawberries, Broccoli, and Green Peas.

Prince George's County

E. A. Parker & Sons
Rod and Chris Parker
12720 Parker Lane
Clinton, MD 20735
(301)292-3940

Open: Spring, summer, and fall.
P-Y-O Selections: Thornless Blackberries, Strawberries, Table Grapes, and a complete selection of vegetables.
Special Comments: Hayrides can be arranged by appointment in the fall; canning supplies and organic grains flour are available.

Johnson's Berry Farm
Rene M. Johnson
17000 Swanson Road
Upper Marlboro, MD 20772
(301)627-8316

Open: Spring and summer.

P-Y-O Selections: Thornless Blackberries, Black Raspberries, Red Raspberries, Blueberries, and Strawberries.

Special Comments: Hayrides can be arranged.

Berry Picking in Virginia

Orange County

Rapidan Berry Gardens
Ned or Anne Coleman
P. O. Box 55
Rapidan, VA 22733
(703)672-4235, (800)552-2379 (toll free)

Open: Mid-May through July.
P-Y-O Selections: Blueberries, Strawberries, and a complete selection of vegetables.

Spotsylvania County

Belvedere Plantation
M. R. Fulks
Star Route TWT, Box 125
Fredericksburg, VA 22401
(703)371-8494, 690-1255 (toll free/dial direct from northern Virginia and Washington, D.C.)

Open: May through October.
P-Y-O Selections: Thornless Blackberries, Strawberries, Pumpkins, and a complete selection of vegetables.
Special Comments: A picnic area is available.

Westmoreland County

Perry's Blueberries
Margaret K. Perry
c/o H. H. Perry Canning Co., Inc.
Montross, VA 22520
(804)224-0440 or (804)493-9049

Open: Mid-June to mid-July.
P-Y-O Selection: Blueberries.

NOTE: A complete selection of vegetables means that the farm offers at least seven vegetables. These usually include green beans, sweet corn, tomatoes, cucumbers, peppers, squash, and pumpkins, as well as cantaloupes and watermelon.

Peach Picking

Peaches 'n cream, peachy keen, she's a peach, and Georgia Peach all attest to the popularity of this fruit. It certainly has become a part of vernacular language.

Georgia peaches are great if you live in Georgia, but home-grown varieties are always best. Even a small yard can accommodate two standard-size trees that will bear heavily if sprayed properly. To have a harvest of any kind, a spray program is absolutely essential.

Far and away the most popular peach is the Elberta peach. The trees come in both standard and dwarf sizes. Advantages of dwarf trees are their smaller size and their early maturity. Not only is the fruit decidedly easier to spray and pick, but impatient gardeners like the fact that dwarf trees bear fruit as early as the second year.

If your interest is in planting rather than picking peaches, check the mail order catalogs. Bountiful Ridge Nurseries in Princess Anne, Maryland, lists approximately 50 varieties of peaches in its catalog. Stark Brothers, another mail order nursery, is world famous for the quality of its planting stock.

Catalogs list two types of peaches—freestone and cling. In most stores consumers of fresh fruit have access only to freestone, as the cling varieties are used primarily for canning. Freestone peaches are best for backyard planting since you can use them for canning as well as eating fresh.

The peach season in the Maryland–Virginia area is roughly from July 5 to September 20. A number of varieties do well in this area. For early bearing July fruit you can grow Red Haven, which is a freestone that is good for eating fresh as well as for canning and freezing. A white-fleshed peach, Raritan Rose is a good freestone for eating fresh. In August, Loring is a good fresh freestone; and Redskin, also a freestone, is good for both eating fresh and for canning. In September, a late peach that does well in this area is Marqueen. Impress your friends with the variety J. C. Hale, which grows half again the size of standard peaches and rivals Elberta in flavor.

Another fruit that can be picked locally is the nectarine, a cross between the peach and plum. Frequently called a fuzzless peach, the fruit has roughly the same growing season and is available locally from July 25 to August 25. The nectarine, however, is not as easy to grow as the peach. If you plan to have a backyard orchard it is best to stick to dwarf and semi-dwarf peaches. The principal problem with nectarines is their tendency to develop brown rot.

Listed below are the farms where peaches and nectarines are available. Keep in mind that to pick peaches and nectarines you will have to climb on ladders available at the farms. This is not recommended for the very young or the elderly. Call before heading out to pick to get specific directions and to inquire about bringing your own container.

For more information on picking peaches in Maryland and Virginia, send for the two guides mentioned in the pick-your-own produce section.

Peach Picking in Maryland

Allegany County

Stegmaier Orchards, Inc.
Jack Stegmaier
R.F.D. 9, Box 355
Cumberland, MD 21502
(301)722-5266

Open: June through February.
P-Y-O Selections: Peaches, Apples, Black Raspberries, and Red Raspberries.
Special Comments: Apple and pear butter are available.

Baltimore County

Armacost Farms Orchard
Eddie L. Armacost
16926 Gorsuch Mill Road
Upperco, MD 21155
(301)239-3440

Open: July through February.
P-Y-O Selections: Peaches, Apples, and Potatoes.
Special Comments: You can arrange a farm tour in October.

Arrowhead Farm
Howard W. Kerr, Jr.
South Offutt Road
Randallstown, MD 21133
(301)922-5465

Open: Late spring and summer.
P-Y-O Selections: Peaches, Strawberries, and Thornless Blackberries.

Moore's Orchard
George F. Moore
5242 E. Joppa Road
Perry Hall, MD 21128
(301)256-5982

Open: July through January.
P-Y-O Selections: Peaches, Apples, Plums, Snap Beans, and White Corn.

Frederick County

Catoctin Mt. Orchard
Harry Black
15307 Kelbaugh Road
Thurmont, MD 21788
(301)271-2737

Open: July through March.
P-Y-O Selections: Peaches, Thornless Blackberries, Black Raspberries, Blueberries, Strawberries, and Sweet and Sour Cherries.
Special Comments: Already picked nectarines are available for sale.

Toomey's Orchard and Farm Market
Thomas J. Toomey
Route 15
Thurmont, MD 21788
(301)271-7382

Open: All year.
P-Y-O Selections: Peaches and Sour Cherries.
Special Comments: You can arrange tours and wagon-rides; a gift shop sells spices, teas, and natural foods.

Howard County

Larriland Farm
G. Lawrence Moore
2525 Florence Road
Woodbine, MD 21797
(301)854-6110

Open: Late May through October and again in December.
P-Y-O Selections: Peaches, Apples, Blackberries, Red Raspberries, Strawberries, and a complete selection of vegetables.
Special Comments: There is a farm festival the first weekend in October; you can arrange farm tours and hayrides, and Christmas trees and firewood are available.

Montgomery County

Hough's Orchard
Forest Hough
20001 Peach Tree Road
Dickerson, MD 20842
(301)349-5330

P-Y-O Selection: Peaches.

Prince George's County

Cherry Hill Farm
William A. Gallahan & Sons
12300 Gallahan Road
Clinton, MD 20735
(301)292-4642, (301)292-1928

Open: April through November.
P-Y-O Selections: Peaches, Apples, Blueberries, Strawberries, and a complete selection of vegetables.
Special Comments: There are wagonrides to and from the fields as well as children's wagonrides in October.

Peach Picking in Virginia

Fauquier County

Hartland Orchard
Henry C. Green
Markham, VA 22643
(703)364-2316

Open: During summer season.
P-Y-O Selections: Peaches, Nectarines, and Summer Apples.

Peach Manor Orchard
W. E. or E. G. Williams
Bealeton, VA 22712
(703)439-3035

Open: July through September.
P-Y-O Selection: Peaches.

Hanover County

Kruger's Orchard
Robert or Barbara Kruger
Rt. 6, Box 238
Mechanicsville, VA 23111
(804)779-3812

Open: July through August.
P-Y-O Selections: Peaches and Butterbeans.

Loudoun County

Hill High Orchards
John Sleeter
Rt. 1, Box 14
Round Hill, VA 22141
(703)338-7997 or 471-1448
(toll free/dial direct)

Open: April through December.
P-Y-O Selections: Peaches, Apples, and Pumpkins.
Special Comments: They have a duck pond for fishing that makes a nice setting for a picnic.

Orange County

Moormont Orchard
J. Goodwin Moore
Rt. 1, Box 464
Rapidan, VA 22733
(1-800)572-2262 (toll free when dialed from VA only), (703)425-9657

Open: June through September.
P-Y-O Selections: Peaches, Summer and Fall Apples, and Table Grapes.
Special Comments: There is a picnic area, and honey, cider, sparkling cider, preserves, jams, and jellies are sold.

NOTE: A complete selection of vegetables means that the farm offers at least seven vegetables. These usually include green beans, sweet corn, tomatoes, cucumbers, peppers, squash, and pumpkins, as well as cantaloupes and watermelon.

Apple Picking

The sight of an orchard of bright red apples is one of nature's delights. No matter whether you pick them, eat them, cook them, or celebrate their special place in the American myth, you can enjoy an excursion into apple orchard country anywhere from mid-August to early November.

Apples are a prolific fruit; there are more than 15,000 varieties. Your choice fortunately is more limited. Some guidelines will help you determine which of the bountiful apple harvests in Maryland and Virginia you want to take advantage of.

First of all, decide how you plan to use the apples. Do you want to put them in lunches, dice them for salads, or cook them? After that decision, you can consider the special features of the various varieties. Jonathan, Golden Delicious, and Stayman can be used any way—for lunches, salads, or cooking. For eating fresh and in salads, choose Red Delicious. To eat fresh and to cook use Grimes Golden, York, Winesap, or Rome Beauty.

For growing apples in the yard, Northern Spy is frequently recommended. In fact, some experts say it's the best apple grown in the United States. A close hybrid of that variety, Red Northern Spy, is not highly regarded. Of course, one will not err in growing Baldwin, Red Delicious, Grimes Golden, Rhode Island

Greening, Yellow Delicious, or Jonathan. In opting for a backyard orchard, keep in mind that most apple trees bear heavily only every other year.

If you want to pick apples yourself, several orchards in the area are easily reached. The same cannot be said for the fruit, as you do have to climb a ladder to reach the apples. This makes it dangerous for young pickers and awkward for some older pickers. Remember to call before you set out. Also, be sure to bring your own container, though some orchards require you to use theirs for picking and weighing.

For more information on picking apples in Maryland and Virginia, send for the two guides mentioned in the pick-your-own produce section.

Apple Picking in Maryland

Allegany County

Stegmaier Orchards, Inc.
Jack Stegmaier
R.F.D. 9, Box 355
Cumberland, MD 21502
(301)722-5266

Open: June through February.
P-Y-O Selections: Apples, Black Raspberries, Red Raspberries, Peaches, and Strawberries.
Special Comments: Apple and pear butter are available.

Baltimore County

Armacost Farms Orchard
Eddie L. Armacost
16926 Gorsuch Mill Road
Upperco, MD 21155
(301)239-3440

Open: July through February.
P-Y-O Selections: Apples, Peaches, and Potatoes.

Moore's Orchard
George F. Moore
5242 E. Joppa Road
Perry Hall, MD 21128
(301)256-5982

Open: July through January.
P-Y-O Selections: Apples, Peaches, Plums, Snap Beans, and White Corn.

Howard County

Larriland Farm
G. Lawrence Moore
2525 Florence Road
Woodbine, MD 21797
(301)854-6110

Open: Late May through October and again in December.
P-Y-O Selections: Apples, Blackberries, Red Raspberries, Peaches, Strawberries, and a complete selection of vegetables.
Special Comments: There is a farm festival the first weekend in October; you can arrange farm tours and hayrides, and Christmas trees and firewood are available.

Montgomery County

Lewis Orchard
Lottie M. Lewis
18900 Peach Tree Road
Dickerson, MD 20842
(301)349-4101

Open: July through December.
P-Y-O Selection: Apples.

Prince George's County

Cherry Hill Farm
William A. Gallahan & Sons
12300 Gallahan Road
Clinton, MD 20735
(301)292-4642 or (301) 292-1928

Open: April through November.
P-Y-O Selections: Apples, Blueberries, Peaches, Strawberries, and a complete selection of vegetables.
Special Comments: There are wagonrides to and from the fields as well as children's wagonrides in October.

Apple Picking in Virginia

Fauquier County

Barton Orchard
Thomas G. Teates
Rt. 4, Box 551
Christiansburg, VA 24073
(703)382-9348

Open: Mid-September through early November.
P-Y-O Selection: Apples.
Special Comments: There are picnic tables, and cider and honey are available.

Hartland Orchard
Henry C. Green
Markham, VA 22643
(703)364-2316

Open: Autumn.
P-Y-O Selection: Apples.

Stribling Orchard
Robert & Mildred Stribling
P.O. Box 116
Markham, VA 22643
(703)364-2092 or (703) 364-2894

Open: September to November.
P-Y-O Selection: Apples.
Special Comments: There is picnicking in the orchard, and cider, fresh jelly, pickles, and homemade bread are available.

Frederick County

Frederick Farm Market
J. Kelly or Sally Robinson
Rt. 4, Box 46
Winchester, VA 22601
(703)667-1743 or (703) 667-0250

Open: Mid-September through October.
P-Y-O Selection: Apples.
Special Comments: Cider, jams, jellies, and preserves are also available.

Fruit Hill Orchard, Inc.
Audrey Fahnestock &
Robert Solenberger
Oak Grove Orchard
Route 654
Winchester, VA 22601
(703)662-2483 or (703) 662-2938

Open: September through October.
P-Y-O Selection: Apples.

Loudoun County

Hill High Orchards
John Sleeter
Rt. 1, Box 14
Round Hill, VA 22141
(703)338-7997 or 471-1448 (toll free/direct dial)

Open: April through December.
P-Y-O Selections: Apples, Peaches, and Pumpkins.
Special Comments: There is a picnic area beside a duck pond, and cider, jams, jellies, preserves, and fresh baked pies are sold.

Shenandoah County

Cooper's Orchard
John Cooper
Rt. 1, Box 390
Toms Brook, VA 22660
(703)436-3849

Open: August through October.
P-Y-O Selections: Apples and Peaches.

Warren County

Harmony Hollow Orchard
Dr. O. O. Van Deusen
P.O. Box 1454
Front Royal, VA 22630
(703)636-2009 or (703)
635-3249

Open: September through December.
P-Y-O Selection: Apples.

Grape Picking

Despite expressions like "sour grapes" and "Grapes of Wrath," grapes can provide a great deal of satisfaction for the backyard gardener. Even if you don't use them, the sight of clusters of luminous berries that laden the typical grape arbor can be enjoyable. If you are not inclined to make homemade jelly, jam, or wine give the grapes to more motivated friends and let them return samples of their efforts. You can also choose to eat them right off the vine and to let the birds and squirrels help harvest them.

Grapes will grow along a fence or on their own arbor. The ever popular Concord variety, which is used frequently for jellies and jams, thrives in this area. Be alert, however, to the mildew threat, a problem shared by all area gardeners because of the high humidity. Another popular grape for making jelly is Steuben, which is noted for its large clusters.

If you are going to eat the grapes off the vine you may prefer the seedless varieties—Interlachen, Romulus, and Himrod. Of course, the birds also favor the seedless grapes and may beat you to the harvest. Paper bags protect grapes from birds. If you have more than four vines it's a big job to bag each cluster of grapes.

Interestingly, the birds unerringly pick the seedless varieties, leaving untouched even the luscious looking Golden Muscat. The huge clusters of this attractive grape average one and two pounds a bunch.

The wine grape varieties—Aurora, Seyval, De Chaunac, and Merlot—need more pampering and produce fewer and smaller clusters. Interest in homemade wine is burgeoning. To embark on this project, at least a dozen vines are needed, 30 are preferred. Before starting a venture of this size, call your area Cooperative Extension Service for advice. Also, consider visiting one of the nearby vineyards to gain some helpful pointers on viticulture.

One can buy one- or two-year-old grape plants from any of the large garden mail order houses. Most catalogs present a wide variety of grapes. Grape growers, however, must be prepared to spray the grapes or a spotty harvest will be the result. If you already have an apple, peach, or pear tree the addition of a few vines will not add substantially to your work load.

If you would prefer visiting someone else's vineyard, however, there are area farms where you can pick-your-own grapes.

For more information on picking grapes in Maryland and Virginia, send for the two guides mentioned in the pick-your-own produce section.

Grape Picking in Maryland

Calvert County

Josef and Donann Seidel
Box 233A, SR #2
Plum Point Road
Huntingtown, MD 20639
(301)535-2128

Open: Summer and fall.
P-Y-O Selections: Wine Grapes, Table Grapes, Thornless Blackberries, Red Raspberries, and Blueberries.

Prince George's County

E. A. Parker & Sons
Rod and Chris Parker
12720 Parker Lane
Clinton, MD 20735
(301)292-3940

Open: Spring, summer, and fall.
P-Y-O Selections: Table Grapes, Thornless Blackberries, Strawberries, and a complete selection of vegetables.
Special Comments: You can arrange fall hayrides and obtain canning supplies and organic grains flour.

Grape Picking in Virginia

Augusta County

Wenger Grape Farms
David Wenger
Rt. 4, Box 237
Waynesboro, VA 22980
(703)943-3751 or (703)
943-4956

Open: Summer and fall.
P-Y-O Selections: Concord and Niagara (Table) Grapes.

Fauquier County

Oasis Vineyard
D. Salahi
Hume, VA 22639
(703)635-7627 or (703)
549-9182

Open: Mid-August through September.
P-Y-O Selection: French Hybrids.
Special Comments: You can have your grapes pressed here as well.

King George County

Camillo Vineyards
Beverly or Tom Iessi
Rt. 2, Box 242
King George, VA 22485
(703)663-2577

Open: August and September by appointment only.
P-Y-O Selection: Vinifera and table varieties.
Special Comments: Crusher and press available; you can take home winemaking lessons.

Madison County

Ward H. Kipps
Rt. 3, Box 422
Rochelle, VA 22738
(703)948-4171

Open: August through September.
P-Y-O Selections: French Hybrids, Vinifera and Concord.

Orange County

Moormont Orchard & Rapidan Berry Gardens
J. Goodwin Moore and Ned Coleman
Rt. 1, Box 464
Rapidan, VA 22733
(703)425-9657 or (1-800)572-2262 (can be dialed toll free only in Virginia)

Open: August through mid-September.
P-Y-O Selection: Table Grapes.

Page County

Guilford Farm Vineyard
John Gerba
Rt. 2, Box 117
Luray, VA 22835
(703)778-3853 or (202) 554-0333

Open: August and September.
P-Y-O Selections: French Hybrids, Vinifera Grapes, and Apples.

Virginia Beach Independent City

Virginia Beach Vineyards & Nursery
Jim Mays or Bob Mays
5320 Gale Drive
Virginia Beach, VA 23464
(804)420-2257

Open: Late July through August.
P-Y-O Selections: French Hybrids and Concord Grapes.
Special Comments: You can also purchase potted vines.

NOTE: A complete selection of vegetables means that the farm offers at least seven vegetables. These usually include green beans, sweet corn, tomatoes, cucumbers, peppers, squash, and pumpkins, as well as cantaloupes and watermelon.

Pick-Your-Own Pumpkin Patches

October's prize harvest is pumpkins and the search for the great pumpkin can become a family tradition that expands the Halloween holiday into more than costumes and trick-or-treating.

Halloween can also include a day's outing, creating an October centerpiece for the table, making tasty snacks from the pumpkin seeds or home made pies and breads from the pulp.

Pumpkin picking at a local patch is just the beginning of the fun. Designing and carving the jack-o-lantern gives the imagination full rein as you decide to carve a pumpkin with either an elongated shape or a more jolly round one. The original Jack was far from happy. Legend has it that the tradition for this Halloween stand-by was started in Ireland by a miser named Jack, whose stingy nature prevented him from going to paradise. Because his pranks made him unwelcome to the Devil, Jack was forced to walk the earth until Judgment Day carrying a lantern to light his way.

Pick a pumpkin early and use it uncut as a fall display before carving it the weekend before Halloween. In fact, select an extra small unbruised pumpkin for use as a centerpiece through November and you might still be able to bake your Thanksgiving pies with it. Make certain it is unblemished since small bruises will frequently cause the pumpkin to rot. Also, once carved, the pumpkin will last only a few days.

Before carving the pumpkin, scoop out the insides and use the pumpkin meat for pies and bread. It is easier to carve if you hollow the pumpkin to about a one inch thickness. This usually provides plenty of pumpkin to use for baking. You will also have a large quantity of seeds that can be salted and toasted in the oven for tasty and seasonal snacks.

The next step is to draw a design with a felt-tip marker. For those with confidence this step can be omitted, but it does give you the chance to get the family's approval before the pumpkin is carved. Woe to the carver who creates a terrifying visage when a happy one was envisioned! Pumpkin carving can be simple or complex. The job can be simple by making a few large cutouts, complex by being creative with small thin line cutouts. The thin quarter inch lines allow far more expression than the standard grinning through crooked teeth type.

To further enhance a pumpkin face, use an assortment of fruit and dried natural embellishments. Acorns, walnuts, and Indian corn can serve as eyes or teeth. Gourds are good for noses and tongues as well as to create a pop-eyed effect. For a crowning touch, use dried grasses, leaves, or corn husks for hair. Use your imagination to create a personalized pumpkin.

It is always best to have an adult supervise the carving since sharp kitchen knives are used. Avoid using a serrated knife as it will make uneven cuts. If you accidently cut off the wrong piece, simply attach it with a toothpick.

If you plan to burn a candle inside the pumpkin, cut a wedge out of the lid to allow the smoke to escape. Otherwise the inside becomes extremely blackened and dries out faster, not to mention the odor of burning pumpkin.

But first you have to find just the right pumpkin. Both Maryland and Virginia have nearby pick-your-own farms. Some also provide hayrides and farm fun for the kids. Check the listings carefully, and remember to call to check the size and conditions of available pumpkins.

For more information on picking pumpkins in Maryland and Virginia, send for the two guides mentioned in the pick-your-own produce section.

Pumpkin Patches in Maryland

Anne Arundel County

Belvoir Berry Farm
Linda Brown
1489 Generals Highway
Crownsville, MD 21032
(301)923-2107

Open: May through November.
P-Y-O Selections: Pumpkins, Thornless Blackberries, and Strawberries.
Special Comments: You can arrange hayrides for birthday parties; you can also cut your own firewood.

Baltimore County

Rutkowski & Taylor Farm
J. Taylor and A. Rutkowski
11211 Raphel Road
Upper Falls, MD 21156
(301)592-8785

Open: May through November.
P-Y-O Selections: Pumpkins, Strawberries, and a complete selcction of vegetables.
Special Comments: Hayrides and farm tours are offered.

Charles County

Cedar Hill Farm
Route 5
Waldorf, MD 20601
(301)843-6801

Open: Summer and fall.
P-Y-O Selections: Pumpkins, Fall Greens, and a complete selection of vegetables.
Special Comments: Cider is sold at the farm.

Frederick County

Glade-Link Farms
Shirley A. Wisner
9332 Links Road
Walkersville, MD 21793
(301)898-7131

Open: Spring, summer, and fall.
P-Y-O Selections: Pumpkins, Blueberries, Strawberries, Broccoli, and Cauliflower.

Howard County

Larriland Farm
G. Lawrence Moore
2525 Florence Road
Woodbine, MD 21797
(301)854-6110

Open: Late May through October and again in December.
P-Y-O Selections: Pumpkins, Apples, Blackberries, Red Raspberries, Peaches, Strawberries, and a complete selection of vegetables.
Special Comments: There is a farm festival the first weekend in October; you can arrange farm tours and hayrides; Christmas trees, country hams, and firewood are also available.

Montgomery County

Butler's Orchard
George H. Butler, Jr.
22200 Davis Mill Road
Germantown, MD 20874
(301)972-3299

Open: Spring, summer, and fall.
P-Y-O Selections: Pumpkins, Thornless Blackberries, Red Raspberries, Strawberries, and a complete selection of vegetables.
Special Comments: There are free hayrides on October weekends.

Rock Hill Orchard
Richard A. Biggs
28600 Ridge Road
Mt. Airy, MD 21771
(301)831-7427

Open: June through November.
P-Y-O Selections: Pumpkins, Red Raspberries, Strawberries, and a complete selection of vegetables.
Special Comments: There are fall pumpkin tours; grapevine wreaths and herbal products are available.

Prince George's County

Cherry Hill Farm
William A. Gallahan & Sons
12300 Gallahan Road
Clinton, MD 20735
(301)292-4642 or (301) 292-1928

Open: April through November.
P-Y-O Selections: Pumpkins, Apples, Blueberries, Strawberries, and a complete selection of vegetables.
Special Comments: There are wagonrides to and from the fields and children's wagonrides during October.

E. A. Parker & Sons
Rod and Chris Parker
12720 Parker Lane
Clinton, MD 20735
(301)292-3940

Open: Spring, summer, and fall.
P-Y-O Selections: Pumpkins, Thornless Blackberries, Table Grapes, Strawberries, and a complete selection of vegetables.
Special Comments: You can arrange hayrides in the fall; canning supplies and organic grains flour are available.

Miller Farms
Henry P. Miller and Charles P. Miller
10200 Piscataway Road
Clinton, MD 20735
(301)297-5878 or (301) 297-4562

Open: May to December.
P-Y-O Selections: Pumpkins, Strawberries, and a complete selection of vegetables.

Robin Hill Farm Nursery
Russell Watson
15800 Croom Road
Brandywine, MD 20613
(301)579-6844

Open: October only.
P-Y-O Selections: Pumpkins, Turnips, and Kale.
Special Comments: Pumpkin Harvest Farm Tours by appointment; hayrides on October weekend afternoons.

Pumpkin Patches in Virginia

Fairfax County

Cox Farms
Gina Richard
2599 Chain Bridge Road
Vienna, VA 22180
(703)281-0165

Open: June through October.
P-Y-O Selections: Pumpkins and Strawberries.
Special Comments: Children can enjoy cider, hayrides and picking pumpkins from mid to late October.

Potomac Vegetable Farms
9627 Leesburg Pike
Vienna, VA 22180
(703)759-2119

Open: March through November.
P-Y-O Selections: Pumpkins, Raspberries, and a complete selection of vegetables.

Fauquier County

Manor Lane Berry Farm
Jack and Louise Vinis
Rt. 2, Box 103
Warrenton, VA 22186
(703)347-4883

Open: May through October.
P-Y-O Selections: Pumpkins and Strawberries.

Frederick County

Raspberry Ridge Farms
Jack K. Jenkins
Rt. 1, Box 273
Winchester, VA 22601
(703)662-4552

Open: June through October.
P-Y-O Selections: Pumpkins and a complete selection of vegetables.

Loudoun County

Chantilly Farm Market
Tim Hutchinson or Clair Crockett
Rt. 2, Box 238-B
Leesburg, VA 22075
(703)777-4041

Open: June through October.
P-Y-O Selections: Pumpkins, Strawberries, Sugar Snap Peas, Eggplant, Corn, and Tomatoes.

Cochran's Vegetable Farm
George B. and Emily B. Cochran
P.O. Box 3
Lincoln, VA 22078
(703)338-7248 or (703) 338-7002

Open: May through October.
P-Y-O Selections: Pumpkins, Strawberries, and a complete selection of vegetables.

Spotsylvania County

Belvedere Plantation
M. R. Fulks
Star Rt. TWT, Box 125
Fredericksburg, VA 22401
(703)371-8494, 690-1255 (toll free/dial direct from northern Virginia and Washington, D.C.)

Open: May through October.
P-Y-O Selections: Pumpkins, Strawberries, Thornless Blackberries, and a complete selection of vegetables.
Special Comments: A picnic area is available.

NOTE: A complete selection means that the farm offers at least seven vegetables. These usually include green beans, sweet corn, tomatoes, cucumbers, pepper, squash, and pumpkins, as well as cantaloupes and watermelon.

Choose-and-Cut Christmas Trees

One of Charles Schultz's most touching cartoons shows Charlie Brown trying to find a real Christmas tree among the garish aluminum trees that seem to be in such abundance. If that cartoon strikes a responsive chord around your house, you may want to visit one of the choose-and-cut tree farms in the area. You can re-create some of the fun of the good old days and cut your own tree.

The idea of bringing a live tree into the house is believed to have started in 16th century Germany. The Eastern Orthodox Church celebrated Christmas Eve as the Feast Day of Adam and Eve and church members decorated a fir tree with apples to honor them. When Prince Albert of Germany married Queen Victoria, he introduced the custom of decorating a tree in the home to England. German immigrants continued the practice when they arrived in America.

Most traditionalists still prefer live trees, but too many trees are cut too early. They become brittle and begin to lose their needles. More than one family has had to remove a needleless tree on Christmas Eve and put up a new one to placate a tearful child.

Misadventures like this lead some to artificial trees. Another alternative is to visit the choose-and-cut tree farms. The trees at these farms are truly fresh. Also, you don't have to hold them up to get a good look at them. The biggest problem will be how to get the tree down. It takes a concerted effort. Some tree farms will saw it down for you. If you decide to cut it yourself be sure to bring a saw or an ax. Some farms supply cutting tools but most do not.

At these farms you may have four options: cut your own tree; buy one already cut; buy a live tree, balled and ready for planting; or dig up your own tree.

Remember, however, that the more the farm hands do for you the more it costs. Cutting your own tree is the most economical in the short run. A broader view is that for a little more money you can have the pleasure of a fresh live tree and the value of a decorative evergreen you have planted in your yard.

With a little planning, plus a little luck, you can plant your own Christmas tree and start a new family tradition. However, there are some precautions to keep in mind if you hope to enjoy a living tree the following summer. First, since the ground is often frozen after the holidays, choose where you want the tree and dig the hole early. It's best to fill it with leaves as this keeps the bottom from becoming too frozen and cushions anyone who might fall in. Also, cover the dirt you remove with leaves so that you can pack it around the tree's root ball when you do plant it. A hole about three feet in diameter and two-feet deep is about right for most balled and burlapped live trees.

One final point to remember about planting your own tree: you will have to shorten its stay inside. An indoor stay of about one week is the best to ensure a successful venture. Ask tree farm personnel for additional hints on planting a live tree.

Plan to visit a tree farm a week or two before Christmas, calling ahead to make sure they have an ample supply of the type you prefer. Scotch pine is always a favorite. Other pines you will find locally are white and Austrian pine. Douglas fir and Norway, as well as blue and white spruce, are also available.

Christmas Trees in Maryland

Anne Arundel County

Masque Farm
Robert C. Giffen, Jr.
Route 387, Spa Road
Annapolis, MD 21401
(301)757-4454 (no calls on weekends)

Open: December weekends.
Selections: Scotch Pine, White Pine, and Norway Spruce.

Baltimore County

Johnson's Farm
John W. C. Johnson
1552 Glencoe Road
Sparks, MD 21152
(301)472-2882

Open: December weekends.
Selections: Scotch Pine and White Pine.

Carroll County

J. C. K. Christmas Tree Farm
John C. Kirby
Mayberry Road
Westminster, MD 21157
(301)837-2320 or (301) 346-7597

Open: December.
Selections: Scotch Pine, White Pine, Austrian Pine, and Norway Spruce.
Special Comments: Wreaths and rope are available as well as free cookies.

Silver Run Tree Farm
E. & E. Trees, Inc.
Route 97
Westminster, MD 21157
(301)751-1237 or (301) 829-2799

Open: December.
Selections: Scotch Pine, White Pine, Austrian Pine, Douglas Fir, Norway Spruce, Blue Spruce, and White Spruce.
Special Comments: Holly, wreaths, and greens are available.

Montgomery County

Cider & Ginger Tree Farm
Barbara D. and Clinton F. Wells
17900 Elmer School Road
Dickerson, MD 20743
(301)349-5693

Open: December.
Selections: Scotch Pine.

Prince George's County

Tanner Farm
William H. Tanner
Bladen-Westwood Road
Brandywine, MD 20613
(301)579-2238 or (202) 659-7528

Open: December weekends.
Selections: Scotch Pine and Norway Spruce.

Christmas Trees in Virginia

Albemarle County

Ash Lawn
Route 795
Charlottesville, VA 22901
(804)293-9539

Open: December.
Selection: Cedar.

Fairfax County

James Thomas's Christmas Trees
1629 Beulah Road
Vienna, VA 22180
(703)938-0562

Open: Second and third weekends in December.
Selections: Sheared Scotch, White Pine, and Virginia Pine.

Fauquier County

Yulelog Christmas Tree Farm
Ralph S. Woodruff
7308 Lois Lane
Lanham, MD 20801
(703)364-2811 (farm) or
(301)577-4316 (home)

Open: December weekends.
Selections: Blue Spruce, Norway Spruce, Scotch Pine, Virginia Pine, and White Pine.
Special Comments: Farm is near Marshall, Virginia.

Frederick County

Danny-Dayle Christmas Tree Plantation
Route 7, Box 259
Winchester, VA 22601
(703)662-9026

Open: Thanksgiving weekend and December weekends.
Selections: Scotch Pine, Spruce, and Fir.
Special Comments: The Trim-a-Tree Shop offers imported handmade ornaments; pine wreaths and cones are available.

Pinehill Christmas Tree Farm
Edward L. Christianson
Route 2, Box 95A
Winchester, VA 22601
(703)877-1643

Open: December.
Selections: Scotch Pine and White Pine.
Special Comments: Imported tree ornaments and Scotch Pine wreaths and boughs are available.

Scuttlebutt Christmas Tree Farm
Robert F. Dresel
Route 689
Winchester, VA 22601
(703)888-3442

Open: December.
Selections: Scotch Pine and White Pine.

Walnut Ridge Farm Nursery
Charles Leight
Rt. 1, Box 145
Clear Brook, VA 22624
(703)667-9537

Open: December weekends.
Selections: Scotch Pine and White Pine.

Loudoun County

Loudoun Nursery
Louis S. Nichols
Rt. 1, Box 175A
Hamilton, VA 22068
(703)882-3450 or (703) 882-3560

Open: Thursday through Sunday in December.
Selection: Scotch Pine.

Rappahannock County

Chestnut Hills Farm
Frank P. McWhirt
Rt. 1, Box 73H
Amissville, VA 22002
(703)937-5461 or (703) 532-4604

Open: December.
Selections: Scotch Pine and White Pine.

Parson Christmas Tree Farm
Nels A. Parson
Box 85
Washington, VA 22747
(703)675-3523

Open: Weekend before Christmas.
Selection: Douglas Fir.

Quail Call Farm
William J. Keim
Route 642
Amissville, VA 22002
(703)937-4696

Open: December.
Selections: Scotch Pine, White Pine, Fraser Fir, and Colorado Blue Spruce.

Warren County

Skyline Evergreen Farm
Jim Frith
4919 N. 14th Street
Arlington, VA 22205
(703)527-2743 (home)

Open: December.
Selections: Norway Spruce, White Spruce, Scotch Pine, and White Pine.
Special Comments: The farm is near Front Royal, Virginia.

Vineyards

Virginia

Meredyth Vineyards

Thomas Jefferson would have felt both vindicated and delighted if he had known that in 1979 a Virginia wine, Meredyth Vineyards's 1976 Seyval Blanc, would be served by President and Mrs. Carter at a White House dinner.

Growing grapes in Virginia is not a new phenomenon; it has been done since colonial times. What is new, however, is the remarkable success that Virginia vineyards are experiencing now. In 1981 a newspaper could report 10 wineries in Virginia, while in 1982 a Vinifera Wine Growers Journal could list 45 vineyards in the state.

Early wine making in the Jamestown Era that produced wine that many settlers considered unpalatable was followed by Jefferson's experimental vineyards. He enjoyed about the same success, or lack of it. He planted the wrong vines, and there was no way to cope with plant enemies in the soil and air. In 1773, Jefferson planned to have an Italian, Philip Mazzie, bring European grapevines to Virginia. The American Revolution halted this project, but had it been carried out, it is unlikely that it would have succeeded. Vines imported from France in those days withered and died.

European vines could not be transplanted unless they were grafted to native roots, or unless they were a hybrid. Vinifera vines that originated in Asia Minor were grafted to American roots proven to be resistant to a root parasite in American soil, the phylloxera, an aphid popularly called a "root louse."

The second method of hybridization of French–American crosses proved very successful in the eastern United States. They were resistant not only to root lice but also to airborne mildews and rot. In fact, the success of these French–American crosses became the basis of Virginia's wine industry, which first produced commercial wine in 1975.

Meredyth Vineyards is the largest table wine vineyard in Virginia with 50 acres of vinifera and French hybrids. Meredyth began in 1972 when Archie M. Smith, Jr. planted 3,300 vines. Today Meredyth has 30,000 vines and a commercial winery.

Many Meredyth vintages of past years have been "estate bottled," wording regulated by the Federal government. This means that almost all the wine so labeled came from grapes owned or controlled by the winery. However, estate bottled wines nowadays must originate in a designated viticultural area. The Meredyth people consider it too soon to designate any part of Virginia such an area and have stopped using the estate bottled label. If an American label reads "Produced and bottled by . . ." it means 75 percent of the grapes came from the vineyard on the label. If the label merely says "Made by . . ." it could mean that as low as 10 percent was made from the producer's own grapes.

Meredyth in 1982 harvested 142 tons of grapes, 20 tons of them from other vineyards. The winery's "staple five" wines, in widest distribution, are Seyval Blanc, Chardonnay and Riesling, all white wines; and two reds, Marechal Foch and de Chaunac. Rougeon Rosé is widely available but in smaller quantities.

Visitors to Meredyth Vineyards are welcome from 10:00 A.M. to 4:00 P.M. daily except major holidays. There is no charge for groups of less than 10. Tour guides escort visitors through the winery explaining the wine-making process. Meredyth wines can be purchased at the winery's hospitality facilities.

In the Middleburg area just down Route 628 from Meredyth is Highbury, an experimental vineyard begun in 1969 by Robert de Treville Lawrence, the editor and publisher of *The Vinifera Wine Growers Journal*. Highbury is not elaborate, but if you are a serious student of wine and wine making stop to talk with Mr. Lawrence, an acknowledged authority in the field. He makes Cabernet Sauvignon, Riesling, and Beaujolais for his own pleasure and that of his family and friends.

Directions: Take Beltway Exit 9, I-66 west. Exit onto Route 50 west. Continue to Middleburg, Virginia. Turn left on Route 626 and proceed to Route 628 and turn left. The Meredyth Vineyards entrance will be on your right off Route 628. For Highbury, turn right just after turning off Route 626 and before coming to Meredyth. The road to Highbury is a one-way dirt road. When leaving continue up this road and make a right on Route 601 and another right on Route 626 at The Plains to get back to Middleburg.

Piedmont Vineyard

Wine making has a venerable record in Virginia, going back to the earliest days of colonization. A vineyard tract, in fact, is still visible in Williamsburg where in the 1770s a Frenchman, André Estave, had a vineyard in James City County. Like other wine producers he was paid a bounty by the Virginia Assembly to encourage the development of a Virginia wine industry.

Now, many years later, that industry is really coming into its own. Piedmont Vineyard was the first commercial vinifera vineyard in Virginia. This means it is a vineyard growing European varieties grafted to native American roots.

Piedmont Vineyard has 19½ acres of Chardonnay, 6½ acres of Semillon and 4½ acres of Seyval Blanc grapes. From these grapes approximately 10,000 gallons of wine are produced annually. Piedmont makes three white wines. The estate-bottled Virginia Chardonnay is a dry white wine aged in American and Yugoslavian oak, as are all the wines at Piedmont. It has a peach-like aroma and nutty flavor. Chardonnay has been compared with the Burgundies of France. Piedmont's second white is the Virginia Semillon, a dry white wine made from the classic Bordeaux grape. The third is Virginia Seyval Blanc, a dry, fruity wine made from French hybrid grapes.

Piedmont is open for tours Tuesday through Sunday from 10:00 A.M. until 4:00 P.M. A tasting room is located adjacent to the winery. Tours include free tastings of all the wines, including the Special Reserve Chardonnay which is available only at the winery. For groups larger than nine there is a $1.00 charge for the tour and tasting and a $3.00 charge if the group would also like fruit and cheese. There is no charge for smaller groups. Advance notice for tours is appreciated. Call (703)687-5134.

Directions: Take Beltway Exit 9, I-66 west. Exit onto Route 50 west and continue to Middleburg, Virginia. Take Route 626 south for three miles. The winery sign is on the left.

Shenandoah Vineyards

In a valley between the Blue Ridge and Shenandoah Mountains is the first vineyard established in this fruit producing region of Virginia, Shenandoah Vineyards. Since 1977 when it was licensed, Shenandoah has been producing wine for the public from its 10 acres of French-hybrid grapes and eight acres of vinifera grapes.

Shenandoah is currently bottling eight selections: Chambourcin, Chancellor, Seyval Blanc, Shenandoah Blanc, Shenandoah Rosé, Vidal Blanc, Chardonnay, and Riesling.

Shenandoah offers tours and free tasting from 10:00 A.M. to 6:00 P.M. year round. Those just beginning to explore the world of wine may benefit from a few pointers on the correct way to appraise a new wine. Wine tasting is an art in itself.

First of all, the wine glass should be held by the stem. Holding it by the bowl warms the wine and distorts the taste. Next, after looking at the color of the wine, which can range from pale straw to deep ruby, test the body of the wine by tilting the glass and watching the wine flow down the side. If it has body or good "legs," the wine will roll down the glass in clinging sheets rather than like a weak-bodied, rain water drizzle.

Another step is accessing the wine's bouquet or aroma. Hold the wine glass and rotate it just slightly to allow the wine to swirl around. This aerates the wine and brings out the bouquet. This is why wine glasses should never be filled to the brim. Determining a wine's aroma is done simply because a wine that smells good usually tastes good.

The last and most important step is tasting. This is done by taking a sip and then rolling it around in your mouth. Even a novice can readily tell if the wine is sweet or dry. The taster will also recognize if a wine has a long or short finish, which means aftertaste.

Samplers of more than one wine should eat something between each variety. Bread and cheese are often served to clear the palate.

With this information the visitor is ready to drive out Skyline Drive to Shenandoah Vineyards. Reservations are not necessary but it is always a good idea to call to avoid unexpected problems. The number for Shenandoah Vineyards is (703) 984-8699.

Directions: Take Beltway Exit 9, I-66 west, to Route 29-211 at Gainesville. Continue west to New Market. Go north on Route 81 to Exit 71 and turn left on Route 675. Then make a right on Route 686. Shenandoah Vineyards will be on the left off Route 686 in Edinburg, Virginia.

Ingleside Plantation Vineyards

Ingleside Plantation is near two important historical sites—George Washington's birthplace at Wakefield and Robert E. Lee's birthplace at Stratford Hall. Ingleside is also a registered National Historical Place, though certainly not as famous as its neighbors.

For wine fanciers the important history is that the first grape vines were planted at Ingleside in 1960. These vines proved that wine grapes would survive and produce well in this part of Virginia. After 1960 French–American hybrids were planted and an experimental wine making venture was begun initially for home consumption until expansion made it possible to produce wine using the European chateau or estate winery methods.

The constantly expanding vineyard now has 25 acres of both hybrid and vinifera grapes, growing 30 varieties of wine grapes and bottling 14 different wines. The winery has a 20,000 gallon capacity.

Ingleside bottles red, white, rosé, champagne, and fruit wines. Its four red selections are Cabernet Sauvignon, Chancellor, Nouveau Red and Roxbury Red. Its six white wines are Aurora, Chardonnay, Ingleside Fraulein, Ingleside White, Riesling, and Seyval Blanc. Ingleside also has a Wirtland Rosé, a Semi-Dry Virginia Champagne, and a Virginia Apple Wine.

After a guided winery tour, the visitor can enjoy tasting some of Ingleside's selections. The tours are offered Thursday through Sunday from 1:00 P.M. to 5:00 P.M. For other times, call for an appointment at (804)224-7111.

Directions: Take Beltway Exit 4 to I-95. At Fredericksburg take Route 3 east to Oak Grove. Go south on Route 638 for 2.5 miles to the winery entrance on the left.

Barboursville Vineyard

On Christmas Day 1884 the mansion designed by Thomas Jefferson for the plantation of James Barbour burned to the ground. The picturesque ruins are now a registered Virginia Historical Landmark.

Most recognize the name not because of its historical significance but because it now graces the label of the Barboursville Vineyard. The vineyard began planting in 1976, with its first commercial bottling in 1980. Barboursville bottles Cabernet Sauvignon, Chardonnay, White Riesling, Rosé Barboursville, Merlot, and Gewurtztraminer.

Tours are by appointment. Make arrangements by calling (703)832-3824.

Directions: Take Beltway Exit 9 west on I-66. Exit at Gainesville onto Route 29, south towards Charlottesville. About 17 miles north of Charlottesville turn left at Route 33 and continue to Barboursville at the intersection of Route 33 and Route 20. Follow signs to the winery.

Oasis Vineyard

You don't have to be much of a wine enthusiast to enjoy visiting the Oasis Vineyard, presently the largest and most modern winery in Virginia. A recently completed tasting room provides a mountain view that's as heady as any of the wine samples served here. The Blue Ridge Mountains could make nectar of the gods out of any wine.

Throughout the year the wine tours offered at the Oasis Vineyard provide a vantage point for a changing perspective on wine making. The pruning of the old vines and the planting of the new shoots, the care and nurturing of the plants as they bear fruit, and the very important harvest time are all fascinating and make a visit worthwhile. A slide presentation at Oasis provides a complete look at the art of wine making.

Oasis has 30 acres that are quite close to scenic Skyline Drive and just an hour from the Washington area. Oasis grows both French–American hybrids and vinifera vines. Currently, Oasis bottles seven white wines: Sauvignon Blanc, Gewurtztrainer, Reisling, Semillion, Seyval Blanc, Rayon d'Or, and Chardonnay plus a French-style Champagne. They also have six red wines: Cabernet Sauvignon, Merlot, Pinot Noir, Chancellor, Marechal Foch, and Chelois. At the 1981 Wineries Unlimited Eastern Wine Competition, Oasis Vineyard won a Best of Class and a Silver Medal for its 1980 Sauvignon Blanc. At the 1982 Competition its 1982 Semillion won the Silver Medal. Chelois 1980 (red) won first place at the 1982 Middleburg Festival Wine Competition and the Chancellor (red) won third prize at the Wine Competition.

The Sauvignon Blanc, though not necessarily the 1980 vintage, may be tasted any weekend or during the week by appointment. To make arrangements to visit Oasis call (703) 635-7627.

Directions: Take Beltway Exit 9 to Route I-66 west to Marshall's second exit. From Marshall take Route 647 and then make a right onto Route 635. Continue on Route 635 for 10 miles to Oasis Vineyard.

Rapidan River Vineyards

The history of German viticulture in Virginia goes back to 1710. It started when Governor Alexander Spotswood encouraged settlers from Germany's Rhine region to a colony along the Rapidan River in Virginia.

For a time these German immigrants were able to successfully grow a large acreage of European grapes at Germana, as they called their new settlement. Their vines grew and thrived. They began selling both red and white Rapidan wine to the Virginia colonists. Unfortunately, this venture was shortlived. The vines fell prey to the triple perils of mildew, black rot, and the root louse, Phylloxera, ending this early chapter of wine making in Virginia.

A sequel to the story followed in the 1970s when Dr. Gerhard W. R. Guth acquired land along the Rapidan River. Remembering the story of his countrymen, Dr. Guth had studies made of the soil structure, climate, and topography of his Rapidan River property. Results indicated the area was good for grape growing.

Today 27,000 vines are planted on 25 acres of Dr. Guth's land. The vinifera varieties include white Riesling, Chardonnay, Gewurztraminer, and Pinot Noir. The Rapidan River Vineyard uses German technicians and methods to produce wine in this country in accordance with the fine tradition of the German wine industry.

Rapidan River Vineyards are open daily year round for tours and tasting. The hours are 10:00 A.M. until 5:00 P.M. For additional information call (703)399-1855.

Directions: Take Beltway Exit 9, I-66 west. Exit onto Route 29 south and continue to Culpeper. Turn south on Route 522 to Route 611 and go left on Route 611 for about 4 miles to the second gravel road on the left. Continue for 1.5 miles to the vineyards on the right.

Other Virginia Vineyards

Bacchanal Vineyards
David Mefford, Prop.
Route 2, Box 860
Afton, VA 22920
(804)272-6937

Growing eight varieties of vinifera on six acres. The winery is on the slope of the Afton Mountain overlooking Rockfish Valley. Tours are conducted on weekends from April through the middle of November.

Blenheim Wine Cellars
John Marquis, Jr., Prop.
Route 6, Box 75
Carter's Bridge
Charlottes-
ville, VA 22901
(804)295-7666

This 10½ acre vineyard has Chardonnay, Riesling, and Merlot grapes. It will begin offering tours in mid-1983. The house at Blenheim is a national historic place. It was built in 1745 shortly after Monticello and Ash Lawn.

Domaine de Gignoux
Fred Gignoux, Owner
Box 48
Ivy, VA 22945
(804)296-4101

Only four acres, this winery styles itself as a "mini-Loire Chateau." A new concern with tours and tastings, it was begun in 1982.

Farfelu Vineyard
Charles Raney, Prop.
Highway 647
Flint Hill, VA 22627
(703)364-2930

With vines planted as early as 1967, this vineyard now has 33 acres of grapes, with 15 different varieties. At Farfelu they grow both vinifera and hybrids. Tours and tasting by appointment.

La Abra Vineyard &
Winery, Inc.
Prof. Al Weed, Prop.
Route 1, Box 139
Lovington, VA 22949
(804)263-5392

This vineyard has 12 acres of French–American hybrids. The wine is bottled under the Mountain Cove Vineyard label. It is located in the picturesque Blue Ridge Mountains. Hours are 1:00 P.M. to 5:00 P.M., Wednesday through Sunday, for tours and tasting.

Melrose Vineyard
William Benton, Prop.
Route 1, Box 191
Middleburg, VA 22117
(Telephone No. not available)

This ancestral farm in the Virginia hunt country began planting grapes in 1978. They have both vinifera and French hybrids. This vineyard is often included on the annual Middleburg Wine Festival Tour.

MJC Vineyard
Karl T. Hereford, Prop.
Route 1, Box 293
Blacksburg, VA 24060
(703)552-9083

This is the principal winery in the specifically designated viticulture district in the Roanoke area. It has 15 acres of vinifera and hybrid grapes. This vineyard also is a major supplier of custom grafted vinifera grapevines. Its wines are available under three labels: North Roanoke Valley, Pearis Mountain, and Appalachian Harvest. Tours are available by appointment.

Montdomaine Vineyard
Michael Bowles, Prop.
Route 6, Box 168-A
Charlottesville, VA 22910
(804)977-6120

Thirty acres of vineyards in the Carter's Bridge area are planted with Chardonnay, Merlot, and Cabernet Sauvignon. This is the first estate winery in Albemarle County since Prohibition. Tours are by appointment.

Naked Mountain Vineyard & Winery
Robert Harper, Prop.
P.O. Box 131
Markham, VA 22643
(703)364-1609

This 4½-acre vineyard is in the heart of Virginia's Blue Ridge Mountains. Though produced in small quantities, the wines are made from classic European grape varieties. Tours are conducted Noon to 5:00 P.M. Wednesday through Sunday, from March through December.

Oakencroft Vineyards
Mr. and Mrs. John B. Rogan
Route 5
Charlottesville, VA 22901
(804)295-9870

Opening by appointment only in late 1983 this seven-acre vineyard grows Seyval, Chardonnay, and Merlot. Expectations are to have wine available in 1985.

Rose Bower Vineyard and Winery
Tom O'Grady, Prop.
P.O. Box 126
Hampden-Sydney, VA 23943
(804)223-8209

At this small 18th century country house, grapes were first planted in 1974. Now there are six acres of vinifera and hybrids. Rose Bower is open on Fridays and weekends from 2:00 P.M. until 4:00 P.M. for tours and tastings. Tours are conducted from Nov. 1–Dec. 20, April 1–May 15, and July 1–Aug. 15.

Tri-Mountain Vineyard
Joseph C. Geraci, Prop.
Route 1, Box 254
Middletown, VA 22645
(703)869-3030

This vineyard is named for the three mountains that form the cradle of the Shenandoah Valley—the Blue Ridge, Massanutten, and the Great North Mountain. Plans are for 23 acres in grape cultivation. Tri-Mountain makes seven wines. Tours and tastings are available Monday through Saturday from 11:00 A.M. until 6:00 P.M. and on Sunday from 11:00 A.M. until 5:00 P.M.

Maryland

Boordy Vineyard

Philip Wagner, founder of Boordy Vineyard, is often called the Johnny Appleseed of the wine industry. In the early 1930s he started to cross the French grapes he so enjoyed with the hardier, more resistant American varieties. In 1939 he established a nursery and began to supply the French hybrids he created to vintners across the country. He once said, "There isn't a state in the union now, with the possible exception of North Dakota, that doesn't have them."

But not all the grapes were dispersed. In 1945 the Wagners established their own small vineyard, Maryland's first commercial winery. Although its size was modest, its reputation was not. In the fall of 1980, when the Wagners sold Boordy to friends, the R. B. Deford family, Boordy was producing its 36th consecutive vintage.

Boordy Vineyard has now moved from Riderwood to Hydes, Maryland. In the Deford's refurbished 19th century stone and wood barn they are continuing to produce the excellent wine so long enjoyed under the Boordy label.

Though there were only five acres of grapes on their 250-acre farm when the Defords began wine making in earnest in 1980, they anticipate a gradual expansion until they reach 30 acres. Following the Boordy Vineyard tradition, the Defords currently obtain grapes from five major vineyards in the state.

About 85 percent of the wine produced by Boordy Vineyard is sold in Maryland and is widely distributed in the best package stores and restaurants. The 1982 vintage consisted of 18,000 gallons, roughly 7,500 cases. The principal wines are Maryland Red, Maryland White, and Maryland Rosé. They also produce four specialty wines: Cedar Point Red, Nouveau, Seyval Blanc, and Vidal Blanc.

Boordy Vineyard hosts seasonal open houses. Interested persons can call (301)592-5015 to make special arrangements to visit this winery.

Directions: Take Beltway Exit 27 to I-95 north to the Baltimore Beltway. Take Exit 29 to Cromwell Bridge Road. Continue to

Glen Arm, where you go left to a four-way stop. Take a left on Long Green Pike and go two miles to the winery sign at 12820 Long Green Pike in Hydes, Maryland.

Provenza Vineyard

American wines are doing well in the rapidly rising wine market. While some people still think of American wine in terms of the west coast, specifically California, here on the east coast vineyards are increasing in popularity.

The White House on occasion has made it a point to serve only east coast wines at formal dinners. There have included Provenze Red and Northern Virginia's Meredyth White. (See Meredyth Vineyards.)

Provenza Vineyard, a popular favorite among those who enjoy vineyard tours, is not only the closest to the Washington metropolitan area, but it is also one of the most hospitable.

What better way to learn about wine than to sip the various types. At Provenza wine making is a labor of love. The tours are conducted by those involved in the day-to-day wine-making process. You will be given the grape-to-cork process in a manner that makes converts of the most skeptical neophytes.

In fact, it's amusing to listen to those who are just becoming familiar with the various grapes and the wines they produce. At Provenza an acronym of the owner's name is used on the labels, as in Batajolo Red. Many a visitor trying to appear knowledgeable has remarked on what a good grape variety Batajolo is in making wines. It's all in good fun and after a few glasses of wine along with cheese and crackers most visitors feel they are among good friends.

Provenza is a small winery and tours are arranged by reservation. They start around 1:00 P.M. on Saturday and Sunday afternoons and usually take about two hours. To make arrangements call (301)277-2447.

Directions: Take Beltway Exit 28 to New Hampshire Avenue, past Brighton Dam Road to Green Bridge Road. It will be a half mile past Brighton Dam. At Green Bridge Road make a sharp right and then a left at the Provenza sign. The vineyard is at 805 Green Bridge Road in Brookville, Maryland.

Berrywine Plantations Winecellars

Anthony Aellen, a young man with both a mission and a message, enthusiastically conducts visitors through his family's Berrywine Plantations Winecellars, explaining the intricate technique of wine making. The tours are so detailed, yet so interesting, that visitors often leave with the idea of trying to make their own wine.

Be forewarned, however; the Aellens are a classic case of a run-away hobby. According to Anthony, his grandfather made wine in his cellar until 1974, when he retired at the age of 82, passing the equipment and helpful hints on to Jack and Lucille Aellen, Anthony's parents.

The Aellens planted experimental French hybrid grapes on their 230-acre farm in Mt. Airy, Maryland, in 1972. They began making wine in 1976. Ironically that qualifies them as the oldest winery in western Maryland. Berrywine Plantations now produces 30 different varieties. They are, says Anthony, "the Baskin-Robbins of the wine industry with everything but fudge-ripple."

They produce, ferment, and bottle all their own wines. The varieties include three agricultural wines: peppermint, dandelion, and honey wine or mead. Listening to 23-year-old Anthony explain how they developed the peppermint wine, the visitor can understand why he is so excited about the wine-making business. He said, "Each time I mowed the back field I enjoyed the smell of the wild peppermint, so I decided to cut it and try to use the leaves in a wine. Because it was picked when the grapes were ready to be harvested I had to freeze bags and bags of mint leaves. But the freezing actually enhanced the taste." This same sense of discovery and delight in experimentation comes across in many of the wines the Aellen's have created.

While the worth of the wine is in the tasting, the process by which it is made is interesting. California winery tours have long been popular and area growers have found a similar curiosity on the east coast. Because Berrywine is a family business the tours are conducted by those who actually do the work. You'll see the huge vats outside where the grapes are crushed and destemmed and the hopper they call the "mechanical feet" because it does the job many still think of as stomping the grapes.

Before the Aellens obtained this machine it would take four people an entire day to process two tons of grapes. Now one person can process that amount in 45 minutes.

The mixture is then tested for sugar content, acidity, alcohol, and spoilage as it is fermented in American white oak casks. A fermentation lock keeps it from blowing its cork. The normal fermentation period is two to two-and-a-half months. The sediment sinks to the bottom and the racking of the wine allows the top layer to be pumped up through a filter.

The final step involves the whole family, the Aellen assembly line. Bottles are sterilized, placed on a machine to be filled, corked, labeled, and capped. As General Manager Anthony Aellen explains, "Wine making is a science, but making excellent wine is an art."

At the gift shop there is a wide selection of wines to taste and purchase. Under the Berrywine label are the fruit and agricultural wines. It is fun to experiment with elderberry, peach, damsen plum, apple, blackberry, cherry, and pear wine. Under the plantation label you will find the classical dry dinner wines.

In early June the winery has a Strawberry Wine Festival. An annual Oktoberfest is held the third weekend in October. Berrywine is open daily except Wednesday and major holidays. The winery tours start at 10:00 A.M. and at 1:00 P.M. on Sunday.

Directions: Take Beltway Exit 35 to I-270 north to the Damascus exit, Route 27. Follow Route 27 to the Mt. Airy Business District and watch for the signs to the winery.

Byrd Vineyards

Grafting of hybrid grapes on native American stock, often mentioned on vineyard tours, is the subject of a 15-minute slide presentation at Byrd Vineyards which shows how this grafting process is done. In addition, tourists learn about the use of the various pieces of modern wine-making equipment from the very people who use it daily.

Byrd Vineyards encompasses 15 acres in the Catoctin Valley in Myersville, Maryland. This is a picturesque locale to explore. Visitors will discover after tasting the wines at Byrd that it is also a good area for grape production. Wines made here include

Chardonnay, Sauvignon Blanc, Seyval Blanc, Vidal Blanc, Gewurztraminer, Rosé, and Maryland apple wine.

Byrd Vineyard is open for tours, tasting, and wine purchasing from June through November. Hours are 1:00 P.M. to 6:00 P.M. on weekends and weekdays from 1:00 P.M. to 5:00 P.M. It is closed Tuesday. Only groups need reservations. A nominal admission fee is charged.

Directions: Take Beltway Exit 35 to I-270 west to I-70. Follow this for 10 miles past Frederick. Take Exit 42 at Myersville and follow Main Street through town to Church Hill Road. Turn right on Church Hill Road and continue to Byrd Vineyards on the left.

Montbray Wine Cellars

Dr. G. Hamilton Mowbray, founder and owner of Montbray Wine Cellars, believes that a great wine is a fortunate combination of the right grape in the right climate in the hands of the right winemaker. Many wine enthusiasts and awards panels have indicated that Montbray Wine Cellars indeed has found this winning amalgamation.

Dr. Mowbray, one of the founding members of the American Wine Society, received the American Wine Society's Award of Merit for sharing his expertise and experience in growing and making wine from vinifera and French hybrid grapes. His work has also been recognized in France, where he was the recipient of the Croix de Chevalier du Merite Agricole.

Dr. Mowbray's winery was founded in 1964 in the planting of 600 vines including Seyve-Villard, Foch, Riesling, and Chardonnay. In 1966 it became Maryland's third bonded winery and the first American winery to produce a varietally labeled wine from the French hybrid grape Seyve-Villard. This wine is now called Seyval Blanc by other vineyards. The Washingtonian Tasting Panel rates Montbray's Seyve-Villard a number one wine, similar to the high quality wine from the Loire Valley of France or the white wines of Burgundy.

Montbray has also established the world's first "clone vineyard." In 1977 it planted a vineyard with vines propagated from a single cell of the Seyve-Villard 5-276 vine.

Another popular wine is Montbray Rosé, made from an Alsatian hybrid that contains in its genetic background a large proportion of Johannisberger Riesling.

In 1974 an early frost caused the Riesling grapes to freeze on the vine. They were picked immediately and pressed, producing America's first "ice wine."

Montbray also grows Cabernet Sauvignon, Cabernet Franc, and Merlot.

This small winery in Silver Run Valley near Westminster in Carroll County, Maryland, is open daily for tours and tastings. Hours are 10:00 A.M. to 6:00 P.M., Monday through Saturday, and 1:00 P.M. to 6:00 P.M. on Sundays. For information on current conditions of the fields call (301)346-7878.

Directions: From the Beltway take Exit 33 to Route 185, which becomes Route 97 to the Westminster area. Montbray Wine Cellars is located at 818 Silver Run Valley in Westminster.

Pennsylvania

Bucks Country Vineyards and Winery

The Bucks Country Wine and Fashion Museum offers visitors a unique experience that the titles of Arthur Gerold help explain—he is president of the vineyard as well as of Brooks-Van Horn, America's leading theatrical costumer.

People can improve their wine expertise and also enjoy the original costumes from some of Broadway's and Hollywood's biggest hits. Outfits include Marlon Brando's *Godfather* garb, Dorothy's costume in *The Wizard of Oz*, Frank Langella's Dracula regalia and Richard Burton's finery from *Camelot*. Costumes worn by such legendary greats as Mary Martin, Katherine Hepburn, and Gertrude Lawrence are a link with America's theatrical past. Both for the fascinating mementos from the theatre and for the arcane lore on Pennsylvania wine making, this is a one-of-a-kind museum.

Visitors to Bucks Country Vineyards can also tour the winery. Tours include a trip through the cool wine cellars, the bottling and aging rooms, and the tasting room. Guides describe how wine is made at Bucks Country. French bread and croissants are baked on the premises daily, and cheeses may be sampled as well.

Bucks Country is located near New Hope, Pennsylvania, in historic Bucks County. The land in this part of the county was given to Jacob Holcombe by the proprietor of the colony, William Penn, in 1717. Holcombe's farm was situated on what would become the Old York Road, well traveled by stage coaches. Now the road leads from New Hope to Lahaska, site of Peddler's Village.

Bucks Country Vineyards and Winery is open year round Monday through Friday from 11:00 A.M. to 5:00 P.M., Saturdays and holidays from 10:00 A.M. to 6:00 P.M., and on Sundays from noon to 6:00 P.M.. There is a nominal admission for adults on the weekends.

Directions: Take Beltway Exit 27 to I-95 north past Philadelphia to Route 32. Proceed on Route 32 along the Delaware River to New Hope. At New Hope go left on Route 202 towards Lahaska for three miles to the winery.

Buckingham Valley Vineyard and Winery

The oldest vineyard producing Bucks County wine is Buckingham Valley Vineyard and Winery. This small family-owned business was established in 1966 as one of Pennsylvania's first limited wineries.

The range of wines available at Buckingham, however, is certainly not limited. One can choose between 12 different wines including four reds, three whites, two rosés, and a rosette plus apple wine and sangria.

Visitors are welcome Tuesday through Saturday to explore the vineyard, tour the winery, and sample the wines. Hours are noon to 7:00 P.M. on weekdays and 10:00 A.M. to 6:00 P.M. on Saturdays. Only groups of more than 15 require reservations.

Call (215)794-7188. While in the area plan a visit to nearby Bucks Country Vineyards and Winery.

Directions: Take Beltway Exit 27 to I-95 north past Philadelphia to Route 32. Proceed on Route 32 along the Delaware River to New Hope. At New Hope go left on Route 202. When you reach Buckingham Valley go south on Route 413 for 2 miles. Buckingham Valley Vineyard and Winery will be on the left.

Adams County Winery

As proven in the Shenandoah mountain area of Virginia, grapes do well in apple country. It's also true in the Adams County Winery in Orrtanna, Pennsylvania. This vineyard extends across the sloping hills of South Mountain in the heart of the fruit-growing region of southeast Pennsylvania.

After extensive experimentation since the winery's opening in 1975, the grapes grown at Adams County Winery include Seyval Blanc, Vidal Blanc, Pinot Chardonnay, Marechal Foch, Gewurztraminer, Chelois, and Siegfried.

Located in a prime fruit growing region, the winery also produces an assortment of fruit wines. These include strawberry, sour cherry, apple, peach, and nectarine wine.

Tours of the winery are by appointment. Be sure to request the informative slide presentation on the wine-making process. Winery hours are Monday, Thursday, Friday, Saturday, and Sunday from 12:30 P.M. to 6:00 P.M. It is closed on major holidays. To arrange a visit call (717)334-4631.

Directions: Take Beltway Exit 35 to I-270 north to Frederick. Turn north on to Route 15 to Gettysburg. Take Route 30 west for 5 miles. Make a left at 2 miles past the Adams County Winery sign and continue for 2 miles to Orrtanna and the winery.

An Additional Pennsylvania Vineyard

Dutch County Wine Cellar
R.D. 1, Box 15
Lenhartsville, PA 19534
(215)756-6061

Tours and Tasting: Monday through Friday 1:00 P.M. to 5:00 P.M.; Saturday 9:00 A.M. to 6:00 P.M.

New Jersey

Gross' Highland Winery

From a modest eight-acre beginning to more than 80 acres today, Gross' Highland Winery has become the largest direct-to-the-consumer winery in the east.

Like so many immigrants 15-year-old John Gross came to America in 1902 with only his knowledge of an old world trade—in his case the family wine business. It was 32 years after his arrival in New York that John Gross was finally able to start his winery in New Jersey. During this formative period he gained firsthand experience at breweries in New York and Philadelphia.

Tourists today can see the original brick winery, opened in August 1934, where oak casks are still used for aging wines in the cool deep cellars that have walls 18 inches thick. At the time of John Gross's death in 1956 he was producing 7,000 gallons of wine a year. The successful vineyard has continued to expand and flourish under the direction of Bernard D'Arcy, under whose label Gross' Highland Wines are now bottled. The entire operation now produces 21 different varieties of wine.

A 10-minute slide presentation is narrated by a guide who will answer the questions of tourists. Free tours operate Monday through Saturday from 9:00 A.M. to 6:00 P.M. They include visits to the wine cellar, bottling room, and the sampling bar where you can taste the white, red, dessert, and sparkling wines.

The gift shop has a wide selection of wine-related items plus a collection of glassware from around the world. Gross' Highland Winery is only a 10-minute drive from Atlantic City. Visits can also include a stop at nearby historic Smithville.

Directions: Take Beltway Exit 27 to I-95 north to Wilmington. Cross the Delaware Memorial Bridge and follow the Atlantic City Expressway east to the Garden State Parkway. Go north to Exit 40, U.S. 30 east. From U.S. 30 make a left onto 6th Avenue to the Gross' Highland Winery in Absecon, New Jersey.

Wildlife Sanctuaries

Battle Creek Cypress Swamp Sanctuary

Urban adventurers can glimpse an unspoiled world little changed since woolly mammoths and prehistoric camels roamed around the area of Battle Creek Cypress Swamp Sanctuary. Established in 1955 by the Nature Conservancy, this 100-acre preserve is still undiscovered by most daytrippers.

The species of trees you will see along the platform trail that winds through the marshy terrain, bald cypress, has been growing here since prehistoric times. This is as far north as these striking trees are found. Today some of the older ones top out at 125 feet. The trees are called "bald" cypress because they lose all their leaves each fall, but it is their knobby knees clustered at their bases that attract the most attention. Some experts feel the knees stabilize the cypress in the swampy terrain in which they thrive. Others believe that the unusual growths supply oxygen to the cypress.

While this sanctuary is interesting year round, flower fanciers will particularly enjoy a spring visit when the trail is bordered by wildflowers. For help in identifying the flowers and wildlife, stop at the Visitors Center. It has live exhibits including a glass beehive that is literally abuzz with bees making honey from the nectar of a nearby tulip poplar. The Center staff offers frequent guided walks, lectures, nature films and field trips to nearby natural attractions. For details and schedule, call 301-535-5327.

You can visit Battle Creek Cypress Swamp Sanctuary at no charge Tuesday through Saturday from 10:00 A.M. to 5:00 P.M. and Sunday 1:00 to 5:00 P.M. from April through September. The rest of the year the sanctuary closes at 4:30 P.M. It is closed on Mondays, Thanksgiving, Christmas and New Year's Day.

Directions: From the Beltway take Exit 11, Route 4 south. Take Route 4 (it is joined by Route 2) until just before Prince Frederick where you will turn right on Sixes Road. From Sixes Road make a left on Gray's Road; there will be a sign for Battle Creek Cypress Swamp Sanctuary. The sanctuary is a quarter of a mile down Gray's Road on the right.

Blackwater National Wildlife Refuge

If you enjoy being an integral part of the natural world rather than observing it on TV or through bars at a zoo, you will love Blackwater National Wildlife Refuge on the Atlantic Flyway. It's hard to capture in words the thrill you can feel from seeing and hearing thousands of Canada geese on the wing. As you approach the fields where the geese are feeding it sounds as if a throng is cheering for the hometown team. It is not uncommon to see 50,000 Canada geese at one time at Blackwater in late November.

Although one customarily thinks of birds as small, delicate creatures these birds weigh as much as ten pounds. As you would expect, they don't cheep and twitter but cry with a honk that resounds across the fields. Blackwater's five mile scenic drive gives you ample opportunity to hear the honks and get a close look at these striking birds, especially if you have binoculars. You can view them from along Wildlife Drive and from the top of the observation tower.

In the spring you can see goslings. Most geese nest and breed at James Bay in Canada, but some do remain year round at Blackwater. Canada geese mate for life, and have five to eight babies in a batch. Geese are social birds. They form groups and fly in formation with the older birds alternating in the lead position.

Although Canada geese are the most numerous residents of this popular refuge, you'll also see whistling swans, snow and blue geese, and approximately 20 varieties of ducks. In fact, the refuge was originally established in 1932 as a home for migratory ducks.

Two endangered species have found a protected environment here. If you hike the refuge's Woodland Trail you're quite likely to see the large, gray Delmarva Peninsula fox squirrel, unique to Maryland's Eastern Shore. You'll have to look harder to spot the other protected species, the bald eagle. The eagles build nests that resemble large bundles of kindling. If you sight a nest, keep your eye on it for a time and you may see an eagle returning to feed its young.

Visitors are requested to remain in their cars except in designated areas. The refuge is open dawn to dusk daily at no charge. The Visitor Center's hours are 7:30 A.M. to 4:00 P.M., Monday through Friday, and 9:00 A.M. to 5:00 P.M. on Saturday and Sunday. The Visitor Center is closed on weekends during June, July and August and on Christmas Day and all federal holidays.

Directions: From the Capital Beltway take Exit 19, Route 50 east across Bay Bridge to Cambridge. At Cambridge go right on Route 16 to Church Creek. At Church Creek take Route 335 for four miles to Blackwater National Wildlife Refuge.

Chincoteague National Wildlife Refuge

When cold weather starts moving down the Atlantic seaboard so do the migratory birds. Several refuges along the Atlantic Flyway seasonally play host to these passing birds. One of the most popular resting spots is Virginia's Chincoteague National Wildlife Refuge. Indeed, it is not uncommon for a large number of geese, swans, ducks and other waterfowl to winter over here.

More than 275 species have been seen at Chincoteague. There are so many that even the most avid bird watchers are advised to bring a field guide to the birds for help in identifying. A park brochure available at the Visitors Center includes drawings of the most frequently seen varieties. Probably the most numerous species is the snow goose, found here from November to March.

Chincoteague is also the home of the wild ponies made famous by Marguerite Henry's children's novel *Misty,* an excellent book to read before visiting. It is thought that these small horses are descendants of ponies that survived from a shipwrecked

Spanish galleon. The best time to get a closeup glimpse of the ponies is during Waterfowl Week in late November. For this special occasion the refuge opens a 13-mile service road providing far more access than is customarily allowed. On this back road the ponies may approach your parked car, but you are advised not to pet or feed these undomesticated animals. At other times of the year the best place to spot the ponies is from the observation platform near the Pony Trail.

The Virginia portion of Chincoteague Island has approximately 130 head so you are quite likely to see one or more . The ponies travel in groups of 2 to 20 animals, If you don't spot any, you can always stop in the town of Chincoteague at the pony farm. Or you can come back on the last Wednesday in July for the annual pony swim and penning when the ponies swim across Assateague Channel to Chincoteague.

If you are hiking or biking through the Chincoteague refuge you are likely to see some other unusual residents, the Sika deer. Transported to the island from Japan in 1923, the deer came from a similar climate, and it was believed they would add an interesting dimension to the wildlife on Chincoteague.

Summer or winter, the unspoiled Atlantic beach has its appeal. At the Oyster Museum, (open weekends only, from 11:00 A.M. to 5:00 P.M.), you'll find an extensive shell collection. In town at the Refuge Motel you can rent bicycles and arrange wildlife safaris through the center of the refuge, an area not ordinarily accessible by car. Sunset cruises around the island are also available. For information call 804-336-6134 or 336-5511.

Directions: Take the Beltway, Exit 19, Route 50 across the Chesapeake Bay Bridge to Salisbury, MD. At Salisbury take Route 13 to Virginia. Five miles past the state line, turn left on Route 175 to Chincoteague. For the Oyster Museum take a left at the red light when you enter Chincoteague, another left on Maddox Boulevard for approximately two miles; the Oyster Museum will be on your left. To reach the Chincoteague National Wildlife Refuge, continue on Maddox Boulevard; the Visitors Center will be on your left as you enter the refuge.

Eastern Neck National Wildlife Refuge

If you want a no-frills exposure to nature, the Eastern Neck National Wildlife Refuge is the place to visit. You won't find a visitors center, elaborate exhibits or audio-visual program, but in late autumn and during winter you will discover one of the world's largest concentrations of Canada geese. The sight and sound of the geese on the wing is unforgettable.

These stately birds seek the more moderate climate of the Chesapeake Bay during the winter and return to Canada each spring. Although the bay area experiences its share of near Arctic weather, it does occasionally have a pleasant day. When one occurs why not take advantage of it and visit this special refuge? Fortuitously the marsh does not assume as stark and austere a look in the cold months as the forest. The best time to observe the striking Canada geese in flight is at dawn or dusk when they begin and end their foraging.

Though the geese are sufficient inducement to visit Eastern Neck, they are not the only birds that winter here. There is a large duck population, and whistling swans from Alaska. Two varieties of snow geese can be observed: white with black wing-tips and the blue-gray with white heads and necks.

Eastern Neck's 2,285 acres are located on the east side of the Chesapeake Bay at the mouth of the Chester River. There are ten miles of roads through the refuge, and self-guided trails wind through the marsh and woodland. Boardwalks, decks and an observation tower provide access to the waterfowl; all you need to bring are your own binoculars. The refuge is open daily at no charge, but the migratory birds don't begin arriving until October and start leaving in March.

During the winter months the sparse vegetation and leafless trees along the woodland trail make it easier to observe the Delmarva fox squirrel, an endangered species. You'll recognize this squirrel by its white belly and feet. You may also see a whitetail deer, raccoon, opossum, muskrat or woodchuck.

Though the waterfowl diminish you'll see ducks and geese at the refuge year round. The advantage to a visit in late spring or summer, in addition to the weather, is that you can try crabbing in the bay. If you don't have a boat you can net the crabs by just wading out. Old hands recommend that you bring an inner tube and a basket. The tube supports the basket leaving your hands free to net the elusive crabs. Blue crabs are caught as early as May, but July is the best month for crabbing at Eastern Neck.

If you have time stop at nearby Remington Farms, owned by Remington Arms Company. Slightly larger than Eastern Neck it too is open without charge daily from dawn to dusk. One section of the refuge, the wildlife habitat tour, does close during hunting season. Upwards of 20,000 ducks have wintered at Remington Farms in years past.

Directions: From the Beltway take Exit 19 (Route 50) across the Chesapeake Bay Bridge. Take Route 301 off Route 50 and follow 301 north until it intersects with Route 213. Follow Route 213 through Chestertown. At the intersection of Route 20 turn left and take Route 20 to Remington Farms. Eastern Neck National Wildlife Refuge is ten miles farther. Continue down Route 20 to Rock Hall and then take Route 445 across the bridge to the island refuge.

Hawk Mountain

Every field has its jargon and bird watching is no exception, but you don't have to be an ornithologist to experience raptor rapture. Even those who don't know that raptors are birds of prey will thrill to the sight of them riding the wind. From mid-August through November you can see them in abundance at Pennsylvania's 2,000-acre Hawk Mountain Sanctuary.

On a good day you are apt to sight 15 species of raptors from your perch atop Kittatinny Ridge. The varieties will vary with the time of your visit. In September the ospreys, bald eagles and broad-wing hawks are plentiful. In mid-September thousands of medium-sized hawks ride the warm air currents around Hawk Mountain. To see sharp-skinned hawks, red-shouldered hawks, Northern harriers, Cooper's hawks, rough-legged hawks, plan an October trek. Towards the end of October when the winds grow colder you may sight a golden eagle; this eagle's seven-foot wing span is a breathtaking spectacle.

For those who need help in identifying raptors to be seen here, the Visitors Center has a collection of mounted specimens. After familiarizing yourself with the various birds you pick one of the two trails up the mountain. The less arduous (three quarters of a mile) leads to South Lookout and the other, more arduous, to North Lookout. Even the three-quarter mile trail may be difficult for armchair birders but it's worth the effort. The view from the massive sandstone heights extends 70 miles on a clear day. Many of the birds actually fly beneath you and on what they call a 'hot' day, a phrase that has nothing to do with the weather, you may see as many as 10,000 raptors. You can call Hawk Mountain's Sanctuary to check on conditions at 215-756-6961.

One thing to keep in mind about raptor watching is that you will spend a considerable amount of time waiting and it is cold in the fall on the mountain top. Wear warm clothes, carry binoculars and a thermos of hot coffee or chocolate. Raptors fortunately travel during daylight and they travel in groups. Hawk Mountain Sanctuary, which is privately maintained, is open from 8:00 A.M. to 5:00 P.M. daily and charges a minimal admission.

Directions: Hawk Mountain is about a four-hour drive from the Washington Beltway. Take Exit 27, I-95 north. At the Baltimore Beltway head west towards Towson. Take I-83 north past Harrisburg where it merges with I-78-US 22. Follow this to the Pottsville/Port Clinton exit which is PA Route 61. Take this for 4.5 miles to PA Route 895, then go east 2.5 miles to Drehersville. From there it is two miles to Hawk Mountain Sanctuary, as the signs will tell you.

Mason Neck Management Area

On an unspoiled peninsula not far from the crowded suburbs of Washington lies a wilderness that is a sanctuary for the bald eagle, our national bird, and home to a large heron population and many other birds. The Mason Neck National Wildlife Refuge and the Mason Neck State Park jointly provide the protection for the wildlife across 10,000 magnificent acres of grassy picnic areas, streams, bay, marsh and woodland.

It is the diversity at Mason Neck that attracts nature lovers. Many parks have interesting woodland trails but few lead to a spot such as the refuge's 285-acre fresh water Great Marsh. This marsh provides a nesting area for eagles as well as a wintering spot for migrating eagles. Because the eagles engage in their courting and mating during the winter, both the refuge's Woodmarsh Trail and the state parks' Kane's Trail are closed to the public then.

But any time of the year you may explore the state's one-mile loop Bay View Trail overlooking Belmont Bay. This trail too is more diversified than most managed trails. It leads first along the bay, then along boardwalks over the marshland before winding through the woods on its return to the picnic area and Visitors Center. By the time you reach the sign at the park's Visitors Center quoting John Burroughs, you are apt to agree with the great nature writer: "I have loved the feel of the green grass under my feet, and the sound of the running stream by my side, and the face of the fields has often comforted me more than the faces of men."

There is an excellent free brochure that identifies more than 225 species of birds that have been sighted at Mason Neck. It lists their relative abundance in each season. Even though eagles may be in residence, you may not be lucky enough to see one, whereas the birds listed as being common and abundant are almost certain to be seen. In the spring you can expect to see mallards, black ducks, blue-winged teals, wood ducks, lesser scaups, ruddy ducks, bobwhites, several species of gulls and swallows as well as a variety of woodland birds. Some uncommon birds found in abundance during the summer include the great blue heron, great egret, wood duck, and the indigo bunting. Fall finds large numbers of great egrets, black ducks and scarlet tanagers. The common species also include a number of birds you're not likely to spot in your back yard. Be sure to bring binoculars.

The refuge is open free of charge but there is a nominal parking fee for the state park. Both park and refuge are open dawn to dusk daily.

Directions: From the Beltway take Exit 1 in Virginia south on Route 1 to State Route 242, just above Woodbridge. Turn left on Route 242 and proceed four miles to the Mason Neck Management Area.

Jug Bay Natural Area—Patuxent River Park

A wilderness awaits explorers less than an hour from downtown Washington in Croom, Maryland, at Patuxent River Park's Jug Bay Natural Area. Guided pontoon tours, quiet canoe trips, a look at life along the water more than a century ago and wildlife aplenty make an outing to this rural retreat an honest-to-goodness getaway.

Visitors should check at the park office when they arrive at Jug Bay Natural Area. Nominally priced special-use permits are issued by naturalists with the Maryland National Capital Park and Planning Commission to provide visitor access without disturbing the natural environment. With advance planning you can arrange canoe rentals, guided nature walks and escorted pontoon tours; call (301) 627-6074.

Two paths lead away from the park office. One takes you to the Black Walnut Creek area and the second to Patuxent Village. Park naturalists lead 45-minute hikes along the Black Walnut Trail. Hiking on your own may be fun but in the company of a specialist you'll pick up some legend and lore about wildflowers and wildlife. A nest, a bird's cry, a track or a plant might not be fully appreciated if you were out on your own; but finds like these can elicit all kinds of fascinating stories from the naturalists, appealing to both young and old.

Boardwalks, an observation tower and a marshland photograph blind allow visitors a close look at the numerous waterfowl. For those who want to get out on the river there are group pontoon outings scheduled from mid-April to mid-October. These 50-minute tours focus on a variety of ecological topics including bird watcher specials and aquatic life. Pontoon participants must be 13 or older.

There are two kinds of canoe trips: either for individual exploration on Mattaponi Creek and Jug Bay or for longer down-river trips. The river trips are led by park naturalists and give canoeists a chance to observe the river change from a woodland stream to a tidal wetlands. Remember, you must arrange rentals in advance.

Jug Bay, in addition to hiking and boating, offers fishing, camping at primitive sites, and riding. There are eight miles of trails, but you do have to bring your own horse. An interesting attraction to explore is the Patuxent Village, just a short walk from the park office. This village reminds us of what it was like to live along the river 100 years ago. Old tools—like the adze and broad ax on display—were used to build rough-hewn log cabins. There is also a smokehouse, hunting and trapping shed and a packing house with a tobacco prize, used in early America to compress tobacco leaves.

You can also learn a great deal about the work done by our forebears from the W. Henry Duvall Memorial Tool Collection displayed in several large barns. The antique tools and farm equipment can be seen on Sunday afternoons from 1–4:00 P.M. and at other times by advance appointment.

Merkle Wildlife Refuge

When you visit Jug Bay, take time to include a stop at the adjacent Merkle Wildlife Refuge. Although not part of Patuxent River Park, it too offers a look at a wide variety of waterfowl. It's most interesting in spring and fall when migratory birds traveling the Atlantic Flyway stop at the fertile fields of Merkle. You're most apt to find the fields crowded with Canada geese at dusk when they stop to feed. A visitors center and observation deck added in 1985 provide a good vantage point from which to view the birds.

Directions: From the Beltway take Exit 11, Pennsylvania Avenue south to Route 301. Proceed south on Route 301 to Croom Road, Route 382. (Do not take Croom Station Road.) Turn left on Croom Road and proceed until you see the sign for Patuxent River Park where you turn left and follow the signs. For Merkle continue on Croom Road another mile to St. Thomas Church Road. Turn left and continue down this road until you see the sign for Merkle.

Tinicum National Environmental Center

Butterflies and birds flock to Tinicum National Environmental Center: more than 288 species of birds and 25 varieties of butterflies. Their abundance has made this unique environmental study area just outside of Philadelphia a popular destination for nature lovers throughout the Mid-Atlantic. The diversity is possible because the 1,200 acres encompass several habitats each supporting different plants and animals.

The most significant area is Pennsylvania's only remaining freshwater tidal marsh. Dikes were built along the tidal rivers of the Atlantic coast by Dutch settlers in the 17th century. You'll see remnants of these old dikes at Tinicum, but the impoundments you see today were begun in the 1930s. A 3 ½-mile trail circles the impoundments, and a boardwalk provides quicker access. Just down the trail from the Visitors Center where you can obtain a bird checklist is an observation tower from which you can observe and photograph the waterfowl.

At the impoundment's eastern edge is a heron rookery where great blue herons may be spotted, black-crowned night herons, and even green herons though they are most often seen in the tall grasses and reeds. Egrets also frequent the rookery.

At the eastern edge the terrain changes and you see extensive fields of wildflowers. These attract butterflies. There are so many you may want to bring a field guide to help you sort out the red admirals, monarchs, viceroys, painted ladies, aphrodite fritillaries and red-spotted purples which are frequently sighted.

The Tinicum National Environment Center is open daily from 8:00 A.M. to sunset at no charge. The trails accommodate both hikers and bikers. Fishing is permitted but a license is required.

Directions: Take Capital Beltway Exit 27, I-95 north to the Philadelphia area. Exit at Island Avenue turning right on Island Avenue and proceeding to Lindbergh Boulevard. At Lindbergh Boulevard make a left turn and continue to 86th Street. At 86th Street you will see the entrance sign. Turn on the gravel road which leads to the parking lot and Visitors Center.

Animals

Albert Powell Trout Hatchery

Nature lovers, fishing enthusiasts, the perennially curious and the young will be particularly interested in the Albert Powell Trout Hatchery, where Mother Nature gets a vigorous assist in stocking the state's rivers and streams. Just how a fish hatchery operates can be discovered at this easily accessible operation near Hagerstown just off I-70 in Maryland's Washington County. Not being a tourist attraction per se, it doesn't have a visitors center or exhibit area, but you are welcome to explore the area around the raceways. There is a central walkway dividing the series of ponds where the young fish are grown.

Each year roughly 500,000 trout eggs are sent from Washington state for incubation. After hatching, the baby fish are transferred to indoor troughs where they stay for about three months until they grow large enough to be put outdoors. This is when they are ready for public viewing.

The fingerling trout remain in the raceways until they reach 10 or 11 inches, at which size they are considered sufficiently mature to move on to Maryland's streams. Stocking begins in the spring. The objective is to raise 150,000 adult rainbow trout each year. Some 15,000 mature fish are held for a second year, permitting them to reach a length of up to 16 inches. These are the specimens that have fishermen visitors wishing they had their rods in hand.

You can visit the Albert Powell Trout Hatchery at no charge from 9:00 A.M. to 4:00 P.M. daily.

Directions: From the Beltway take Exit 35 (Route 270) to Frederick, then I-70 to just south of Hagerstown. From I-70 take exit 35 (Route 66, north). You will see the fish hatchery on your left as soon as you get on Route 66.

National Aquarium of Baltimore

Although everybody knows it's there—even *Time* Magazine has given it cover-story treatment—it would be a genuine oversight for any review of local nature attractions to omit the National Aquarium of Baltimore. Built and owned by the city, it was designated by Congress as a National Aquarium in 1979. Some observations and practical suggestions are in order to help you get the most out of your visit to this outstanding institution.

The aquarium houses roughly 6,000 specimens, and if you visit on a weekend it may seem as though there are just as many visitors waiting in line. It is better to schedule your outing on a weekday. It will take you about three hours to do justice to all the exhibits. Visitors are directed through the aquarium in one direction; you can't start at the top and work backwards because escalators linking certain areas go only one way.

The first exhibits you see require close attention if you want to read the accompanying information on the small tanks. This means that on days when the aquarium is crowded, bottlenecks occur where visitors wait their turns to peer through the glass. The waits are worth the time because the displays are interesting and well designed, but if you get impatient you might try moving on, completing the circuit and returning later for a second look.

Visitors always want more than a quick look at Anore and Illamar, the beluga whales acquired in 1985. Only five other North American aquariums have beluga whales, and this playful young pair are real crowd pleasers. Though they don't perform tricks, their natural behavior is entertaining to watch. Just as they would at sea, they lob-tail, or smack the water with their tails, and present their tail flukes. They will eventually grow to 13 feet and weigh 2,000 pounds each. Over the next few years repeat visitors can chart their growth.

Approximately half the space at the aquarium features large exhibits where viewing is no problem. At the top of the aquarium there is a glass pyramid 64 feet high which has been transformed into a tropical rain forest, an environment that appropriately depends on water for support. This complex includes exotic birds, a wide variety of lush vegetation, a waterfall and tropical fish.

First timers may think it's all down hill from here, but the best is yet to come. The Atlantic Coral Reef, the largest exhibit of its kind in the country, is probably the most popular at the National Aquarium. A 335,000-gallon, doughnut-shaped tank has 3,000 specimens and an amazingly complete arrangement of coral. The tank's design, with its descending viewing ramp, allows you to look down on the fish, to get up close for eye-level viewing, or to look up at them from below. It's a view of the sea that heretofore only scuba divers could enjoy, an experience which in itself is worth the price of admission. A final thrill awaits as you descend below this reef and that is the Open Ocean Tank where sharks and rays swim.

The National Aquarium of Baltimore is open from mid-May through mid-September on Monday through Thursday from 9:00 A.M. to 5:00 P.M. and on Friday through Sunday from 10:00 A.M. to 8:00 P.M. During winter, it is open daily from 10:00 A.M. to 5:00 P.M. except Fridays when it stays open until 8:00 P.M. Admission is charged.

Directions: Take Beltway Exit 22, the Baltimore-Washington Parkway, which leads into Russell Street. Then turn right on Pratt Street which will lead to the Inner Harbor and the National Aquarium on the right. There are public parking lots across the street.

Baltimore Zoo

The third oldest zoo in the United States, established in 1876, is in Baltimore's Druid Hill Park. More than 1,000 birds, reptiles and mammals can be seen in this 150-acre parkland setting. Some of the facilities—the Mammal House and the caged cats to mention two—are dated, but others like the lion enclosure and the open-air giraffe exhibit reflect the latest in zoo styling. The lions roam the perimeter of their large enclosure, often peering through the windows in the stockade fence and giving visitors a face-to-face confrontation with their magnificence.

Although the National Zoo in Washington has a larger collection and more modern facilities, the Baltimore Zoo is known for its unusually charming setting. A hillside gazebo provides an ideal picnic spot. A path winds through the zoo to each of its 14 major animal exhibits. If you visit in the afternoon be sure to catch the 3:00 p.m. feeding at Penguin Island. The Children's Zoo, undergoing a face-lift in 1986–87, reopens in 1988. It has both wild and domestic animals. Children can also ride a Safari Train that runs through the park in the spring and summer.

At the entrance you pay a nominal admission fee and receive a park map which includes an explanation of the symbols you'll see at each exhibit. It is worth taking time to look this over; it reveals a lot about the animal's home in the wild, what time of day the animal is most active, what the animal eats and how it lives with others in the wild. Some animals live alone while others form life-long partnerships. Still others live in male- or female-led groups.

The Baltimore Zoo is open daily from 10:00 A.M. to 4:20 P.M. On summer Sundays the hours are 11:00 A.M. to 5:20 P.M. Throughout the year the zoo has educational programs for children; call 301-467-4387 for information. Before leaving Druid Hill Park stop at the Baltimore City Conservatory (see selection) or come back another day. You should give yourselves at least 30 minutes to see the Conservatory.

Directions: Take Beltway Exit 27 to I-95 north to the Baltimore Beltway, I-695. Take the Baltimore Beltway towards Towson and exit south on the Jones Fall Expressway (I-83) going towards town. Turn right on Druid Park Lake Drive to the Baltimore Zoo and City Conservatory.

Gettysburg Miniature Horse Farm

The horses you see at the Gettysburg Miniature Horse Farm are no carnival-style freaks. They are the end products of a successful downbreeding program conducted since the 1860s at the Falabella breeding farm in Argentina. They are proportionally correct, just far smaller than the norm.

The Gettysburg farm began in the early 1970s with 51 of the small Falabella horses. This modest beginning excited interest all across the United States and travelers came from all over to visit the farm in combination with a tour of the battlefield and the Eisenhower farm. Hollywood personalities and international royalty have vied for possession of these rare miniatures. Farabella horses have been owned by the Queen of England, Princess Grace of Monaco, Lord Mountbatten, the Aga Kahn, Charles de Gaulle, Aristotle Onassis and Frank Sinatra.

The miniature marvels range in size, color and breed. Some are no larger than Great Danes, some are pintos and others palominos. You'll see both quarterhorses and thoroughbreds; breeds include Clydesdales, Arabians, Appaloosas and English trotters.

The farm has an 800-seat arena where at four daily shows visitors can enjoy the antics of these trained performers. Children under 80 pounds are even allowed to ride them. Although some of the stallions may nibble a bit, the horses have gentle dispositions. There are usually several in the field for youngsters to pet and the stables may also be visited.

Gettysburg Miniature Horse Farm is open from April through mid-November from 9:00 A.M. to 5:00 P.M. daily. In summer the farm stays open until 6:00 P.M. Shows are given at 11:00 A.M., 1:00, 3:00 and 5:00 P.M. from Memorial Day to Labor Day. During the spring and fall there is no 5:00 P.M. show. Admission is charged and rides are extra. There is a refreshment stand or you can bring a picnic.

Directions: From the Beltway take Exit 35, I-270 to Route 15 north. Continue on Route 15 to Gettysburg. Where Route 15 intersects with Route 30, go west. On Route 30 about 3 miles past Gettysburg, you will see a large sign directing you to the farm.

National Zoological Park

Of course it's best to enjoy wildlife in its natural element—floating, flying, running free. But today's zoological parks at least create an illusion of freedom. The frisky if not fertile pandas, stars of the National Zoo since their arrival in 1972, cavort in a large enclosure complete with play equipment. Confinement doesn't seem too restrictive to them.

Visitors to the Great Ape House may find themselves remembering Charlton Heston's confinement in "The Planet of the Apes." Some of the giant creatures give the impression that they are contemplating matters of giant importance. The small monkeys in the Monkey House seem more carefree, swinging and leaping from ropes to platforms.

The National Zoo was established by Congress in 1890, slightly more than 30 years after the first zoo in the United States was opened in Philadelphia. Animals were first kept in Washington in a pen close to the White House. A herd of buffalo was exhibited, then several other animals presented by foreign countries. It was soon obvious that this was not a good location for the growing collection and the National Zoo was set up on 175 acres along Rock Creek. Highly regarded, the collection now has roughly 3,500 animals representing about 480 species.

Despite its size the National Zoo is easy to cover because of the six-color coded trails that lead off the main pathway, Olmsted Walk. The main walkway is being improved and will eventually be a red paved road. The time needed for each trail varies from 45 minutes on the green Crowned Crane Trail to the orange Lion Trail that can be done in 10 minutes.

You'll want to spend time just watching the animals. The antics of the prairie dog keep visitors entranced. The seals vying for room on their rocks captivate onlookers. The free flying aviary is also a popular exhibit, and of course any visitors in the park at 11:00 A.M. and 3:00 P.M. should try to be at the Panda House to watch them being fed.

When you arrive at the zoo check at the information booth for the schedule of the seal and sea lion training sessions, the elephant training demonstration and the special programs. Educational programs and exhibits can be explored at the ZOOlab in the Education Building from noon to 3:00 P.M. Tuesday through Sunday during the summer and Friday through Sunday in the winter. The BIRDlab in the Bird House is open noon to 3:00 P.M. Friday through Sunday and the HERBlab in the Reptile House is open noon to 3:00 P.M. Wednesday through Sunday. The zoo itself is open daily except Christmas. Hours are 8:00 A.M. to 8:00 P.M. with the buildings opening 9:00 A.M. to 6:00 P.M. from May through mid-September. The rest of the year the grounds close at 6:00 P.M. and the buildings at 4:30 P.M. Admission is free but there is a parking fee. Picnic tables are available and there are refreshment stands and gift shops.

Directions: From the Beltway take Exit 33 (Connecticut Avenue) towards Washington. The National Zoo is in northwest Washington in the 3000 block of Connecticut Avenue. There is also a zoo entrance off Beach Drive (the Rock Creek Parkway) and at the junction of Harvard Street and Adams Mill Road.

District of Columbia Parks

(Listed Alphabetically)

Anacostia Park

A 1355-acre park, extending along the Anacostia River and accessible from the Anacostia Freeway, offers recreational opportunities and the Kenilworth Aquatic Garden (see p. 23).

Battery-Kemble Park

This small wooded park lies in northwest D.C. between Foxhall Road and MacArthur Boulevard. It covers the site of a Civil War battery overlooking the Potomac River and the Virginia shore. Includes playground equipment.

Dumbarton Oak Park

A 27-acre wooded park nestled above bustling Georgetown. Along the stream that winds through the park, rocks interrupt the flow and create both tranquil pools and rushing falls. The park is especially popular in the spring when wildflowers bloom in profusion along the trails. Enter the park by the Lovers Lane footpath off R Street.

Fort Dupont Park

Off Randle Circle east of the Anacostia River is another park with a reminder of the Civil War; one of the many defensive forts protecting the capital was located here. Now the emphasis is on recreation; the park has athletic fields, indoor courts and hiking and biking trails.

Lady Bird Johnson Park and Lyndon Baines Johnson Memorial Grove

This park, named in honor of the first lady who did so much to beautify America, does its part to beautify Washington. In the spring more than 2500 dogwoods and more than a million daffodils bloom here. At the south end of the park there is a 15-acre grove of white pines, dogwood, rhododendron and azaleas. Located between Memorial Bridge and the 14th Street Bridge along the west bank of the Potomac and the George Washington Memorial Parkway.

Lafayette Square Park

This peaceful oasis across Pennsylvania Avenue from the White House has been the scene of many protests but it reveals none of that turbulence. Indeed the squirrels are friendly, and in moderate weather the benches are inviting. Statues honor statesmen, but it is the stately trees that attract nature lovers.

Meridian Hill Park

A little bit of France and Italy can be found in this park's terraced landscape. European touches like water terraces, wall fountains and long promenades remind visitors of old world elegance. Flowering trees add a touch of color in the spring. The park is off 16th Street, N.W. above Florida Avenue.

Montrose Park

Between Dumbarton Oaks Park and Rock Creek Park is a 16-acre woodland park where youngsters enjoy sledding on the hills during the winter. A rose garden and boxwood maze offer areas of formal charm. This park, like Dumbarton, is accessible from Lovers Lane off R and 31st Streets, N.W.

Potomac Park

When you combine East and West Potomac Parks you have 700 acres of unique beauty including the never-on-schedule cherry blossoms around the Tidal Basin. No matter when they bloom they are always a special treat for Washingtonians. West Potomac Park also encompasses the Constitution Gardens with its 7½ acre lake. Hains Point is at the southern tip of East Potomac Park. As you picnic or relax at this river side park you can watch a fountain that shoots a 100-foot spray into the air. Ohio Drive, along the Potomac east bank, links both parks from the Lincoln Memorial down to Hains Point.

Rawlins Park

General John A. Rawlins was President Grant's Secretary of War (he was also his Chief of Staff during the Civil War). The park named for this relatively unknown political figure is small but worth your attention. Water lilies bloom in the two tranquil pools, and rows of magnolias have their waxy flowers reflected in the calm water in late March and early April. The park is between 18th and 19th Streets, N.W. two blocks west of the White House. The north and south boundaries of Rawlins Park are formed by a divided E Street, N.W.

Rock Creek Park

This large (4,500 acre) park borders Rock Creek both in the District and in Maryland, providing quiet wooded paths along the 12-mile creek. Wild flowers can be found along the paths, blooming in greatest profusion in the spring. Bird enthusiasts find this a year-long refuge for numerous species. At the Rock Creek Nature Center (below Military Road) you can discover both historical and botanical information on the park. Beach Drive follows the length of Rock Creek and can be reached by more than a dozen roads that feed into the park.

Maryland State Parks

(Listed by Region)

APPALACHIAN REGION:

Herrington Manor State Park

In Garrett State Forest five miles northwest of Oakland is Herrington Manor's 53-acre lake. Activities include boating, swimming, fishing, hiking and camping.

Swallow Falls State Park

The Youghiogheny River flows through tree-shaded gorges offering spectacular scenery. Muddy Creek Falls is an impressive 51-foot drop. There are nature trails and campsites at Swallow Falls nine miles northwest of Oakland.

Deep Creek Lake State Park

Only ten miles northeast of Oakland, Maryland, but easily mistaken for upper state New York. A six square-mile man-made lake provides the opportunity for a variety of watersports.

New Germany State Park

This 210-acre park five miles south of Grantsville is on the site of a once thriving milling center. A 13-acre lake offers swimming and boating and the hiking trails are used for cross-country skiing.

Big Run State Park

A 300-acre undeveloped wilderness park with primitive camping. Located at the northern tip of the Savage River Reservoir about 10 miles northwest of Piedmont.

Dans Mountain State Park

Nine miles south of Frostburg you can hike and fish in a 480-acre rugged mountain park. From nearby Dan's Rock, a 2,898-foot precipice, you'll have a panoramic view of Garrett County. The park also has an olympic-size pool.

Rocky Gap State Park

Amid the mountain scenery seven miles northeast of Cumberland you can swim, boat, hike and camp during the summer and skate and sled during winter.

Fort Frederick State Park

Located 15 miles west of Hagerstown near Indian Springs, this fort was built in 1756 during the French and Indian War. It is the best preserved pre-Revolutionary fort in America. Two barracks and the surrounding stone wall have been restored to their appearance in 1758. During the summer months authentically dressed personnel interpret the fort's history. Hikers and bicyclists take advantage of the C&O canal towpath that runs through the park.

Gathland State Park

This park 15 miles west of Frederick was the mountain retreat of Civil War reporter George Alfred Townsend. A historical walking tour introduces visitors to the unique facility he created, which includes an impressive arch dedicated to war correspondents.

South Mountain Natural Environmental Area

A 7,035-acre area stretching from just east of Harper's Ferry north to the Pennsylvania border. It includes 40 miles of the Appalachian Trail. The area is popular with hikers who can camp at primitive and improved sites.

Greenbrier State Park

The Appalachian trail passes through this 1275-acre park ten miles southeast of Hagerstown. There is swimming and canoeing on a 42-acre man-made lake. Hiking trails skirt the lake.

Washington Monument State Park

Here citizens of nearby Boonsboro built the first monument dedicated to George Washington. Visitors can climb the monument's rugged stone tower. There are also hiking trails and a history center in the park.

Gambrill State Park

Scenic overlooks, a small fishing pond and hiking trails make this park six miles northwest of Frederick one of Maryland's most popular parks.

Cunningham Falls State Park

Cascading 78 feet through a rocky gorge, these falls are only one of the appealing features in this 4,950-acre park 15 miles north of Frederick in the Catoctin Mountains. You can hike through shaded glens, follow streams and climb winding mountain trails.

PIEDMONT REGION:

Seneca Creek State Park

History and nature combine to make this a popular park. An old mill, stone quarries, Indian grounds and a quaint schoolhouse are located within the park. A 90-acre lake offers boating, fishing and a water boat tour. This 5,150-acre park between Gaithersburg and Germantown also has hiking and riding trails.

Patuxent River State Park

Hiking, fishing and riding can be enjoyed within Patuxent's 6375 acres. A self-guided nature trail highlights the special features of the Patuxent River Valley in Howard and Montgomery counties east of Damascus.

Patapsco Valley State Park

Five separate recreational areas can be found in this 11,500-acre park that sprawls along the Patapsco River from the Liberty Dam on the North Branch and Sykesville on the South Branch down to the river's mouth near the Baltimore harbor.

Soldiers Delight National Environment Area

Hiking and riding trails let visitors explore the only undisturbed serpentine barren, a slightly elevated unspoiled setting with brush and shrubs, in Maryland seven miles west of I-695 in Baltimore County on Route 26.

Rocks State Park

The Susquehanna Indians used these deeply indented rock seats for ceremonies. The King and Queen seats offer a royal view of Deer Creek flowing far below. Rocks State Park is eight miles northwest of Bel Air.

Susquehanna State Park

Nature and history come together at this 2,540-acre park three miles north of Havre de Grace. Steppingstone Museum is a working 19th-century farm. Cornmeal is ground at the Rock Run Grist Mill. Other historic sites are the Jersey Toll House and the Archer Mansion. Fishing and hiking are also popular here along the Susquehanna River.

COASTAL PLAIN:

Cedarville Natural Resources Management Area

Located several miles east of Waldorf, Cedarville's 3,500 acres encompass part of the Zekaih Swamp where the Piscataway Indians once hunted and fished. Visitors can still enjoy freshwater fishing as well as hiking, picnicking and camping.

Smallwood State Park

Smallwood's Retreat was the home of William Smallwood, Revolutionary war officer and governor of Maryland. House tours and craft demonstrations are given during the summer months at this 405-acre park west of La Plata along the Potomac River.

St. Mary's River State Park

Five miles east of Leonardtown is a 250-acre lake where fishing and boating can be enjoyed.

Point Lookout State Park

During the Civil War Confederate soldiers were held here in a Union prison camp. Today visitors can enjoy swimming, boating, crabbing and camping. The park is at the end of Route 5 on Point Lookout where the Potomac River meets the Chesapeake Bay.

Calvert Cliffs State Park

Fossils from the Miocene period, 15 million years ago, are still being found in these steep cliffs overlooking the Chesapeake Bay. There is a hiking trail and playground area at this 1,185-acre park 14 miles south of Prince Frederick.

Sandy Point State Park

This 785-acre park on the Atlantic Flyway attracts migratory birds and water sport enthusiasts. Activities include birdwatching, swimming, fishing and boating. The park is at the western terminus of the Bay Bridge.

Gunpowder Falls State Park

Between Harford and Baltimore Counties 11,475-acres of parkland is divided into several areas providing swimming, picnicking, hiking and other family recreational activities.

Elk Neck State Park

Sandy beaches, verdant marshlands, wooded bluffs all can be found within Elk Neck's 1,765 acres nine miles south of North East. Nature lovers will enjoy the abundant bird population and the diverse wildlife. Sports enthusiasts will appreciate the swimming, fishing and boating. Cabins and campsites are available.

EASTERN SHORE:

Wye Oak State Park

Maryland's state tree has its own 29-acre park. More than 400 years old, this huge white oak tree is the largest and finest of its species in the country. The park is near Wye Mills off Route 213 on the Eastern Shore.

Tuckahoe State Park

Tuckahoe also has a national champion tree: the largest Overcup Oak in the United States. Other trees indigenous to Maryland are being propagated at the park's 500-acre Adkins Arboretum. Tuckahoe Creek flows through this 3,400-acre park and there is a 20-acre lake for boating and swimming. It is located six miles north of Queen Anne.

Martinak State Park

This park two miles south of Denton may once have been the site of an Indian village. Now it offers fishing, picnicking and camping.

Janes Island State Park

At the mouth of Crisfield Harbor you can go swimming, crabbing and fishing at this 3060-acre park. Boaters can explore the island portion of the park.

Pocomoke River State Park & Milburn Landing Area

Eight miles west of Snow Hill within the Pocomoke State Forest is a 370-acre park with camping, fishing, picnicking, hiking and a boat launch.

Shad Landing Area

Four miles southwest of Snow Hill is a second park in the Pocomoke State Forest. Boat tours, nature study and self-guiding nature trails provide a close-up look at the creeks, tributaries and marshland. The park has a large swimming pool. Other activities include boating, canoeing, fishing and camping.

Assateague State Park

This 755-acre park six miles south of Ocean City is Maryland's only ocean park. Swimming, surfing, crabbing, fishing can all be enjoyed along this two mile stretch of the Atlantic. During the summer there are guided interpretative walks and campfire programs.

Virginia State Parks

(Listed by Region)

MOUNTAINS:

Claytor Lake State Park

Claytor's 472 acres offer a sandy beach, launch ramps, campsites and lakeside picnicking. There are bridle trails and riding horses. The park is off I-81 near Radford.

Clinch Mountain Wildlife Management Area

A 25,500-acre wilderness environment atop a high plateau five miles west of Saltville offers primitive camping, trout fishing and hunting.

Douthat State Park

Within the Allegheny Mountains near Clifton Forge this 4,493-acre park offers a 50-acre lake stocked with trout, a restaurant overlooking the lake, a sandy beach, boats for hire, campgrounds and hiking trails.

Goshen Pass Natural Area

Three ridges radiate from the southwest face of Little North Mountain and drop as much as 1,800 feet to the Maury River. This rugged terrain makes an impressive natural area. The park is 12 miles northwest of Lexington.

Grayson Highlands State Park

Rugged peaks and alpine-like scenery can be enjoyed on Grayson's hiking trails. The visitor center has displays on frontier life. This park has campgrounds and adjoins the Mount Rogers National Recreation Area in southwestern Virginia.

Hungry Mother State Park

Three miles north of Marion is a lovely wooded park with a 108-acre lake. Swimming, boating, fishing, hiking, riding, camping and picnicking can be enjoyed.

Natural Tunnel State Park

This geological phenomenon is 850 feet long and as high as a 10-story building. Both man and nature move through the tunnel—a stream shares space with the railroad line. The park also has scenic pinnacles, or 'chimneys.' There is a swimming pool, fishing along the stream, picnicking and camping. The park is just outside Weber City in the southwest corner of the state.

Shot Tower Historical State Park

Overlooking the New River in southwest Virginia just off I-77 is this shot tower built to make ammunition for the early settlers. The 75-foot tower is a National Historic Mechanical Engineering Landmark. There is a hiking trail plus picnic facilities, and when an attendant is on duty you can climb the tower.

Sky Meadows State Park

Sky Meadows' 1,132 acres in the Blue Ridge Mountains west of Middleburg offer hiking, picnicking and primitive camping convenient to the Appalachian Trail.

Southwest Virginia Museum

A collection encompassing the culture and industry of southwest Virginia is housed in a four-story mansion in Big Stone Gap. Closed on Mondays, from March 1 to Memorial Day and September 2 to January 1.

PIEDMONT:

Bear Creek Lake State Park

A swimming beach and lakeside picnic tables make this a popular central Virginia park. The park is 45 miles west of Richmond.

Fairy Stone State Park

A 168-acre lake and lucky fairy stones add picturesque appeal to facilities for camping, hiking, swimming, riding and picnicking. The park is accessible from the Blue Ridge Parkway, 50 miles south of Roanoke.

Twin Lakes State Park

Just three miles southwest of Burkeville are two lakes (formerly Goodwin Lake-Prince Edward) that offer swimming, boating, fishing, picnicking and camping.

Holliday Lake State Park

Adjacent to Appomattox Court House, site of Lee's surrender to Grant, Holliday Lake's wooded setting provides overnight and daytime recreation: boating, fishing, camping, swimming and picnicking.

Lake Anna State Park

Located 22 miles southwest of Fredericksburg, Lake Anna's 2,058 acres offer hiking trails, fishing, picnicking and camping.

Occoneechee State Park

Across Buggs Island Lake from Clarksville in south-central Virginia is a park named after the Occoneechee (pronounced O-ko-nee-chee) Indians. Water sports, fishing, picnicking and camping.

Pocahontas State Park

Close to Richmond and Petersburg within a state forest is a park ideal for hiking and camping. Swift Creek Lake provides a chance for boating and fishing, and one of Virginia's largest pools is ideal for swimming.

Sayler's Creek Battlefield Historical Park

When General Lee's Confederate force retreated from Petersburg 7,700 men were killed or wounded at Sayler's Creek, the last major battle of the Civil War in Virginia. The park on this historic ground is just east of Farmville.

Smith Mountain Lake State Park

Nestled in a scenic setting near Lynchburg and Roanoke is this 1,506-acre lakeside park featuring boating, fishing, hiking, picnicking and camping.

Staunton River State Park and Historic Battlefield

Here on June 25, 1864, a determined group of old men and boys repelled a large Federal force at a railroad bridge. A swimming pool, picnic area, boat launching ramp and camping facilities offer recreation opportunities, making this lakeside park just east of South Boston a dual delight.

Tabb Monument Historical State Park

West of Richmond, a one-acre park on Route 609 in Amelia County commemorates the poet/philosopher Father John B. Tabb.

COASTAL:

Charles C. Steirly Heron Rookery Natural Area

This National Natural Landmark, a dense swamp, just five miles northeast of Waverly in Sussex County preserves one of the few remaining heron rookeries in Virginia. Access is restricted due to its isolated location; for details call 804-294-3625.

Chippokes Plantation State Park

Across the James River from Jamestown, this has been a working farm since 1646. This National Historic Landmark also offers recreational options: bicycle/hiking trails, and a swimming pool.

False Cape State Park

A coastal park on the Atlantic Flyway which attracts a huge migratory bird population. Located 15 miles south of Virginia Beach on the North Carolina state line. Access is limited to hikers and bikers.

Grist Mill Historical State Park

George Washington once operated the grist mill on Dogue Run three miles west of Mount Vernon.

Mason Neck State Park

Located next to Mason Neck National Wildlife Refuge this 1,804-acre park 7 miles northeast of Woodbridge offers interpretative programs, hiking trails and a picnic area.

Parkers Marsh Natural Area

The unique plants and animals of the marsh can be observed at this park bordered by Onacock Creek, Back Creek and the Chesapeake Bay on Virginia's Eastern Shore near the town of Onacock.

Seashore State Park and Natural Area

Located on Cape Henry in Virginia Beach, this 2,770-acre natural area offers camping, hiking, bicycling as well as an amazing array of wildlife and plantlife. Giant sand dunes and languid lagoons make it a fascinating area.

Westmoreland State Park

Between George Washington's Birthplace and Robert E. Lee's birthplace on the Potomac River is a park with a wealth of recreational options: swimming, boat launching ramps, hiking trails, camping facility and picnic tables.

York River State Park

Fresh water and salt water, with their very different plant and animal populations, meet here a few miles north of Williamsburg. There is hiking, boating, fishing and picnicking.

Annual Calendar of Events

January

Cylburn Arboretum—Winter Garden Symposium—(301)542-3109 MID

March

Norfolk Botanical Gardens—Orchid Show—(804)853-6972 ALTERNATE YEARS
Norfolk Botanical Gardens—Camellia Show—(804)853-6972 MID
London Town Publik House and Gardens—Tavern Days—(301)956-4900 MID
Cylburn Arboretum—Spring Garden Symposium—(301)542-3109 MID
Longwood Gardens—Easter Conservatory Display—(215)388-6741 LATE
Brookside Gardens—Easter Spring Flower Show—(301)949-8230 LATE
U.S. Botanic Garden—Easter Show—(202)225-8333 LATE
Gunston Hall—Kite Festival—(703)550-9220 LATE
Williamsburg Garden Symposium—(703)229-1000 LATE
St. Mary's City—Maryland Day Celebration—(301)994-0779 LATE

April

Norfolk Botanical Gardens—Shower of Flowers Show—(804)853-6972 EARLY
London Town Publik House and Gardens—Daffodil Show—(301)956-4900 EARLY
The U.S. National Arboretum—Daffodil Show—(202)472-9100 MID
Norfolk Botanical Gardens—Azalea Festival—(804)853-6972 MID
Fort Ward Park—Azalea Festival—(703)838-4343 MID
The U.S. National Arboretum—Camellia Show—(202)472-9100 MID–LATE
White House—Garden Tour—(202)456-2323 MID
Colonial Pennsylvania Plantation—Civil War Reenactment—(215)353-1777 MID

London Town Publik House and Gardens—Horticultural Day—(301)956-4900 MID
Historic Garden Week in Virginia—(804)644-7776 or (804)643-7141 or write Historic Garden Week Headquarters, 12 East Franklin Street, Richmond, VA 23219 MID
Maryland House and Garden Pilgrimage—(301)821-6933 or write to 600 West Chesapeake Avenue, Baltimore, MD 21204 MID
House and Garden Tour of Historic Shepherdstown, Martinsburg, Charles Town and Harper's Ferry—(304)876-6273 or write TOUR, P.O. Box 40, Shepherdstown, WV 25443 MID
Woodend—Spring Open House and Plant Sale—(301)652-9188 LATE

May

Cylburn Arboretum—Market Day—(301)396-0180 EARLY
Colonial Pennsylvania Plantation—Craft Fair—(215)353-1777 MID
William Paca Gardens—Roses and May Flowers Weekend—(301)267-6659 or (301)269-0601 MID
London Town Publik House and Gardens—Market Day—(301)956-4900 LATE

June

Berrywine Plantations—Great Maryland Strawberry Wine Festival—(301)662-8687 EARLY
U.S. Botanic Garden—Cactus & Succulent Show—(202)225-8333 MID
Gunston Hall—Arts and Crafts Celebration—(703)550-9220 MID
Colonial Pennsylvania Plantation—Revolutionary War Reenactment—(215)353-1777 MID

July

Maymont Park—Old Timey Fourth of July—(804)358-7166 EARLY
Lilypons Water Gardens—Lotus Festival—(301)874-5133 MID
Chippokes Plantation—Pork, Peanut, and Pine Festival—(804)294-3625 MID

St. Mary's City—Children's Festival—(301)994-0779 or (301)994-2943 MID
St. Mary's City—Early American Crab Feast; Militia Days—(301)994-0779 or (301)994-2943 LATE

August

Oatlands—Children's Day—(703)777-3174 EARLY
Leesburg—August Court Days—(703)777-2000 MID
Middleburg Vineyards—Wine Festival—(703)687-6833 or (703)754-8564 LATE
National Colonial Farm—Corn Feast—(301)283-2113 LATE

September

Claude Moore Colonial Farm—Pre-Revolutionary War Day—(703)442-7557 or (703)471-7382 MID
Oatlands—Needlework Exhibit—(703)777-3174 MID
National Colonial Farm—Harvest Festival—(301)283-2113 MID
Gunston Hall—Car Show—(703)550-9220 MID
Shenandoah Vineyards—Harvest Festival—(703)984-8699 MID
Norfolk Botanical Gardens—Aquarium Show—(804)853-6972 MID
Brookside Gardens—Chrysanthemum Showcase—(301)949-8230 LATE
Fairmount Park—Historic Tours—(215)686-1776 LATE

October

Byrd Vineyard—Wine Harvest Festival—(301)293-1110 EARLY
Shaefer Innstead Farm—Fall Pumpkin Festival—(301)972-7247 EARLY
U.S. National Arboretum—Orchid Show—(202)472-9100 EARLY
Norfolk Botanic Garden—Bird Show—(804)853-6972 EARLY
Robin Hill Farm—Pumpkin Harvest Farm Tour—(301)579-6844 MID
Berrywine Plantations—Oktoberfest—(301)662-8687 MID
Gunston Hall—The First Virginia Regiment of the Continental Line Encampment—(703)550-9220 MID

London Town Publik House and Gardens—Needlework Show—(301)956-4900 MID
Chancellor's Point Natural History Center—Aboriginal Day—(301)994-0779 MID
Cylburn Arboretum—Fall Symposium—(301)542-3109 MID
Norfolk Botanical Gardens—Rose Show—(804)853-6972 MID
Oxon Hill Farm—Fall Festival—(301)839-1177 LATE

November

Oatlands—Christmas at Oatlands—(703)777-3174 EARLY
Longwood Gardens—Thanksgiving Conservatory Display—(215)388-6741 LATE

December

Norfolk Botanical Gardens—Christmas Flower Show—(804)853-6972 EARLY
St. Mary's City—Christmas Madrigal Evenings—(301)994-0779 or (301)974-2943 EARLY
National Colonial Farm—Herbal Christmas Shopping Weekend—(301)283-2113 EARLY
Morven Park—Christmas Celebration—(703)777-2414 EARLY
Longwood Gardens—Christmas Conservatory Display & Christmas Tree Drive—(215)388-6741 MID
Brookside Gardens—Christmas Poinsettia Display—(301)949-8230 MID
Gunston Hall—Carols by Candlelight—(703)550-9220 MID
London Town Publik House and Gardens—Christmas Candlelight Tour—(301)956-4900 MID
Colonial Williamsburg—Grand Illumination—(703)229-1000 MID
William Paca House—Christmas Celebration—(301)267-8149 MID
Maymont Park—Torchlight Christmas Open House—(804)358-7166 LATE
Rising Sun Tavern—Christmas Open House—(703)373-1176 LATE
White House—Candlelight Tours—(202)456-2323 LATE

Index

THE BEST GUIDE BOOKS TO THE MID-ATLANTIC COME FROM EPM . . . PLAN AHEAD AND ORDER NOW:

	No. Copies	Price
THE WALKER WASHINGTON GUIDE. The sixth edition of the "guide's guide to Washington", completely revised by Katharine Walker, builds on a 25-year reputation as the top general guide to the capital. Its 320 pages are packed with museums, galleries, hotels, restaurants, theaters, shops, churches, as well as sights. Beautiful maps and photos. Indispensable. $6.95	______	______
INNS OF THE SOUTHERN MOUNTAINS. The first comprehensive guide to the 100 best hostelries of the Appalachians between the Shenandoah and the Great Smoky Mountains National Parks. Author Pat Hudson, a native of Tennessee, has personally visited each place. To meet her standards an inn must offer not only quality hospitality but also introduce guests to the heritage and/or natural beauty of VA, WV, KY, TN, NC and GA. $8.95	______	______
WASHINGTON ONE-DAY TRIP BOOK. 101 fascinating excursions within a day's drive of the Capital Beltway—out and back before bedtime. The trips are arranged by seasons and accompanied by calendars of special events, map and notes on facilities for the handicapped. $7.95	______	______
PHILADELPHIA ONE-DAY TRIP BOOK. And you thought Independence Hall and the Liberty Bell were all Philadelphia had to offer? Norman Rockwell Museum, Pottsgrove Mansion, Daniel Boone Homestead, Covered Bridges and Amish Farms are among the exciting trips featured. $8.95	______	______
ONE-DAY TRIPS THROUGH HISTORY. Describes 200 historic sites within 150 miles of the nation's capital where our forebears lived, dramatic events occurred and America's roots took hold. Sites are arranged chronologically starting with pre-history. $9.95	______	______
THE VIRGINIA ONE-DAY TRIP BOOK. The fifth and newest of Jane Ockershausen Smith's series for day-trippers. One of the most experienced travel writers in the Mid-Atlantic area admits to being surprised by the wealth of things to see and do in the Old Dominion. You will be too. $8.95	______	______

(See next page for a convenient order blank)